For Marissa and Michael—
through whose eyes I first discovered the wonder of picture books.

And for Ed—
who never once refused them a story
(although he was snagged for trying to skip a page
on more than one occasion).
I love you all with all my heart.
—SE

For my little munchkins, Riley and Mairead—
who share my love of books and inspire me every day.
I love you more than words can say.

For my patient husband Alex—
the love of my life, my best friend, and world's greatest dad.
—KG

I can write like that!

A Guide to Mentor Texts and Craft Studies for Writers' Workshop, K–6

INTERNATIONAL
Reading Association
® 800 BARKSDALE ROAD, PO BOX 8139
NEWARK, DE 19714-8139, USA
www.reading.org

Susan Ehmann
Kellyann Gayer

The International Reading Association attempts, through its publications, to provide a forum for a wide spectrum of opinions on reading. This policy permits divergent viewpoints without implying the endorsement of the Association.

Executive Editor, Books   Corinne M. Mooney
Developmental Editor   Charlene M. Nichols
Developmental Editor   Tori Mello Bachman
Developmental Editor   Stacey L. Reid
Editorial Production Manager   Shannon T. Fortner
Design and Composition Manager   Anette Schuetz

Project Editors   Tori Mello Bachman and Rebecca A. Stewart

Cover   Design: Lise Holliker Dykes; photographs: © 2009 JupiterImages Corporation (bottom left), © 2009 Shutterstock Images LLC (all others)

Library of Congress Cataloging-in-Publication Data

Ehmann, Susan, 1949-
 I can write like that! : a guide to mentor texts and craft studies for writers' workshop, K-6 / Susan Ehmann and Kellyann Gayer.
    p. cm.
 Includes bibliographical references and index.
 ISBN 978-0-87207-708-9
 1. Creative writing (Elementary education) 2. Children's literature--Study and teaching (Elementary) I. Gayer, Kellyann, 1971- II. Title.
 LB1576.E345 2009
 372.62'3--dc22
                                                                                    2009017642

Craft Elements

Susan Ehmann has been teaching in the Smithtown Central School District on Long Island, New York, for 17 years—the last 14 years as an elementary reading teacher. She has served as a staff developer in several district literacy initiatives and was selected by her peers to receive the Torch Award for her continuing efforts to "pass on the torch" of learning to her fellow teachers. She has presented at local conferences and workshops on reading and writing instruction. Susan lives in Stony Brook, New York, with her husband, Ed. They have two grown children, Marissa and Michael, and a new son-in-law, Derick. You can reach Susan by e-mail at sehmann@smithtown.k12.ny.us.

Kellyann Gayer has been teaching in the Smithtown Central School District on Long Island, New York, for the past 15 years. She spent the first 5 years of her career as a first-grade teacher, and for the past 10 years, she has been an elementary reading teacher. She has served as a staff developer in several district literacy initiatives and has presented at various local conferences and workshops on reading and writing instruction. Kellyann lives in Northport, New York, and spends much of her free time with her husband, Alex, and two young daughters, Riley and Mairead. You can reach Kellyann by e-mail at kgayer@smithtown.k12.ny.us.

Here we are—four years after conceiving the idea for writing this book. There were many moments along the way when we questioned whether we would ever reach this point. More than once we asked each other, "What have we gotten ourselves into?" But WE DID IT! The book is finished and has evolved into much more than we planned from our original inspiration. There's a kind of bittersweet feeling about actually finishing this project, which has been such a huge part of our lives. Working side by side through all these hours has been rewarding on so many levels and is something that we will treasure always.

There are so many people who helped us in so many ways and we would like to thank each and every one of you. If you haven't been named here, know that we are nevertheless grateful for your assistance.

We have been fortunate throughout this project to have the support of administrators who share our passion for literacy instruction and who have provided the encouragement, freedom, and opportunities to make it all happen.

Thank you to our former principal at St. James Elementary School, Lew Baranello, who always supported us unconditionally in our efforts to expand our knowledge base and try new instructional approaches. You trusted our judgment without question and never once used "the stamp" on us!

Thank you to our current principal at St. James, MaryGrace Lynch, whose expertise in the field of literacy instruction serves as a constant inspiration to the teachers in our school. Your love of the children and of teaching is always apparent and it never surprises us to see you in a classroom conferring with children or modeling a lesson for writers' workshop. You have been behind us in this project since the day we conceived the idea.

Thank you to Arlene Wild, principal at Mills Pond Elementary School, also an expert in literacy instruction, whose excitement about this book has been infectious. You never missed an opportunity to inquire about our progress along the way and have expressed many times how proud you are of our accomplishment.

A huge thank you to all the teachers at St. James and Mills Pond schools. Thank you to those of you who years ago joined us as we began our study of this instructional approach to the teaching of writing. You have continued that journey by learning and sharing with an ever-widening circle of teachers. You have opened your classroom doors, shared your students' writing, gotten excited about newfound mentor texts, and given a most precious gift to your students. We especially want to thank the following teachers who offered samples of their children's writing to be used in this book: Robin Baker, Kim Chacon, Kathy DeBono, Sara Long Harte, Lisa Hennessy, Kristi Hoenes, Mark Jaklitsch, Louise Mahler, Marianne Marquart, Lisa Mozian, Christy Petruzzelli, Kristen Quail, Christie Simonton, and Joe Amendolia, who provided comic relief when we were most stressed.

Thank you to the parents who graciously gave permission to have their children's work appear in the book.

Thank you to Kathy Martin, our beloved teaching assistant, who reshelved the mentor texts. And then reshelved them again...and again...and again...and always with a smile on her face.

Thank you to Diane Widmer (Mrs. Doubtfire) and Dana Link, our computer gurus, who were always available for technical support and never once made us feel like we were asking a stupid question.

Thank you to Amy Arnberg who planted the seed. You introduced us to the words of Katie Wood Ray and taught us to read like writers.

Thank you to MaryGrace Lynch, Arlene Wild, Joyce Tyree, and Marianne Marquart for reading the earliest versions of the manuscript and making much needed suggestions.

Thank you to Katie Wood Ray who graciously accepted an unfinished manuscript from two virtual strangers and not only read it, but offered suggestions and words of support in our search for a publisher.

Thank you to Judy Davis, Lynn Herschlein, and Lois Bridges, all of whom offered us early support on how to go about getting our book published. A further thank you to Judy, for opening your classroom at the Manhattan New School and for coming to *our* schools to share your expertise.

Thank you to our anonymous peer reviewers who offered so many constructive suggestions in the early stages of our manuscript development.

Thank you to the publishing houses and authors who so graciously offered permission to reprint text from the children's picture books. Special thanks to Joie Nobisso who seemed as excited about our book as we were!

Thank you to Sue's sister, Kathi Reilly, high school English teacher extraordinaire, who sat with Sue on the beach and looked through stacks of picture books in search of craft elements.

Thank you to Kellyann's parents, Kathy and Gerry Holly, and mother in-law and father-in-law, Bernadette and Ed Gayer, for countless hours of free babysitting services. The girls always enjoy spending time with their grandparents.

Thank you to Riley Gayer for your insight and contributions. You're well on your way to being a great writer.

Thank you to our husbands, Alex and Ed, who painstakingly pored through the final manuscript in search of typos and grammatical errors (of which there were many). We know we haven't been easy to live with during the final stages of this project but we appreciate your patience and support and realize every day just how lucky we are.

Thank you to everyone at the International Reading Association, especially Corinne Mooney who first showed confidence in our manuscript and held our hands as we began this process as two complete novices in the field of book publication.

An **ENORMOUS** (thought you'd appreciate the print features!) thank you to our editor, Tori Mello Bachman. We're suddenly at a loss for words to express our gratitude for all of your support throughout this project. Your calm and positive attitude kept us from "stressing out" many times over. You constantly pushed us to make our book better, while always respecting our opinions and ideas. You are insightful, smart, and creative. It's amazing to us that you seem to know our book as well as we do. Thank you, thank you, thank you!

Lastly, and perhaps most importantly, thank you to the children whose writing inspires us each and every day.

Almost from the beginning of my journey as a writing teacher, I imagined leisurely Saturday afternoons in the children's section of the bookstore poring over picture books and poems. I'd search for those treasures that met my criteria…that my young readers and I would fall in love with the writing, that hearing these stories of accomplished writers would generate grand conversations, and that these conversations might fill our heads with the possibilities for our own stories. Then, returning to these texts, we'd once again savor the words, and in fact, be jealous of the author's power to make us fall in love. When life and time constraints invariably got in the way of this "lovely fantasy," I imagined a national chain of bookstores stocked with books chosen by teachers for teachers with young writers in mind. Well, sometimes fantasies do come true, and here it is, the teacher's bookstore that comes to you.

I absolutely love this book and so will you if you have known for a long time the power of mentor texts. And you'll love it if you're just discovering the impact a great picture book can have on your writing workshop. So, it is with great pleasure that I write this foreword. From all teachers of writing who will undoubtedly treasure this text, I send a collective "thank you" to Sue and Kellyann. Thank you for the years of searching the shelves of bookstores, libraries, and classrooms; for listening to teachers and knowing what we needed; for listening to the kids who first uttered, "I love this book. Listen to this…." Thank you from all the young writers for this incredible gift of knowing how to read like writers, young writers who will certainly be heard saying, "I can write like that!"

I Can Write Like That! is the ultimate mentor text. In my work with teachers, I'm constantly asked, "What can I teach that will lift the quality of my students' writing?" Kellyann and Sue have identified 27 different craft elements and explained the important role they play in teaching students to be better writers. Question answered. Next, with the expertise that accompanies years of teaching experience, Sue and Kellyann have lain out a sampling of some of these craft studies that help us understand the components of a purposeful study. Finally, in what they call the "heart" of their book, they extend an invitation into a magnificent annotated library, rich with choices of picture books and poetry collections, and spell out the possibilities each holds for our craft studies.

And finally, a collective thank you for the clear, concise manner in which Sue and Kellyann present this practical book, sure to become essential reading for elementary and middle school writing teachers. Thank you for taking the guess work…and the leg work…out of the search. When I first met Kellyann and Sue, I wondered what I could teach these two well-informed, well-read, gracious teachers. In fact, it is they who have taught me so much. I look forward to sharing this gem of a resource with teachers, administrators, librarians, coaches, and fellow consultants. I am certain they will be grateful for the find.

Congratulations on a job well done!

Judy Davis
Literacy consultant and coauthor of
The No-Nonsense Guide to Teaching Writing

Samuel Johnson once noted, "The greatest part of a writer's time is spent in reading in order to write; a man will turn over half a library to make a book." Having just finished going through hundreds of children's books overflowing with beautiful language, similes, voice, wordplay, and powerful opening lines that immediately engage the reader, we are struck by the irony of our struggle to find the right words to begin this book: "Shouldn't we now be experts on this subject?" we ask ourselves.

And so we have decided that the best place to start is at the beginning, to tell you what brought us here. We both began our teaching careers as elementary classroom teachers, but chance and circumstance brought us together as reading teachers at St. James Elementary School in the Smithtown School District on Long Island, New York. A bit like college roommates who enter the arrangement with a certain amount of trepidation, neither of us knew how our partnership would fare. But here we are, nine years later, and a generation apart—colleagues who have grown into friends.

One fuel for the fire of our friendship is our passion for books and the role they play in our students' education. In fact, we often laugh when we find ourselves getting overly excited about a new piece of children's literature or a new professional book that either confirms or brings new insight to our teaching.

As lifelong avid readers, we both considered ourselves to be experts on the subject of children's literature. We were able to recognize quality literature and come up with creative ideas on how to use these books in the classroom. *The Snowy Day* by Ezra Jack Keats (1962) is the perfect springboard for students to write about the season's first snowfall. *Welcome to the Green House* by Jane Yolen (1993) is packed with information about the rainforest. *Rosie and Michael* by Judith Viorst (1974) teaches children about the true meaning of friendship. But had we ever considered using these books to teach students *how* to write? The answer, we have to admit, was *no*—at least not until the Spring of 2000 when we met Amy Arnberg, a teacher trained through Columbia Teachers College, who had written an article for *Primary Voices K–6* about a memoir study she had conducted with her fifth graders (1999). We approached her about doing some professional development with our teachers and she graciously agreed. The rest, as they say, is history.

In the two years that followed, we immersed ourselves in the words of Lucy Calkins, Ralph Fletcher, and Katie Wood Ray, and the way we look at books completely changed. We found ourselves reading like writers. Words and terms that were once foreign to us— author's craft, mentor texts, voice, touchstone texts, small moments, zooming in—were suddenly part of our everyday vocabulary. The more we learned, the more we realized that we had even more to learn and more work to do.

Collegial circles were formed, a professional library was started, and teachers began to take what they were learning into their classrooms. Our students were learning to write in a whole new way—they, too, were reading like writers and writing like readers. Soon it was no longer enough just to read the words of the experts in the field; we wanted to see the theory in action so we began taking teacher field trips. The Teachers College Reading and Writing Project Saturday Reunion at Columbia University has become an annual event, complete with coach bus, food, drink, and laughter. In addition, every classroom teacher at St. James Elementary has had the opportunity to board the Long Island Railroad and head in to New York City to spend a day with teachers and students at the Manhattan New School. There, we have seen many of the authors whose books grace the shelves of our professional library. But rather than seeing them as authors, we were seeing them as classroom teachers—the same as all of us, doing what they love best. Our administrators took this to the next level and arranged for Judy Davis, a now-retired fifth-grade teacher from the Manhattan New School and coauthor of *The No-Nonsense Guide to Teaching Writing* (2003), to come to Smithtown to provide professional development to all intermediate-grade teachers.

We were steadily building upon our knowledge of writing instruction and thus recognized the need to acquire the materials necessary to run a successful writers' workshop. Foremost among these materials would be books. In our capacity as reading teachers, we are constantly sought out by classroom teachers looking for book suggestions. "Do you have a book I could use to teach onomatopoeia?" "How about one with a circular ending?" Questions such as these have become a regular part of our day.

Our teachers needed a collection of books that would serve as mentor texts. The collection needed to be readily accessible and comprehensive. We set upon the task of building such a collection. Our school library and classroom libraries have a wealth of children's literature. We began by dissecting the books we already had in an effort to identify the unique and meaningful techniques the authors used to tell their stories. That was a start. However, to build upon our collection we needed to research and purchase even more books to serve as mentor texts to our students. We spent hours thumbing through the tattered copies of some of our old favorites, as well as some of our more recent acquisitions.

Our next stop was the public library. We went to the public libraries in each of our hometowns and spent days sifting through the stacks looking for children's books that were cited as good mentor texts in professional books about writing instruction. Along the way, we discovered books that were not on any lists but were filled with examples of author's craft. How excited we became with each new discovery! We still laugh about a snowy afternoon we spent together in the Smithtown Public Library, unaware that a blizzard was raging outside until the librarian came over and politely asked us to leave so she could close the library and go home.

We also spent a great deal of time browsing through publishers' catalogs and visiting publishers' websites, always on the lookout for just the right books to complement our collection. The more time we spent in our search, the more we realized how much time and effort could be saved if teachers had access to an extensive bibliography of children's books that identified the elements of author's crafts contained within each book. From there, our idea grew into creating a comprehensive resource that included not only a bibliography but also descriptions of the craft elements with exemplar mentor texts to teach each author's craft, served up with easy-to-implement craft studies. And so here it is, and here we are. This book is our attempt to help you, elementary-grade teachers, to give your students a most precious gift—books and authors to use as models for their own writing. How rewarding it is when our students can listen to a well-written story, identify the author's craft, and say, "I can write like that!"

The Importance of Establishing a Philosophy of Writing

The starting point for any teacher of writing is to understand one's own philosophy of writing. Our mentor in this journey of self-reflection was Lucy Calkins. In her book *The Art of Teaching Writing* (1994), Calkins eloquently writes:

> as human beings we write to communicate, plan, petition, remember, announce, list, imagine...but above all, we write to hold our lives in our hands and to make something of them. There is no plot line in the bewildering complexity of our lives but that which we make for ourselves. Writing allows us to turn the chaos into something beautiful, to frame selected moments, to uncover and celebrate the organizing patterns of our existence. (p. 8)

This statement summarizes our belief in the importance of written expression.

For us, the framework that supports this philosophy is the writers' workshop. As Fletcher and Portalupi (2001) state,

> The writing workshop does not place the teacher under the bright lights on center stage. Rather, the teacher sets up the structure, allows students plenty of choice, and gets [students] writing. You work off the energy students create. (p. 3)

Reading and writing instruction in our school district is structured through a balanced literacy approach. The readers' workshop and writers' workshop power this instruction and support the gradual release of responsibility from teacher to student that is at the heart of balanced literacy. To establish a unified foundation among our district's nine elementary schools, our central administration purchased *Units of Study for Primary Writing: A Yearlong Curriculum* (Calkins & The Teachers College Reading and Writing Project, 2003) for all primary teachers. For intermediate grade teachers, *The No-Nonsense Guide to Teaching Writing* (Davis & Hill, 2003) was purchased. Over the ensuing years, our teachers have built upon this foundation, learning from experience, from one another, and most of all, from the students.

There are also, however, unseen teachers at the heart of this instruction—the authors whose words line the shelves of our classroom libraries. In *Wondrous Words*, Ray (1999) has devoted an entire book to the importance of learning to write from writers. In her opening chapter, she writes, "Writing well involves learning to attend to the *craft* of writing, learning to do the sophisticated work of separating *what it's about* from *how it is written*" (p. 10). We believe there is no better way to accomplish this than to immerse ourselves and our students in the words of authors through the use of mentor texts within the writers' workshop. Fletcher and Portalupi (1998) sum up this idea beautifully: "The writing you get out of your students can only be as good as the classroom literature that surrounds and sustains it" (p. 10). This is why a teacher's underlying knowledge of children's books and how they can serve as mentor texts is an essential element in becoming an effective teacher of writing.

Picture Books as Mentor Texts

In describing the importance of teaching students to write from writers, Ray (1999) states that "teaching students to do this is the instructional challenge faced by teachers who want to help students to write well" (p. 11). Our experience has shown us that a further challenge faced by teachers is finding just the right books to support this instruction. Although we have attempted to compile a comprehensive bibliography of titles to address this challenge, it is important to note that we do not claim it to be an all-inclusive list. It's important to note, too, that although we have included only picture books, we do not intend to imply that children's novels, newspapers, magazines, brochures, and so forth should not be used as mentor texts. These are invaluable models of outstanding writing. They can and *should* be used for writing instruction, particularly in the intermediate grades. However, picture books, by their very nature, are shorter, usually just 30 or so pages. It is easier to show students what an author is doing when the format is simple. And so, picture books have become our tools of the trade.

There are countless exemplary children's picture books. No list can encompass them all. There are picture books that tell wonderful stories with meaningful messages that make great read-alouds, but may not lend themselves to writing instruction. Those titles are not included here. Libraries are filled with picture books noted for their illustrations (many with a Caldecott designation to prove it). Although we appreciate beautiful artwork, we believe that for the purpose of teaching children to write, the illustrations are secondary to the words. Thus, many of those titles are not included here. We selected books that we feel will make our students better writers, following Ray's guidance from *Wondrous Words* (1999):

> The bottom line for why I select the text is that I see something in *how that text is written* which would be useful for my students to also see. I see something about the text that holds potential for my students' learning. I am looking for texts that have something in them or about them that can add to my students' knowledge base of how to write well. (p. 188)

Although there is no template for selecting mentor texts, we did have some specific criteria that guided us through our particular selection process. We attempted to seek out a variety of multicultural literature. We attempted to select books whose characters and settings address the broad range of lifestyles experienced by children across the United States. We selected books that reach our youngest readers and books that will capture the interest of our more mature students. And finally, we attempted to select books that represent a balance of genres, including fiction, personal narrative, memoir, literary nonfiction, poetry, how-to books, letter writing, and journals or diaries. Most important, we selected books that we feel will make our students better writers.

We have included many authors whom you will find mentioned time and time again in books about writers' workshop. These are the authors who exemplify outstanding writing and serve as accessible models for our students. We, as teachers of writing, owe them a huge debt of gratitude. We also have included books and authors that may not be so well known, gems that we've discovered along the way that add sparkle to our library. Yet, we recognize that there are many others—authors and books that may be among your favorites—that we haven't had the good fortune to experience. So, although we hope the bibliography will serve as a useful tool, keep in mind that it is not exhaustive. Our hope is that you will use everything we have provided to further your own discovery of children's literature and its applications in the writers' workshop.

Teaching Author's Craft

Twenty-seven different craft elements are highlighted within this book. Before listing the individual elements, we would like to clarify our definition of *author's craft*. We believe that any purposeful and meaningful technique that an author uses to capture the reader's attention may be considered an element of craft. As you explore this book, you will find that our definition extends beyond the traditional literary devices and applies to works of both fiction and nonfiction.

We have purposely chosen only those craft elements that we feel are appropriate for elementary-age students. We believe that our students should be exposed to all of the 27 craft elements by the time they complete elementary school. They should be given ample opportunity to study these techniques and should have the opportunity to try them in their own writing. It is important to note that although all of the craft elements highlighted should be studied, some will be beyond the reach of certain students' abilities as writers. We do not want to discourage our young writers from trying out different writing styles and crafting techniques, but we also do not want to set them up for failure. Writing is a means of personal expression. There are many times that students need to complete an assigned writing lesson not of their choosing, but our goal as writing teachers is to expose them to the many crafting techniques available, encourage them to experiment, and show them how to incorporate the ones that work best for them as part of their repertoires. It is important to tread carefully in deciding when to push our students to experiment and when to leave the decision to them. To make those choices effectively, you must understand the crafts you are teaching and you must know your students as writers. We never want to create reluctant writers who are frustrated by unrealistic demands.

Among the literary devices in this book are several that you already know. Terms like *metaphor* and *simile*, as well as others like *onomatopoeia*, *alliteration*, and *personification* are universally recognized. For this reason, we choose to teach our students the accepted terminology. In other cases, authors and publishers use techniques or styles (such as the layout of the print on a page or the choice of font) that may not have established names but which, nevertheless, should be deemed as craft. For the purpose of consistency, we have assigned names to these craft elements. You and your class may choose to name these elements for yourselves as the students discover them in the authors' works. For example, what we refer to as *Wordplay* has been called *Mixed-Up Language* by a third-grade class in our building. We have used the term *Breaking the Rules* to encompass several different techniques that contradict accepted rules of grammar but which are often used by authors to create a particular effect.

Use terminology that works best for your students, but bear in mind the importance of a consistent instructional vocabulary that your students will use year after year with each grade's new teacher. Also keep in mind that our list is not intended to be all-inclusive. If you and your students discover a craft technique that we have not included, celebrate that discovery and add it to your list!

How to Make This Book Work for You

To help you navigate your way through this book and to help you decide how best to use it to suit your specific instructional needs, the remainder of this Introduction provides a brief synopsis of all the tools and resources available to you in this book, as well as our ideas for how you can use them. We hope you will come to view this book as an essential resource for your writers' workshop and turn to it when seeking to accomplish the following:

- To build a library of mentor texts
- To uncover all that you can teach from each book in your growing mentor library, whether it be from an old favorite or a new discovery

- To find the perfect mentor texts to teach specific craft elements
- To locate age-appropriate craft studies that support your writing curriculum and further serve as models as you develop craft studies of your own

Turn to Part 1 to get an overview of each craft element as well as to view the different craft techniques you might choose to teach within your writers' workshop. Part 1 describes each of the craft elements you'll find in this book, listed alphabetically. Included with each craft element is a definition, elaboration on its use by writers, and a list of four or five picture book titles that *exemplify* this craft. This is where you can turn to find the perfect book to serve as a mentor text for a particular craft. And if you are just starting out with writers' workshop, these are some books you might want to include as you begin to build your library.

When selecting the exemplar titles for each author's craft, we tried to include books that used a craft in a variety of ways. This necessitated omitting some exceptional texts to keep each list of exemplars to a reasonable length. Keep in mind that there are additional titles in the Annotated Bibliography that *you* might like to include as *your* exemplar mentor texts for any given craft.

In Part 2 we have included craft studies using some of our favorite mentor books. These craft studies are meant to provide guidance, not to serve as prescriptive teaching formats, so please feel free to adapt them to fit your writers' workshop. We have designed the craft studies following a consistent format that we hope will serve as an easy-to-follow model for future lessons you develop as you and your students expand your study of author's craft. Sprinkled throughout are examples of authentic writing from the students in our school. You also will find some suggestions for ways to celebrate your students' writing through publication and display.

And now we come to the heart of our book—the annotated bibliography—the seed from which this book has grown. The large charts and extensive bibliography that make up Part 3 are the culmination of many, many hours of study, research, and reading, and we hope they provide a quick guide that you can turn to time and again. Our goal is to help you find titles that serve well as mentor texts and to identify the craft elements that are contained within each book.

First you will find two charts. The first, organized alphabetically by title, allows you to choose a particular craft element and cross-check an alphabetical listing of titles wherein that craft can be found. This will serve as a handy tool when you have a particular picture book in mind and want to discover the craft elements that can be taught through it. The second, organized alphabetically by author, allows you to quickly find titles by a favorite writer. This second chart will prove useful when planning an author study or when selecting mentor authors. After the charts, you will find the bibliography to which you can turn for more detail about quality picture books with rich examples of author's craft.

We have taken the traditional idea of an annotated bibliography a step further to provide information that will be useful to you as you structure your writers' workshop: We have listed 150 picture books that exemplify numerous examples of author's craft, and we have provided you with a list of the craft elements that are contained within each book. For ease of navigation, all craft elements are listed alphabetically and not in order of importance or frequency of use within the book. When copyright permission allowed, we have provided examples of the craft from the book. These are representative examples and are not meant to include every example of an author's use of a particular craft.

You also will find a number of additional resources in the appendixes of this book. The five reproducible recording sheets included in Appendix A will serve as models as you design the Explore phase of your craft studies. Photocopy them for your students or use them as models for your own recording sheets. Regardless of whether you use our sheets or ones that you design, we encourage you to complete a sample entry for your students to use as a model as they begin their research. Recording sheets are included for the following six crafts:

- Descriptive Language
- Hyperbole
- Lead
- Onomatopoeia
- Print Features and Print Layout

We've included two lists in Appendix B: Children's Books About Writing and Suggested Professional Readings. The Children's Books About Writing list provides you with titles of some of our favorite books that speak to young writers about the process of writing. Some of these titles are works of fiction, some are informational, some are autobiographical—but are all specifically written for young writers and give insight to the writing process. Student writers are often surprised to discover that professional authors experience many of the same stumbling blocks that they do. Understanding this serves as validation that writing can be hard and it also provides encouragement to young writers who may be experiencing frustration. Additionally, these books can be useful in reaching those students who *never* feel frustrated—the ones who dash off a piece of writing, think it is perfect as is, and refuse to go through the process of revision. Reading about the amount of time that authors devote to revision can be a humbling eye-opener for these reluctant revisionists. Enjoy sharing these books with all of your budding authors.

The Suggested Professional Readings list (in addition to the references cited within the pages of this book) reflect the professional resources we pull off our shelves time and again because of the wealth of information they impart about teaching students to write well. We hope this and all the other tools in this book will help you expand your own writers' workshop and help you in your efforts to nurture your student writers.

Finally, to get you excited about what you'll find in the remaining pages of this book, we thought it apropos to include a finished piece of student writing. The following poem, written by Sara, a third grader, reveals a child who has taken to heart her four years of writing instruction from Kindergarten through Grade 3. She has listened to poetry with a writer's ear and has learned to weave craft elements effectively into her writing. Enjoy…

The Sun

A blaring hot flare of light
Casting bright shadows
On the depths of Earth

A yellow-orange ball of fire
Rising in the sky
For a new day to shine in the morning

And sinking down for a rest at night
With colors that dawn in the evening air
Impeccable

Colorful streaks shine
Like carnival lights

It turns plain ordinary grass
Into rays of…
Shining pieces of sun!

PART 1

Craft Elements

Words are an author's tools and, like any good craftsman, an author chooses his or her tools with great care. As Fletcher and Portalupi (1998) put it, "craft is the cauldron in which the writing gets forged" (p. 3). There are many reasons why an author might choose a particular craft: to create a sensory image that invites the reader to see, hear, taste, smell, or feel; to find that perfect opener that will hook the reader and reel him or her into the pages of the book; to teach or impart factual information in an interesting way; to play with the visual appearance of the words to create a desired effect; or simply to combine words to create a pleasing sound or rousing rhythm.

The following is an alphabetical list of the author's craft elements that fill the pages of the picture books that we know and love. After each description of a craft element, we have listed our favorite books that exemplify that craft element. For purposes of brevity and accessibility, we have limited these lists of exemplary texts to no more than five, but in the annotated bibliography in Part 3, you will find many more quality picture books that you can use for each craft. You can use the chart in Appendix A, also, to match books and crafts. And of course you will find your own favorite books for each craft as you continue on your search for quality mentor texts.

ALLITERATION

Alliteration is the purposeful repetition of an initial sound—most often a consonant or a consonant cluster—in two or more words of a phrase in order to set a mood, to establish a rhythm, to capture the beauty of language, or simply to have fun.

Example: The sunlight sparkled and shimmered on the sandy shore.

Alliteration is all about sound. Students need to focus their attention not only on the meaning of the words, but, more important, on how the words sound.

Alliteration is one of those crafts we all know and love. Like simile and onomatopoeia, it's a craft we remember learning somewhere in our educational careers. Examples are plentiful. There are countless books that are devoted solely to alliteration and there are even more that incorporate a beautifully crafted alliterative line or phrase.

Although alliteration is one of the more familiar crafts, it is often underappreciated. Alliteration does not have to be heavy handed. At its best, alliteration is subtle and, quite simply, makes words more powerful by combining them with other words. Alliteration can be mellifluous or intense and oftentimes creates its aural effect without the reader even noticing how it was done.

Because alliteration is so closely linked to phonemic awareness, it is typically the first craft to which a student is introduced. Even our youngest authors can recognize this craft and have fun with it. As students grow as writers, they will experiment and grow in their use of alliteration. Students who have been having fun with alliteration and using it in playful ways since the primary grades need to take this craft to the next level. With effective modeling through mentor texts such as the following, you can guide your students to make the most of alliteration.

- *Ellsworth's Extraordinary Electric Ears: And Other Amazing Alphabet Anecdotes* by Valorie Fisher
- *H Is for Home Run: A Baseball Alphabet* by Brad Herzog
- *Journey Around Chicago From A to Z* by Martha Day Zschock
- *Some Smug Slug* by Pamela Duncan Edwards
- *Watch William Walk* by Ann Jonas

BREAKING THE RULES

Breaking the rules as a craft of writing constitutes any intentional misuse of sentence structure, grammar, or punctuation that contradicts traditionally accepted rules of grammar.

Example: And with a crack of the bat the 12-inning game came to an end.

Breaking the rules: The very words send shivers up a teacher's spine. We spend countless hours teaching our students grammatical rules, proper sentence structure, and punctuation conventions. How, then, do we give them permission to break the rules? Nevertheless, we cannot ignore authors' regular use of this craft, nor can we ignore its effectiveness in many instances. Is it fair for us to deny this license to our aspiring writers?

Students should have a solid foundation in the conventions of written English before selectively shunning those conventions for stylistic reasons. Young writers need the maturity to understand their audience and purpose for writing. Although it is acceptable to make these stylistic choices in a piece of creative writing, it is not acceptable in most other forms. You, as the writing teacher, will know whether your students are ready to make these distinctions, and you will guide them to knowing when such rule breaking is appropriate. The following are some examples of books in which this craft is used to good effect.

- *Over and Over* by Charlotte Zolotow
- *The Snow Speaks* by Nancy White Carlstrom
- *When Marcus Moore Moved In* by Rebecca Bond
- *Where Once There Was a Wood* by Denise Fleming
- *the wonderful happens* by Cynthia Rylant

CIRCULAR ENDING

The structuring of a story wherein the action comes full circle so that the story ends up where it began.

Circular ending may be a misnomer to a degree, because books with circular endings actually have no ending. The very concept of a book ending up where it started gives a sense of infinity to the story because the whole idea is that it will happen again and again and again.

Like the other structural crafts covered in this book, such as cumulative text and see-saw pattern, the circular story is popular in books for very young readers. Students are able to recognize the circular pattern and understand the implication that the story will repeat.

Although students will find this structure easy to identify at a young age, they will need more experience with writing to craft their own circular piece. Students who are interested in structuring a piece of writing with a circular ending should be encouraged to give it a try, perhaps using some of the following as a model, but you may find this craft to be one that's not conducive to whole-class instruction.

- *Last Night at the Zoo* by Michael Garland
- *Parade* by Donald Crews
- *Psssst! It's Me...the Bogeyman* by Barbara Park
- *Puddles* by Jonathan London
- *Roller Coaster* by Marla Frazee

CUMULATIVE TEXT

Cumulative story structure is one wherein lines of text repeat and are built upon until the story reaches its end.

Because of its patterned predictability, this method of structuring a story is popular in songs and stories for preschoolers. It's a craft that is easily recognized by and often targeted toward our youngest learners, but don't let this fool you. Cumulative texts are not easily crafted.

It is important for students of writing to recognize this craft and study its different applications by various authors. As with circular endings, students who are interested in crafting a piece of cumulative text should be encouraged to do so, but it would be an unrealistic expectation to have your entire class working on cumulative stories at a young age. As writing instructors, we constantly must make decisions about which of the crafts that we study are within the reach of our students as writers. The following are some examples of cumulative texts.

- *Fishing in the Air* by Sharon Creech
- *Rain* by Manya Stojic
- *What's Up, What's Down?* by Lola M. Schaefer
- *The World That We Want* by Kim Michelle Toft

DESCRIPTIVE LANGUAGE

Descriptive language is the purposeful choice of words made by an author to bring images to life for the reader. The image may be created with a few

well-chosen words or through multiple well-crafted passages.

Example: The gently swaying burnished leaves cast an autumnal glow on the lake's quiet surface.

Descriptive language is a broad term that can range from a kindergartner's addition of a "color word" to describe something in his or her writing to an elaborate intertwining of multiple crafts that meld together to paint a picture in the reader's mind. Descriptive writing is often linked to sensory details as there is no surer way for a reader to connect to a piece of writing than to experience it through one or more of the five senses. The important thing to remember is that the ultimate goal for using descriptive language is to transport the reader into the piece of writing so that he or she can "live" the experience.

As your students become more sophisticated writers, you will want them to focus on different aspects of descriptive language. For example: How does an author use descriptive language to create the setting? How does an author use descriptive language to develop a character? To slow down a moment? To zoom-in on a detail? To "show" instead of "tell"? To create an effective lead? These are but a few of the many ways that this craft enriches our writing. Some examples of descriptive language can be found in the following texts.

- *Butternut Hollow Pond* by Brian J. Heinz
- *Come On, Rain!* by Karen Hesse
- *The Storm Book* by Charlotte Zolotow
- *Twilight Comes Twice* by Ralph Fletcher
- *White Snow, Bright Snow* by Alvin Tresselt

EFFECTIVE ENDING

Authors purposely select a style in which to craft the ending to a piece of writing to maximize the final impression on the reader.

How often we have heard someone say, "I really loved the book until the end. It was such a letdown!" The last words you read in a book are the ones you take with you. Your immediate reaction upon reading that last line and closing the book is what will prompt you either to recommend the book or forget it.

As we study the craft of effective endings it is important to make sure that our students understand that we are looking not only at *how* the story ends, but also at the unique and creative ways in which the author crafts his or her words. Effective endings and leads share similar opportunities for construction. A book can end with a question, an exclamation, or a line of dialogue. It can be a single word, a sentence fragment, or a long, breathless run-on. It can echo the title or a line that has appeared once, twice, or repeatedly throughout the book. It can end on a note of finality, or it can end with an ellipsis, allowing the reader to draw his or her own conclusions. It can even circle around so that the reader understands "this all will happen again."

As with all stylistic choices, modeling effective endings is essential if we want our young writers to become adept at this craft. Select books that demonstrate a variety of techniques, such as the following suggestions, and let these serve as your mentors. Encourage your students to recraft the endings to their pieces of writing in different styles and then share them with their peers to determine which ones work most effectively.

- *Bat Loves the Night* by Nicola Davies
- *Just Like Daddy* by Frank Asch
- *The Little Yellow Leaf* by Carin Berger
- *Rain* by Manya Stojic
- *Treasures of the Heart* by Alice Ann Miller

FLASHBACK

A flashback is an interruption in the continuity of a story to relate some earlier episode.

It is sometimes important to the story for the reader to be privy to background information. There are several ways for a writer to impart these necessary details. Most often, an author will simply provide the needed information through the narration or by having a character relate the details within the story's dialogue. But another extremely effective method is to allow the reader to go back in time and read through the historical content as it happened. This flashback technique of telling a story within a story can take many forms. Flashback can be used to supply a single incident from the past that's needed to tell the story in the present; it can be used in an alternating pattern wherein the story moves back and forth between the past and present; or it can be the dominant aspect of the story with the present action secondary.

Students need a certain degree of maturity to follow an author's transitions between past and present, especially when the transitions are seamless and subtle. It follows, therefore, that an even greater degree of maturity and a certain amount of writing experience are needed before a student can experiment with this craft effectively. A good place to begin is with personal narrative. If you feel you have a writer who is ready to try out this technique, suggest that he or she select a piece of personal narrative that might be more complete with some historical perspective and encourage that writer to craft a flashback scene. Study mentor texts such as those in the following list to discover ways to incorporate flashback within present-tense writing.

- *Aunt Flossie's Hats (and Crab Cakes Later)* by Elizabeth Fitzgerald Howard
- *Bigmama's* by Donald Crews
- *Dear Willie Rudd,* by Libba Moore Gray
- *Grandpa Loved* by Josephine Nobisso
- *Storm in the Night* by Mary Stolz

HYPERBOLE

Oftentimes linked to quantitative embellishment or idiomatic expressions, hyperbole is any purposeful use of exaggeration to emphasize a point or

create a desired effect. It is understood that the exaggeration is not intended to be taken literally.

Example: <u>I am so hungry I could eat a horse!</u>

It's always amazing to us as teachers that students who can recount vivid detailed stories about incidents in their lives can sit down with pencil in hand and have nothing to write about. It is up to us as teachers of writing to harness all that excitement in sharing an oral account and help to channel it into the written word. There are certain crafts that are particularly fun to play with and which lend themselves to teaching reluctant writers. Hyperbole is one of those crafts.

Children are prone to hyperbole in their everyday speech, so it is not a far reach for students to learn to incorporate this technique effectively into their writing. The use of hyperbole brings voice to a piece of writing. As our students capture the hyperbolic details of their spoken language we should show them how these same details can bring voice to their writing. Some good examples of hyperbole can be found in the following books.

- *Dear Mrs. LaRue: Letters From Obedience School* by Mark Teague
- *Dogs Rule!* by Daniel Kirk
- *Earrings!* by Judith Viorst
- *Someday* by Eileen Spinelli
- *Whoosh Went the Wind* by Sally Derby

INTERESTING FORMAT

Books are sometimes structured in nontraditional ways. An interesting format in children's picture books would encompass any means of telling a story that is not in traditional prose or poetic form.

Authors sometimes choose to tell a story in nonprose form. Most often, this alternate format is illustrated poetry; however there are many other unique and interesting designs through which an author can tell a story. Students love to discover and try out new and different ways to structure their narration. Some formats with which young writers can experience success include, but are not limited to, letters, journals, and diaries. Keep a chart in your classroom as your students discover the many unique and distinctive structures that authors use to tell their stories, such as those in the following books.

- *Dear Mrs. LaRue: Letters From Obedience School* by Mark Teague
- *Diamond Life* by Charles R. Smith, Jr.
- *Diary of a Worm* by Doreen Cronin
- *Journey Around Chicago From A to Z* by Martha Day Zschock
- *My Map Book* by Sara Fanelli

LEAD

The first line or lines of a book, when effectively crafted, can draw in the reader from the opening page.

Example: Crack! The bolt of lightning split the night sky as we huddled wide-eyed and trembling in our makeshift shelter.

There are those who would argue that writing an effective lead is the most important craft because it is the hook that draws the reader into the book. Of course, the truth is that even the greatest lead will not carry a poorly written book; however, a weak start can discourage a reader from moving forward to discover the writing that lies within.

Authors, recognizing the importance of crafting an effective lead, employ a variety of techniques to do so. A lead can be in the form of a question, an exclamation, or a line of dialogue. It can be a single word, a sentence fragment, or a run-on. It can incorporate another craft—onomatopoeia, alliteration, simile, metaphor, hyperbole. It can introduce a character, stage the setting, or establish the theme. It can echo the title or announce a line that will repeat throughout the book, sometimes reappearing as an effective ending. The possibilities are too numerous to list.

Students need plenty of opportunity to study the many ways that authors craft effective leads and then try them out in their own pieces of writing. The following texts might serve as good examples for this craft element.

- *Mud* by May Lyn Ray
- *Night Rabbits* by Lee Posey
- *Puddles* by Jonathan London
- *Shortcut* by Donald Crews
- *Walk On! A Guide for Babies of All Ages* by Marla Frazee

LISTS

A list is a series of related words, names, numbers, or other items that are arranged in order, one after the other, and used in writing to create an effect.

Example: The garden was a profusion of color with roses and zinnias and daisies and dahlias and petunias and salvia and lilies.

There are many ways for an author to create imagery. One of the lesser used but highly effective methods is to craft a list. Lists work to create vivid mental pictures, not through beautiful language, but through quantity. When a list is crafted effectively, whether it's a list of nouns (as in the example above), verbs, or adjectives, the string of words underscores the image that the author is creating.

Our youngest writers can craft simple lists to bring imagery to their writing. "I like toys" can become "I like jump ropes, dolls, coloring books, crayons, teddy bears, pogo sticks, and dress-up clothes." As students mature as writers they can study the many ways that authors use lists for effect. Students typically enjoy experimenting with this craft and find success in bringing imagery to their writing. Some examples of the use of lists can be found in the following suggested texts.

- *Out of the Ocean* by Debra Frasier
- *Over and Over* by Charlotte Zolotow
- *A Quiet Place* by Douglas Wood
- *Treasures of the Heart* by Alice Ann Miller
- *When the Sky Is Like Lace* by Elinor Lander Horwitz

METAPHOR

A metaphor is a direct or implied comparison of one thing to another without using the word <u>like</u> or <u>as</u> to evoke an image in the reader's mind.

Example: <u>After the storm, the road was a sheet of glass.</u>

Unlike the easily recognizable simile, its partner in the world of literary comparison, the metaphor is not so readily identified. When a *direct* metaphor is crafted, linking an object explicitly with its metaphor, it is easier to pick out than when the comparison is implied. With *implied* metaphor, the reader must use context to determine what the metaphor represents. Notice the difference:

- *The autumn leaves were a patchwork quilt draped across the hillside.* (direct)
- *A patchwork quilt was draped across the hillside.* (implied)

Because the use of metaphor is a sophisticated technique, it is best reserved for intermediate-grade students who have experience in recognizing and writing various craft elements. Younger students who are taught to recognize choices that an author makes will notice metaphors but are likely to see them as *descriptive language*. Generally, by the third or fourth grade, direct metaphors may be introduced with success. By the fifth and sixth grades, implied metaphors may become part of some students' writing repertoires. You, as the writing teacher, will make these instructional choices because you know your students best. The following books provide some good examples of metaphor use.

- *Come On, Rain!* by Karen Hesse
- *Creatures of Earth, Sea, and Sky* by Georgia Heard
- *Up North at the Cabin* by Marsha Wilson Chall
- *Water Music* by Jane Yolen
- *White Snow, Bright Snow* by Alvin Tresselt

ONOMATOPOEIA

Onomatopoeia—often referred to as <u>sound words</u>—brings sound to the page, allowing the reader to experience writing through yet another sense.

Example: <u>The pitter-patter of the rain on the roof and the whoosh of the wipers on the windshield created a hypnotic effect.</u>

An amusing anecdote from one of our teachers introduces this craft element perfectly: The teacher asked his students for a volunteer to explain *onomatopoeia* to the rest of the class. Without hesitation, one of the boys raised his hand and responded, "I'm not sure...but I think it's a kind of Mexican food!"

Onomatopoeia is the craft that's hard to spell, difficult to pronounce, and although sometimes confused with enchiladas and tortillas, it is easy to recognize and fun to use. Our world is filled with sound. Doesn't it make sense that our writing should be, as well? Visual images tap only one of the reader's five senses. An effective author will craft his or her writing to engage the other four as well. Onomatopoeia allows us to hear a story as well as see it.

As with alliteration, examples of onomatopoeia in children's picture books are numerous. Also as with alliteration, there are entire books dedicated to this craft. Students readily recognize onomatopoeia in an author's writing and experience early success when trying it on their own. Some good examples can be found in the following books.

- *Crocodile Listens* by April Pulley Sayre
- *The Listening Walk* by Paul Showers
- *Max Found Two Sticks* by Brian Pinkney
- *Snow Sounds* by David A. Johnson
- *Vroomaloom Zoom* by John Coy

PERSONIFICATION

Personification is the craft technique wherein a thing, quality, or idea is given human characteristics, emotions, or actions, thereby bringing it to life.

Example: <u>The wind whispered and danced through the leaves.</u>

The goal of an author is to craft words so that the reader connects with the writing. What better way to accomplish this than to give human qualities to an inanimate object, feature, or idea so that the reader identifies with the subject?

In the early grades, students can be taught this technique in its most basic form. As they become more experienced writers they can be taught to recognize and experiment with more subtle and nuanced examples of personification.

Guide your students to enjoy this craft as it *leaps* and *soars* off the pages of countless picture books, such as the following, on your shelves.

- *Atlantic* by G. Brian Karas
- *Gilberto and the Wind* by Marie Hall Ets
- *long night moon* by Cynthia Rylant
- *Mojave* by Diane Siebert
- *Twilight Comes Twice* by Ralph Fletcher

POINT OF VIEW

A book's narrator tells the story from a particular point of view. Sometimes authors allow the reader to see the world through unexpected eyes by choosing a nontraditional narrator, and thereby, presenting the story from a unique point of view.

Years ago, writing from a particular point of view was considered the height of creativity in students' writing. As the teaching of writing moved toward the writers' workshop structure with students keeping writers' notebooks, the genre of choice became personal narrative. There is good reason for this shift in that there is no subject so filled with writing possibilities as one's own life. Nevertheless, there is room for creative writing in the elementary curriculum. Frowning upon a student writing from the point of view of a pencil may have been giving short shrift to a craft with many opportunities for success.

There are crafts that inevitably seem to be linked. Point of view is a craft that is often linked with voice. It seems a natural connection—if a narrator is expressing his or her point of view, voice is bound to come through. When teaching students to write from the point of view of an animal, place, or thing, encourage them to find the subject's voice—to spend some time thinking as the subject before putting pencil to paper. There are countless picture books told from a unique point of view, some of which can be found in the following list. Many are light-hearted and fun to read, but others are powerful and beautifully crafted. Use them as models to help your students try out this craft in their writing.

- *Atlantic* by G. Brian Karas
- *Dear Mrs. LaRue: Letters From Obedience School* by Mark Teague
- *Diary of a Worm* by Doreen Cronin
- *Dirty Laundry Pile*: *Poems in Different Voices* selected by Paul B. Janeczko
- *Loki & Alex: Adventures of a Dog and His Best Friend* by Charles R. Smith, Jr.

PRINT FEATURES

Authors often manipulate the print to create a desired effect. Boldface print, a change of font size or color, use of italics, and variations in uppercase or lowercase letters all may be used for this purpose.

One of the more playful crafts that students enjoy learning about is an author's use of print features. The purposeful use of print features can be as simple as writing the word *green* in green ink or as creative as writing the word *terrified* in a spooky font or the word *tilt* in an italicized font. This versatile craft can be studied and applied by students in all grades. The following books contain good examples of different print features.

- *Crocodile Listens* by April Pulley Sayre
- *Diamond Life: Baseball Sights, Sounds, and Swings* by Charles R. Smith, Jr.
- *Freight Train* by Donald Crews
- *Psssst! It's Me...the Bogeyman* by Barbara Park
- *Vroomaloom Zoom* by John Coy

In addition to altering the font, authors sometimes choose purposeful and unique placement of the print on the page to create a particular effect.

Print features and print layout seem to go hand in hand. Equally important to how the text looks is where it appears on the page. Authors and illustrators make careful choices about print layout. The reasons for these choices are numerous and can affect the placement of a single word or determine the placement of the text on a page or multipage spread.

The effect is a visual one, such as when the print bends and stretches and takes on shapes to reflect the author's intended meaning or in the way a page of text is woven with the illustration to draw the reader's eye to different points on a page.

```
       l
   S      i
              d
                 i n g
```

Print layout also can be used to control the reader's pacing. In the following example the author forces the reader to slow down and pause on the word "flutter," bringing a poetic effect to a piece of prose:

White, sparkling snowflakes
   flutter
   to the snow-swept ground.

Print layout can be subtle, creating a desired effect on the mood of a piece of writing. A selection intended to convey a serious or somber subject would not likely have text scattered about the page in a playful way. It's important to impart to students that deciding how the text will lay out on the page is a conscious choice that an author makes. Students must use care when making these same choices in their own writing. Some good examples of print layout variations can be found in the following list.

- *Autumnblings* by Douglas Florian
- *Diamond Life: Baseball Sights, Sounds, and Swings* by Charles R. Smith, Jr.
- *Doodle Dandies: Poems That Take Shape* by J. Patrick Lewis
- *Earthdance* by Joanne Ryder
- *Roller Coaster* by Marla Frazee

PUNCTUATION

Punctuation is the system of standardized marks in writing to separate sentences or sentence elements to make the meaning clear.

Punctuation is much more than the definition above. Punctuation is not only the use of markers to separate words into sentences, clauses, or phrases. When an author intentionally uses punctuation to create a desired effect, the punctuation is no longer a tool, but a craft that breathes life into the words, as in the following example:

The cat ever so silently crept up behind the tiny bird...slowly...s-l-o-w-l-y...and then...the bird sensed his presence and flew off to freedom!

Punctuation is a tricky craft to teach to elementary-age students because we, as teachers, constantly work so hard to teach our students to use conventional punctuation in their writing. For this reason, it is important that students have a solid foundation in the rules of standard punctuation before teaching them to experiment with punctuation as a craft. Again, you are the best judge of your students' readiness to play with punctuation. You may find the examples in the following books to be good models for those students who are ready.

- *All You Need for a Snowman* by Alice Schertle
- *Earrings!* by Judith Viorst
- *Journey Around Chicago From A to Z* by Martha Day Zschock
- *The Little House* by Virginia Lee Burton
- *Roller Coaster* by Marla Frazee

REPETITION

Repetition is the purposeful recurrence of a word, phrase, or line to create a desired effect.

Example: <u>The rain soaked the trees, soaked the flowers, soaked the streets, and soaked me to the bone!</u>

An author might choose to use repetition for a variety of reasons: for emphasizing something, for creating rhythm, for building an emotional connection between the reader and the text, or for tying the story together with a common thread. There are a number of ways that this can be accomplished. The author may repeat a single word in succession (e.g., *the dark dark night*); use a single word that repeats in a sentence but not in succession (e.g., *She ran past the big oak tree, past the red barn, past the old tire swing*); or employ a single word that repeats in several sentences (e.g., *Tigers snarl. Tigers stalk. Tigers pounce*).

An author also might choose to repeat a phrase or entire sentence. The repeating line may be found interspersed randomly throughout the text; in a set pattern, such as at the start of each page; or even simply, as the opening and closing line of a story. The following books provide examples of the use of repetition.

- *Earrings!* by Judith Viorst
- *Just Like Daddy* by Frank Asch
- *Over and Over* by Charlotte Zolotow
- *Snow Is Falling* by Franklyn M. Branley
- *Welcome to the Green House* by Jane Yolen

RHYME

Rhyme is the correspondence of terminal sounds of words or of lines of verse.

Example: The snowfall paints

A peaceful scene

While on my windowsill

I lean

Any of us who has taken an undergraduate poetry class will recall terms like *iambic pentameter* and *trochee* and *dactyl* that kept our heads spinning. For the purposes of this book, we will view the craft of rhyme (and its accompanying rhythm) in a much simpler light. Rhyme, like alliteration, is associated with phonemic awareness and, therefore, is one of the earliest instructional tools. It is no coincidence that preschool, kindergarten, and first-grade teachers fill their days with poems and songs to promote language development in their students. Young students enjoy the rhythmic pattern of rhyming verse long before they understand the concept. Likewise, they can recognize rhyme before they are able to generate it.

And so it is with rhyme as an author's craft. Many children's picture books are written in a variety of rhyme schemes because picture books are meant to be read aloud. There are books that are written entirely in verse, books that are written with occasional lines of verse, and books that incorporate internal rhyme by pairing rhyming words. Elementary school students should be given plenty of opportunity to study rhyme as an author's craft. What is the rhyming pattern? What is its effect on the book? Is it playful, serious, or simply lovely language that delights the ear? Why might the author have chosen to use this particular craft for this particular book? Would the book have lost something if it were written in straight prose? How does the use of rhyme in one book compare with the use of rhyme in others? These are the questions we want our young writers to be asking.

Teaching students to rhyme as a means of creating phonemic awareness is an important instructional tool for learning to read. Teaching students to write in verse is an entirely different matter and is an unrealistic goal for many young writers (or adult writers, for that matter). When students are asked to write in verse, the result oftentimes is forced and unsuccessful. Even some of the most proficient writers in your classroom will find it daunting to craft rhyming verse. For this reason, as with some of the other more sophisticated crafts, we recommend that students learn this technique but try it in their own writing only if *they* chose to give it a whirl. As writing teachers, we should encourage students to consider rhyme as an option; however, it is one of those crafts that we feel works best when it is student initiated. Once a student decides to take the plunge, you should help that student develop the craft to his or her greatest potential. Good examples of rhyme can be found in the following books.

- *Bats at the Beach* by Brian Lies
- *Dogs Rule!* by Daniel Kirk
- *Farmer's Garden: Rhymes for Two Voices* by David L. Harrison
- *H Is for Home Run: A Baseball Alphabet* by Daniel Herzog
- *Mojave* by Diane Siebert

SEE-SAW PATTERN

A predictable pattern is created when an author structures a book so that there is a back-and-forth balance between portions of the text. This back-and-forth pattern is much like riding a see-saw.

When riding a see-saw there is a constant sense of expectation. When on the ground, one awaits the thrill of ascent and when at the top, the delight of descent. Books containing a see-saw pattern similarly create a sense of anticipation in the reader. It is this predictability that makes see-saw books popular as read-alouds for preschoolers. Young students readily recognize the pattern and enjoy using see-saw books as models for their own patterned writing. If given mentor texts that employ obvious use of this technique (such as those in the following list), our youngest writers demonstrate surprising success with this craft.

- *Grandad Bill's Song* by Jane Yolen
- *I Am the Dog I Am the Cat* by Donald Hall
- *Rosie and Michael* by Judith Viorst
- *Someday* by Eileen Spinelli
- *When I Was Little: A Four-Year-Old's Memoir of Her Youth* by Jamie Lee Curtis

SEQUENCING

When a book spans a finite period of time with the actions chronicled at explicit intervals, the author has used the craft of sequencing to relate a story.

All books have a sequence. There is a clear beginning, middle, and end. So when is a sequence unique? When does it become a craft?

When an author uses some established chronology as a means of sequencing a book, this unique format becomes the craft of sequencing. Any explicit chronology can serve as the thread that propels the story forward to its end—seconds, minutes, hours, days, weeks, months, years; dawn to dusk, morning to night, breakfast to dinner, summer to fall to winter to spring; the phases of the moon; the stages of a life—the possibilities are endless.

Sequences can be obvious or subtly woven into a story. Our youngest writers can craft a simple sequential piece, such as a personal narrative that spans the four seasons of the year. More mature and experienced writers can study the many creative ways that authors sequence texts and experiment with sequencing in their own writing. The following books provide some good examples of sequences.

- *Birthday Presents* by Cynthia Rylant
- *Dear Mrs. LaRue: Letters From Obedience School* by Mark Teague
- *The Little House* by Virginia Lee Burton
- *Sky Tree: Seeing Science Through Art* by Thomas Locker
- *When the Moon Is Full: A Lunar Year* by Penny Pollock

SIMILE

Simile is the craft technique in which an author compares one thing to another using the words <u>like</u> or <u>as</u> to evoke an image in the reader's mind.

Example: <u>He was as quiet as a mouse.</u>

Authors often use comparison as a means of evoking sensory images. Perhaps the most frequently used comparison is the simile. Simile is another one of those terms that rattles around in our brains from some long-ago high school English class. Many of us would have little difficulty providing an example, but how many of us actually have looked closely at authors' use of this familiar craft?

Similes can be simple or sophisticated. They can be obvious or subtle. They can make you grimace, make you laugh, or simply take your breath away. Because the simile is easily recognized by our youngest students, it is one of the earliest crafts to be introduced. Don't be discouraged if your students' first attempts are clumsy or inappropriate. Don't be surprised if your students tend to insert this newly discovered technique into every second sentence of their writing. These seem to be part of the natural developmental process of using similes. Guide your students toward effective use of this craft by providing the examples needed to take their use of similes to the next level, such as those found in the following books.

- *All the Colors of the Earth* by Sheila Hamanaka
- *All the Places to Love* by Patricia MacLachlan
- *Gentle Giant Octopus* by Karen Wallace
- *My Dog Is as Smelly as Dirty Socks: And Other Funny Family Portraits* by Hanoch Piven
- *Tigress* by Nick Dowson

TEXT FEATURES

Most often found in works of nonfiction, text features help the author to present information in an organized way. Text features may include such components as a table of contents, an index, diagrams, pictures with captions, headings, or a how-to page.

We tend to think of craft as being associated with narrative writing, but literary nonfiction is a popular genre for children's picture books. (It should be noted, however, that text features are not limited solely to informational books.) In addition to the more common examples cited in the definition above, there are many unique text features that authors employ. Oftentimes these text features are not found within the pages of the book but may be found on the endpapers inside the covers, on the title page, or on the copyright page.

Students in the intermediate grades enjoy experimenting with text features in their writing. Teachers who are constantly looking for ways to get it all in should seize the opportunity to combine content area curricula with reading and writing workshops. Allowing students the opportunity to write literary nonfiction that incorporates text features is an important use of writing workshop time that links well to social studies and science. Good examples of text features can be found in the following books.

- *Hairs/Pelitos* by Sandra Cisneros
- *Journey Around Chicago From A to Z* by Martha Day Zschock
- *Out of the Ocean* by Debra Frasier
- *The Pumpkin Book* by Gail Gibbons
- *Scoot!* by Cathryn Falwell

VERBS AND VERB FORMS

A verb is any word expressing action, existence, or occurrence and constitutes the main element of a sentence's predicate.

Example: <u>The skittering mouse scampered and scurried in an effort to avoid Farmer Tucker's broom.</u>

Teachers of grammar often follow the unwritten tenet: *Begin with the verb!* There is good reason for this instructional approach. The verb is the most easily identified part of speech and arguably the most important word in the sentence because it specifies the action. It is no surprise, then, that authors take great pains to craft the perfect verb or verb form when defining the action within their writing. Although the verb defines the action, verb forms can also bring action to other parts of speech. Infinitives and gerunds serve as nouns, while participles become action-packed adjectives.

Students need to be taught to distinguish among verbs, nouns, and adjectives. Once they have mastered this most basic foundation of sentence structure, they should be encouraged to expand their vocabulary to make their word choices more meaningful. Provide your students with plenty of opportunity to study the ways authors craft verbs and verb forms and then have them go back into their writing notebooks to beef up their verbs. A thesaurus is an excellent and underutilized resource for vocabulary expansion. Make a word wall of especially effective verbs and verb forms that students use successfully in their writing. The following texts provide good examples of the use of verbs.

- *Come On, Rain!* by Karen Hesse
- *Scoot!* by Cathryn Falwell
- *Twister* by Darleen Bailey Beard
- *Water Hole Waiting* by Jane and Christopher Kurtz
- *Whoosh Went the Wind* by Sally Derby

VOICE

An author's use of voice allows the reader to gain insight, through the words on the page, on the character's (and oftentimes, the author's) personality, thoughts, and feelings.

Many authors provide their characters with narration, but not all characters have voice. When an author gives voice to a character, that character comes alive. Have you ever watched someone reading silently when suddenly he or she begins to chuckle aloud? Chances are, the author was using voice to present something in an amusing way. Interestingly, a character's (or a writer's) voice comes from the written, not the spoken word. Unlike in plays, where the characters' words are meant to be interpreted and then acted out, in narrative writing the voice of the character must come through to the reader even if the words are never spoken aloud. This is no easy feat.

For this reason, voice is often considered a craft that's easy to recognize but hard to define and even harder to teach. Voice requires immersion before a student begins to have a clear understanding of what it's all about. Point out voice to your students as often as possible. Select books for your read-alouds that contain good examples of voice, such as those in the list that follows. It is through listening to you reading with appropriate expression and intonation that your students will learn to read with voice. Students must be able to read with voice before they can write with voice. A certain amount of maturity is needed before a student begins to find his or her own voice as a writer and then it takes a lot of practice before that voice can be conveyed through written words.

- *Earrings!* by Judith Viorst
- *Gila Monsters Meet You at the Airport* by Marjorie Weinman Sharmat
- *Psssst! It's Me...the Bogeyman* by Barbara Park
- *Walk On! A Guide for Babies of All Ages* by Marla Frazee
- *Whoosh Went the Wind* by Sally Derby

WORDPLAY

Wordplay is the subtle or clever creation of words, including puns. The derivation of the word is appropriate because it defines some essential feature of the thing being described.

Example: <u>The rollercoaster took a scalp-tingling, stomach-dropping, eyelid-scrunching plummet before coasting to a stop.</u>

As the term implies, authors sometimes play with words in order to craft new words and to create a desired effect. This might include a twist on the meaning, rhythm or rhyme, light-hearted fun, or a made-up word that perfectly captures a significant image. Another relatively sophisticated technique, wordplay can be used with surprising success by elementary school students if they are provided with ample opportunity to study its use in exemplar texts, such as the following:

- *Autumnblings* by Douglas Florian
- *My Mama Had a Dancing Heart* by Libba Moore Gray
- *Psssst! It's Me...the Bogeyman* by Barbara Park
- *This Place in the Snow* by Rebecca Bond

PART 2

Selected Craft Study Lessons

Whatever craft an author chooses, there is one constant: The choice is purposeful and precise. Laminack (2007) writes,

> Craft is the intentional use of techniques—including word choice, imagery, sound, rhythm, cadence, the placement of words on the page, use of white space—to create a desired impact upon the reader and to evoke a response from the reader. It is important to note that writers use craft with care. It isn't done randomly or without thought. (p. 17)

In the sampling of craft studies that follow, we will share with you lessons that are designed to impart this understanding to your students. Although each lesson is targeted to a specific age range, we hope you will find them all valuable regardless of the grade level you teach. Each concludes with some suggestions for ways to adapt the lessons for students of various grades and levels of writing experience. Some lessons are directed toward our youngest writers, and others are developmentally appropriate for older children only. We have attempted to make these distinctions clear. When we use the designation *primary* we are referring to students in grades K–2. Intermediate students are those in grades 3–6. We hope that the format and samples provided will help you in developing your own craft studies.

Remember that the goal of any craft study in your writing workshop is to empower your students to experiment with different styles, techniques, and craft elements to become better writers. Some of you are in schools where children have been studying craft since kindergarten and have reached a level of sophistication in their writing. We recognize that your study of craft may be incorporated within genre studies rather than as craft studies in isolation. Feel free to pick and choose whatever portions of our lessons best suit your needs.

A list of *suggested* mentor texts accompanies each sample craft study found in this section. The books are listed in alphabetical order, not in order of importance, nor in the order in which they are referenced in the craft study. For some of the craft studies, any or all of the books listed can be used regardless of your students' level of proficiency with a specific craft. For other craft studies we felt it was important to distinguish between books that would be appropriate at each level: writers who are new to the craft and writers who are familiar with the craft. We hope that you will find several lessons that meet your needs. Please also consider other books from the Annotated Bibliography in Part 3, as well as ones you discover on your own.

We have designed these craft study lessons to span several days. We want you to pace your study according to your own students and their needs, so we purposely have not structured the lessons day by day. In other words, some craft studies may be accomplished in a few days; others may span a week or more. Adapt these lessons to fit your personal teaching style. The important thing is that students have the opportunity to experience and recognize well-crafted writing, discover what the author is doing that makes the writing good, explore additional examples, and then try the craft on their own.

For the sake of clarity and consistency, we have organized each craft study lesson into the following distinct parts, which we will explain in detail:

- Notice and Name
- Explore
- Give It a Try
- Celebration
- Adaptations

Notice and Name

It is always more meaningful for students to have ownership in their learning. This makes Notice and Name a significant step in their ultimate understanding of the craft. In this part of the study, students have the opportunity to hear a particular craft, notice what the author is doing, and name it. The *teacher* plays the key role in the success of this investigation through the careful selection of mentor texts.

In choosing the appropriate mentor texts, it is important to be mindful of the lesson's focus and clear as to the objective. Once you have established your vision, you're on your way. First you'll select the books from which you plan to model the craft and mark the excerpts for quick reference. Then, gather the students and explain that you will be reading some examples of great writing. Explain whether you will be reading the entire book or only parts. Invite students to listen carefully with their writers' ears to notice what common techniques the authors have used in their writing. Finally, once the students understand what the authors are doing, name the craft. If you prefer, you can allow students to come up with a name for the craft on their own.

Explore

At this point in the study, it is crucial for the students to be immersed in the craft. The purpose of this phase is for the students to acquire a deeper understanding of the craft. Why does the author choose this particular craft for this particular place in the book?

Allow students time to do their exploration. Good research takes time. Students should not speed through this process. Lots of practice with this type of exercise will encourage students to do slow and careful research to find the best examples. Depending on the age and chemistry of the students, as well as on their experience in researching mentor texts, determine how many sessions of your Writing Workshop you wish to devote to this phase of the study. Exploration can be done in different ways. The age of your students, as well as their experience with craft study, will guide you in deciding which method is most appropriate.

One suggestion is to use your daily read-aloud time. Read books that contain examples of the craft. Once again, a clear objective is essential: Know what you want your students to achieve and provide them with rich examples to steer them toward that goal. A good starting place is with the books you've already introduced during Notice and Name. Students should have the chance to hear the books in their entirety (perhaps more than once) to think about the authors' crafting decisions. Discuss the authors' use of craft and record the class findings on a chart.

If your students are more proficient readers, you can share this exploration with them. Model how you would go about searching for and charting examples of the craft. Then give them the opportunity to pore through books, reading like writers. Assemble baskets of books that demonstrate the craft. Students can work in pairs or small groups depending on the structure of your writing workshop and on the number of mentor texts available for this exploration. Students should look for examples of the craft and then consider the authors' crafting decisions. In Appendix B, we have provided suggested recording sheets on which students can chart their findings. Provide time to share what the students have discovered.

In addition, encourage students to notice examples of the craft in their independent reading. Celebrate those discoveries as a class.

Give It a Try

Be mindful that the ultimate goal of craft study is for students to internalize the craft and incorporate it effectively into their *own* writing. This does not happen quickly. Set your expectations based on the age and experience of your student writers.

For our youngest or least experienced writers, the craft is best practiced in isolation. Depending on the craft element and the make-up of the class, a realistic goal for these young writers might be to simply recognize what the author is doing. We can guide our more experienced writers to find places in their writing where they can incorporate a particular craft, while our most sophisticated writers will adopt several crafts as their own and will work them into their writing with fluidity and intention. Regardless of where your student writers are on this continuum, it is your responsibility as a teacher of writing to continually assess your students and provide explicit and meaningful instruction that will challenge them to take their writing to the next level.

Celebration

Authors write for a purpose and for an audience. This should be the case for your student authors, as well. Although not every piece of writing will go to publication, there should be some forum in which the students' writing is celebrated. This could be as simple as reading a well-crafted line to the class or as big an event as inviting parents to an authors' tea to hear their students' published books. At the end of each craft study presented in this chapter, we have included a suggestion for celebration.

Adaptations

For the sake of balance, some craft studies are targeted to students who are new to a particular craft while others are geared toward those who have some familiarity with the craft. In either case, we offer adaptations to take the study either up or down a level so that you will have options from which to choose, regardless of your students' grade or level of proficiency.

We hope you will find the ideas on the following pages to be both effective and practical and that the examples of authentic students' writing included within the studies will bring a smile to your face and show you what is possible, even from the youngest writers.

As teachers we want to empower our students with the ability to integrate higher-level thinking and inquiry into their writing. Although we provide ideas for teacher-directed craft studies and celebrations, we must emphasize the importance of limiting the use of these types of activities as students mature as writers. Instead, provide plenty of opportunity for them to generate their own topics for research and discovery while you confer with and guide them through the process of stylized writing.

ALLITERATION

Suggested Grade Levels: 1–2

Students need to be immersed in a craft to recognize its existence within a piece of writing as well as the author's purpose for using it. Is every string of words that begins with the same sound an example of alliteration, or is purposeful alliteration something more? Can a student recognize that the phrase *"the bee buzzed around my head"* does not necessarily qualify as purposeful use of alliteration but that the following phrases from some of our favorite mentor texts are clearly purposeful? These alliterative phrases create a visual image as well as an aural effect that is unmistakable:

> Lightning licking the navy-blue sky (*Storm in the Night,* by Mary Stolz)
>
> Tide that tickles with splashing spray, squishy, sandy, soggy ground, slippery seaweed that wraps around (*Hello Ocean,* by Pam Muñoz Ryan)

First graders at St. James Elementary use their own names to come up with alliterative sentences. Kevin in Christy Petruzzelli's class wrote, "Kevin was a king carrying kittens to the kitten store, and carrying kangaroos too!" Ally, a third grader, had a more subtle touch with her alliterative metaphor: "A giant white ball bounces into space every starlit night and adds a special glowing touch to the weary world." And consider it all a success when you have a fifth grader who writes, "My piano plays tunes that will make your sweet soul sing."

You can create many lessons to encourage students to deepen their understanding of this craft. As students discover the nuances of alliteration, you must create plenty of opportunities for them to go back into their writing and find places to use this craft in different ways. In one piece the student may want to be obvious and heavy-handed; in another, he or she may want to be subtle with a light touch. This is how we learn to write.

MENTOR TEXTS

For Writers New to This Craft

Clara Caterpillar by Pamela Duncan Edwards

Ellsworth's Extraordinary Electric Ears: And Other Amazing Alphabet Anecdotes by Valorie Fisher

Four Famished Foxes and Fosdyke by Pamela Duncan Edwards

Potluck by Anne Shelby

Some Smug Slug by Pamela Duncan Edwards

The Wacky Wedding by Pamela Duncan Edwards

Walter Was Worried by Laura Vaccaro Seeger

Watch William Walk by Ann Jonas

Willie's Word World by Don L. Curry

The Worrywarts by Pamela Duncan Edwards

For Writers Familiar With This Craft

H Is for Home Run: A Baseball Alphabet by Brad Herzog

Journey Around Chicago From A to Z by Martha Day Zschock

A Swim Through the Sea by Kristin Joy Pratt

Note: *H Is for Home Run* is published by Sleeping Bear Press as part of an entire series of alphabet books on a variety of topics. *Journey Around Chicago From A to Z* is published by Commonwealth Editions and is part of a series of alphabet books that highlight U.S. cities. All of these books would be excellent resources for this craft study.

Notice and Name for Writers New to This Craft

Gather your students on the carpet and explain that you are going to read them a book titled *Potluck* by Anne Shelby. Unfortunately this book is out of print, but is a popular book that can be found in many school and public libraries. (*Willie's Word World* by Don L. Curry is a good substitute if you cannot get your hands on a copy of *Potluck. Ellsworth's Extraordinary Electric Ears* by Valorie Fisher works well for this lesson, also.) Ask the students to listen very carefully and describe what they notice about the book.

Read the book aloud, sharing the illustrations. Encourage students to share what they notice. Anticipate that some may notice that the book goes in ABC order; some will notice that it's a book about children's names. You will likely have some who will catch onto the fact that each child in the story brings a type of food that begins with the same letter as the initial letter in his or her name. If no students in the class point out these things, go back and reread, enunciating each beginning sound as you point to the words.

Once the students understand what the author is doing, name the craft and tell them that over the next few days they will have the chance to use alliteration with their own names.

Explore

During your next writers' workshop, once again gather your students on the carpet. Reread *Potluck* and review the craft of alliteration. Then ask the students for names of family members or friends. (It's important that you don't use the name of any student in the class during this part of the lesson.) Write the names on chart paper or an interactive whiteboard so that students can see the beginning letter.

Select one of the names. As a class, develop an alliterative sentence. You will need to facilitate your students' thinking and prompt them to keep building on the sentence. For example, if the class says, "Lisa ate a lollipop" guide them to find a new word for *ate* that begins with the letter *L*. You might then encourage them to describe the lollipop. You may end up with something like this: "Lisa licked a luscious lemon lollipop." Do several of these as a class.

Give It a Try

It is now time for the students to apply this technique on their own. Explain that you will be creating a class book just like *Potluck*, the book that Shelby wrote. Send each student back to his or her seat with a sheet of white drawing paper and crayons. Each student should begin working on a self-portrait. Stress that they will be the illustrators for your class book so it is important to take their time and do their best drawing. Encourage them to think about words that begin with the same letters as their names. Spend time conferring with each student. Some will need more support than others. Provide as much support as necessary, leading the student toward a level of alliterative sophistication you think appropriate for the individual. Students should record their sentences with their self-portraits.

Devin, a first grader in Mrs. Petruzzelli's class, created a playful image with "Devin's dog danced all day!" And Christopher in Kim Chacon's class came up with an alliterative sentence that would make a great lead: "Christopher was confused when a cricket cancelled Christmas!"

Celebration

When all students are finished, invite each to come up before the group to display his or her drawing and read the alliteration. Encourage students to listen and check to see if the words begin with the same sound as the name. Applaud each author's use of craft.

Design a cover, laminate and bind the book, and add it to your classroom library. It will be a guaranteed favorite for your students to pull during readers' workshop!

Adaptations

For Writers New to This Craft

A slightly more simplified version of this lesson for kindergartners or early first graders asks students to use what they have learned about alliteration to pair either alliterative adjectives or alliterative verbs with their names. Choose whichever you think will be easier for your students to do. Follow the lesson described above, but in this simplified format. Once a student has decided on his or her adjective or verb, write the word at the top of the self-portrait and then draw a line on which the student will write his or her name. For students who are not developmentally ready to take on this task, provide three alliterative adjectives or verbs and allow him or her to choose. If you choose to use adjectives, your pages might read something like this: *Beautiful Brianna! Diving Dylan! Exciting Emily!*

Jumpy John! If you choose to use verbs, your pages might read as follows: *Christopher climbs! Jason jumps! Rebecca runs! Sarah sings!*

For Writers Familiar With This Craft

Don't rule out alphabet books for intermediate-grade students. Alphabet books provide the perfect opportunity to combine alliteration with informational research projects and report writing. First give students several days to study books in which authors have combined research of factual topics with the craft of alliteration to create alphabet books for older children or adults. The alphabet books that will serve as the mentor texts for this lesson are better enjoyed and analyzed with a partner, so we suggest students work with a writing partner. Have students chart their findings. (A word of caution as you are selecting mentor texts for this lesson: There are many alphabet books that are written around factual topics, but not all of them include alliteration.)

The ultimate objective is to have your students make a class book that is modeled after the mentor texts they've been researching—an alphabet book that revolves around a single topic. Begin by selecting a broad topic that ties in with your science or social studies curriculum. When choosing to do a structured writing project like the one suggested here, you will need to employ considerable teacher direction in order for the study to run smoothly. We strongly recommend that you determine not only the topic but also the subjects within the topic (one for each letter of the alphabet). Students will need time to research their topics. They then will combine the factual information they have compiled, along with their study of the craft, in order to create a work of literary non-fiction. Remember, your goal is to move your students toward independence in the use of this craft by having them consistently return to their writing to incorporate newly learned techniques or to refine their use of already known craft elements. A thesaurus is an invaluable tool for helping intermediate-grade students find alliterative words to describe their topics. Mark Jaklitsch's fifth-grade students at St. James Elementary created beautiful pages for an alphabet book on rainforest animals. If you choose to try out the lesson we've described for taking alliteration to the next level, the pages of your published book might look something like the example in Figure 1.

FIGURE 1. Intermediate-Grade Alphabet Book

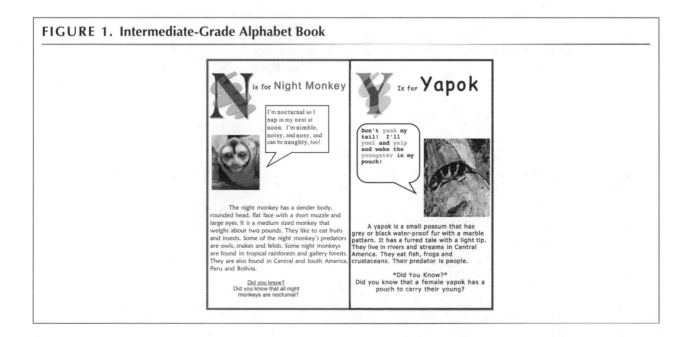

DESCRIPTIVE LANGUAGE

Suggested Grade Levels: 3–6

A quality of good writing lies in the author's ability to *show* important story elements such as feelings, setting, and mood rather than to *tell* the reader explicitly. For example, instead of writing, "The boy felt nervous," an author might write, "His face turned pale. He felt his stomach churn, his body trembled, and he felt a bead of perspiration trickle down his face." How boring writing would be if authors did not use this technique to engage us as readers and allow us to be swept away by their words!

Notice and Name for Writers Familiar With This Craft

Gather your students on the carpet. Remind them that you have been focusing a lot on how authors use descriptive language to paint a picture in the reader's mind. Explain that today you are going to show them a special way that authors use descriptive language by reading some authors' writing about the seasons of the year. Go on to explain that you will not be reading the books in their entirety, but only parts. Ask them to listen carefully with their writers' ears to determine the season about which the author is writing.

Read the following excerpts one season at a time (without sharing the title), allowing students to guess the season after you have read both excerpts for that season.

MENTOR TEXTS FOR ALL YOUNG WRITERS

Butternut Hollow Pond by Brian J. Heinz

Candy Corn by James Stevenson

Fireflies by Julie Brinckloe

Grandpa Loved by Josephine Nobisso

Hello, Harvest Moon by Ralph Fletcher

In November by Cynthia Rylant

The Little House by Virginia Lee Burton

The Lonely Scarecrow by Tim Preston

Sky Tree: Seeing Science Through Art by Thomas Locker

The Snow Speaks by Nancy White Carlstrom

Summersaults by Douglas Florian

Sun Dance Water Dance by Jonathan London

When the Fireflies Come by Jonathan London

White Snow, Bright Snow by Alvin Tresselt

Winter: An Alphabet Acrostic by Steven Schnur

Summer

When the Fireflies Come by Jonathan London

The *thong-thong* of backyard badminton.
The *slap-slap* of bare feet on the blacktop
Bird chirp and bee buzz.
The *woof-woof* of a big dog at our heels.
Ching-a-ling. Ching-a-ling.
"Here comes the Ice Cream Man!" I shout.

Summersaults by Douglas Florian

Skipping stones
Ice cream cones
Double plays
And barefoot days.

Fall

Sky Tree: Seeing Science Through Art by Thomas Locker

The leaves of the tree
turned gold, orange, and
red. Squirrels hurried to
store nuts and
acorns.

Hello, Harvest Moon by Ralph Fletcher

The crops have been gathered.
The pumpkins have been picked.
The silos are filled to bursting
with a million ears of corn.
Tired farmers are fast asleep.

Winter

Winter: An Alphabet Acrostic by Steven Schnur

Just as the
Evening lights come on,
White flakes begin falling
Earthward, glittering
Like diamonds.

The Snow Speaks by Nancy White Carlstrom

When words freeze
in the thin, brittle air
and nostrils stick together,
The snow speaks
in squeaks and crunches
under the children's feet.
Cold Cold Cold

Spring

The Little House by Virginia Lee Burton

when the days grew longer
and the sun warmer,
she waited for the first robin
to return from the South.

Candy Corn by James Stevenson

It's a friendly time of year—
Soft air, and lilacs bending
Low enough to sniff.
Even the beech tree
Has sent a branch
To pay a visit to my porch.

The students will quickly recognize the four seasons from these excerpts. It is important that you guide them toward an awareness of how the author never names the season. Ask the students to identify particular words or phrases that helped them recognize the season. Explain that writing is much more interesting when an author *shows* the reader a subject rather than just *tells* the reader.

Explore

Students should work in pairs or small groups, depending on the structure of your writers' workshop and on the number of mentor texts available for this exercise.

First, assemble baskets of books that demonstrate the concept of Show—Don't Tell in describing the seasons of the year. The books listed in the Mentor Texts box are just a few good choices. Instruct students to look through the books to find places where the author describes a season without actually naming it. In Appendix B, we have provided a reproducible recording sheet on which students can chart their findings. Walk around the room and confer with the various research teams throughout the search.

Once students have completed their research, assemble the class and allow time for them to share their findings. Again, it is up to you to decide how many examples will be shared with the entire class. The format should be the same as your initial read-alouds, wherein the selected students will read the excerpt aloud and the others will determine the season being described.

Give It a Try

It is now time for the students to apply this technique. Before they incorporate it into their own writing, it is best to practice this craft in isolation. Tell the students that it is now their turn to Show—Don't Tell. Instead of describing the weather or seasons of the year, the students will use the technique to describe a time of day.

Select *just one* book that demonstrates this imagery. Keep the example short and specific so that children feel confident that the task is not out of their reach. One good such example is from *Butternut Hollow Pond* by Brian Heinz. When describing the night, Heinz writes:

The water shimmers under moonglow, and wisps of fog
dance over the pond like ghosts.

Now, on a piece of chart paper or on an interactive whiteboard, brainstorm with your students a list of possible times of day that might be described. Your list might include:

- Morning
- Sunrise
- Dawn
- Afternoon
- Noon

- Evening
- Sunset
- Twilight
- Night
- Midnight

Students can work independently or with partners and write in their writer's notebooks about specific times of day they would like to convey. The students should then use descriptive language to show the times they have chosen. The trick? The student cannot use the specific time of day in the description. Explain that these descriptive images will be available to incorporate into future writing pieces.

Confer with students throughout this process.

Celebration

Helping students to become effective critics of their own writing, as well as the writing of their peers, is a constant goal of the Writing Workshop. Have each student or group select their three favorite examples from their lists. The class should then discuss and critique the examples and decide, as a class, which example from each writer or writing partnership should be included in the celebration.

Create a "Guess What Time of Day?" bulletin board display outside your classroom. Make it an interactive guessing game so that passersby will be drawn to read and be dazzled by your students' writing. Decorate with clocks, roosters, suns, stars, moons, and so on. Here's how:

- Give each writer or writing partnership two pieces of paper.
- On the first sheet, the writer(s) should write the beautifully crafted image.
- The second sheet will serve as the answer sheet and should state the time of day being described and should include a colorful illustration to accompany the image.
- Staple the first sheet to the top of the second sheet so it can be flipped up for the answer. Hang on the themed bulletin board for all to admire and play along.

Adaptations for Writers New to This Craft

For younger students who are not yet able to explore the books on their own, you can modify the lesson as follows. For several days during the daily read-aloud, select books that demonstrate this craft element by showing the season of the year. Invite students to listen with a writer's ear to identify the craft and the season being described. Create a chart with three columns—Title, Author, Season—and as a class, record the information.

This chart will serve two purposes. It introduces students to the research process and it also serves as a reference. Students who are able to read the books independently may use the chart as they revisit the books. For the students who are not yet able to read on their own, you can use the chart as a reference model while revisiting the texts with the students. If you feel that your younger writers are able to imitate this craft, by all means, allow them to experiment. Some of our second graders gave it a try; Robin Baker's second graders at St. James Elementary School wrote:

Morning: *The sun is gradually rising like a beautiful ballerina all orange and red.*

Sunset: *The sun slowly floating to the ground like a paper airplane.*

Noon: *The sun like a hot air balloon floating in the big, beautiful blue sky.*

Evening: *While the sun goes down, the light fades into the dark sky.*

Night: *You can almost see the man in the moon wearing a tuxedo and playing the guitar.*

HYPERBOLE

Suggested Grade Levels: 3–6

MENTOR TEXTS FOR ALL YOUNG WRITERS

Dear Mrs. LaRue: Letters From Obedience School by Mark Teague

Diamond Life: Baseball Sights, Sounds, and Swings by Charles R. Smith, Jr.

Dogs Rule! by Daniel Kirk

Earrings! by Judith Viorst

Hot City by Barbara Joosse

Someday by Eileen Spinelli

Whoosh Went the Wind by Sally Derby

For those of us prone to exaggeration, it's hard to imagine a world without hyperbole. Just as we use exaggeration to tell the stories of our everyday lives, authors often use hyperbole to tell their stories, oftentimes bringing voice to their writing in the process.

Hyperbole is a craft that is fairly easy to recognize and is within the reach of most students in their own writing. Of course, the level of sophistication in the hyperbole your students produce will vary depending on their maturity as writers. Young writers enjoy experimenting with hyperbole, so have fun with this craft study!

Notice and Name for Writers Familiar With This Craft

Gather your students in your meeting area and explain that you are going to read some authors' writing. Go on to explain that you will not be reading the books in their entirety, but only parts. Ask them to listen carefully with their writers' ears.

Listed below are some excerpts that would serve as effective models. For more options, you can use the Craft Study Charts and the Annotated Bibliography found in Part 3 to locate additional books that include hyperbole. You also may have some favorites of your own.

A few of our favorite excerpts—and possible introductions to them—are listed below. Read some or all of these excerpts slowly and with dramatic flair to emphasize the use of hyperbole:

> In *Dear Mrs. LaRue: Letters From Obedience School*, Mark Teague describes how hard life is for Ike after he is sent to Dog Obedience School. (Read Ike's letters of October 7th and/or October 11th. Be sure to show the illustrations so that children get a sense of Ike's dramatic exaggeration of his situation.)

> In *Dogs Rule!*, Daniel Kirk uses a series of poems to look at life from the point of view of several different dogs. (Read the stanza about Great Danes in the poem "Dogs Rule!" Then read the following lines from the poem "Squirt": *My head's too big. It weighs a ton.* Conclude by reading stanzas two, three, and four from the poem "Howlin'Time.")

> In *Earrings!*, Judith Viorst presents a young girl trying to convince her parents that she's old enough to get her ears pierced. (Read the eighth page of the story as the book's narrator tries to explain to her parents that she is the *only* girl who does not have pierced ears.)

> In *Whoosh Went the Wind*, Sally Derby writes about a young boy who is late for school and tries to explain to his teacher that it is the wind's fault. (Read the portion that starts *"The post office flag was flapping so hard its stars fluttered down to the sidewalk. I picked up stars till my pockets were full...".*)

> In "To The Moon" from *Diamond Life*, Charles R. Smith, Jr. lets us eavesdrop on a conversation among a bunch of Little Leaguers as they describe their batting power. (Read the selection in its entirety.)

Allow students to talk about what they've noticed. Students zero in on this technique quite readily when they've been exposed to multiple examples. Ask them to react to the various examples of hyperbole. Discuss the mental imagery each creates. Talk about why the author may have chosen to write each excerpt in this way. Name the craft for the students.

Explore

If you have enough books that include examples of hyperbole, assemble them in baskets for students to explore over the next few days. Students should work in pairs or small groups and write down examples of hyperbole they find as they explore the books. If you do not have a sufficient quantity of books or if your students are not ready for independent exploration, select just a few to highlight during your read aloud time over the next few days. Encourage students to listen for examples of hyperbole in the authors' writing. Talk about the different uses of hyperbole. Are there similarities? What effect does each hyperbole have on the reader?

Give It a Try

Model for your students how to turn an ordinary sentence into a hyperbolic sentence. A teacher in our building uses visual graphics to underscore the difference for her young writers. The ordinary sentence has a graphic of someone yawning in boredom. The hyperbolic sentence has a graphic of a flashy smiley face flexing his muscles. Try something like this on chart paper or an interactive whiteboard:

> Ordinary: I dropped the glass on the kitchen floor and it broke.
>
> Hyperbolic: I dropped the glass on the kitchen floor and it shattered into a million pieces with a crash that made me jump out of my shoes!

Discuss the different effect each sentence has. Then try a shared writing experience. During a minilesson in Lisa Hennessy's fifth-grade class, a teacher-written sentence was displayed on the board:

> Ordinary: It's very cold out today.

The children then worked together to build the following sentence using the newly acquired craft:

> Hyperbolic: It's so cold outside that my skin turned blue, I got frostbite on my toes, my teeth turned into icicles, and my tears froze.

Students now need the opportunity to practice using this craft independently. Have them go back into their writing notebooks and find one place or several places that hyperbole would make their writing even better. Confer with students as they craft their revisions.

Celebration

Ask students to share their revisions with their writing partners, allowing for feedback and additional revision if necessary. Bring students together and invite them to share their ordinary and hyperbolic sentences. If you would like, make a bulletin board display of these transformations from ordinary to hyperbolic.

Lisa Hennessy's fifth graders certainly added muscle to their ordinary sentences in the following examples:

> Ordinary: The wave was big.
>
> Hyperbolic: That wave was as tall as the Empire State Building.—Joseph
>
> Ordinary: It was really hot outside.
>
> Hyperbolic: It was so hot outside that I felt as if I would melt into a puddle and sink into the ground.—Luke

Ordinary: I love ice cream.

Hyperbolic: I love ice cream so much I would eat it every day for my entire life if I could.—Dylan

Ordinary: It was a windy day.

Hyperbolic: The wind was so strong that it blew the whole city into a different country.—Daniel

Adaptations for Writers New to This Craft

The Notice and Name portion of this craft study can remain essentially the same for your primary students. The humor in *Dear Mrs. LaRue* might be above the understanding of your little ones but the other excerpts should work well. The Explore phase would consist of having your students listen for examples as you read dramatically during read-aloud time. Determine whether your students are capable of crafting independent hyperbole. Students in kindergarten and first grade should be able to experiment with this craft through shared writing as a class. Many first and second graders will be able to craft simple examples of hyperbole on their own, using the Ordinary Sentence versus the Hyperbolic Sentence model. You might want to provide the ordinary sentence and let each student work on adding hyperbole or you may find that it's easier if students are given free rein.

Suggested Grade Levels: 3–6

MENTOR TEXTS FOR ALL YOUNG WRITERS

Bigmama's by Donald Crews

Crocodile Listens by April Pulley Sayre

Earrings! by Judith Viorst

Last Night at the Zoo by Michael Garland

Mud by May Lyn Ray

Night in the Country by Cynthia Rylant

Night Rabbits by Lee Posey

Psssst! It's Me...the Bogeyman by Barbara Park

Puddles by Jonathan London

Shortcut by Donald Crews

Walk On! A Guide for Babies of All Ages by Marla Frazee

When the Fireflies Come by Jonathan London

An effective lead is important. However, we as teachers must convey to our students that a lead is not needed to get started on a piece of writing. Oftentimes, the lead is crafted when a piece is completed.

If we are to expect students to become adept at this craft we must provide them the opportunity to discover and study the many varied ways that authors construct effective leads. With plenty of modeling from mentor texts, you might expect your students to craft leads like some of the following that were written by the young writers at our school:

Well, it all started when I woke up that day, September 6th.—Jesse, Grade 4

The dead silence of my family felt eerie like a haunted mansion ripping at my insides. The storm was approaching and the day turned into night and in five minutes passing, it had all gone black.—Joseph, Grade 5

Billy asked my mom, "Will you marry me?"—Mackenzie, Grade 1

It was as if the world had frozen, the clock hands of time had stopped, and it was just me, on the ground... sprawled out in pain. I felt like a T.V. movie on pause. No words. No motion. Nothing.—Brianna, Grade 5

Imagine coming home from a long night. It's dark, it's late, and the front door (that you know you locked) is open.—Ally, Grade 4

There I was driving a $200,000 boat I don't even own.—Patrick, Grade 4

In Autumn, everything is silent, except for the trees blowing back and forth. Listen...whoosh, whoosh.—Erika, Grade 3

Bark! Bark! I have a dog.—Adriana, Kindergarten

It was so hot outside that even the sky was sweating.—Andrew, Grade 4

Now reader, have you ever been nervous and excited at the same time?—Michaela, Grade 4

Notice and Name for Writers Familiar With This Craft

Gather students in your meeting area. Explain that you are going to read opening lines from a variety of picture books. Read the lead from each of the Mentor Texts listed. After you have read through all of them, go back and reread each lead one at a time. Stop and ask the students what they've noticed about each lead. Chart their observations on chart paper or interactive whiteboard. Discuss your findings. What leads do they like and why? Guide your students to categorize the different techniques that authors use to craft effective leads, such as use of simile, question format, suspense, hyperbole.

Explore

Students should work in pairs or small groups, depending on the structure of your writing workshop and on the number of mentor texts available for this exercise. First, assemble baskets of books that contain a variety of effective leads. You can use the Craft Study Chart and the Annotated Bibliography found in Part 3 to find books that contain great leads. You also may have some favorites of your own.

Students should analyze the different leads that authors use to draw in the reader. Many of these will be techniques you have discussed during the Notice and Name portion of this study. The goal is to have students find examples of these techniques and expand upon the list. They can record their findings in their writing notebooks. They should chart the title, author, lead, and the technique the author used in crafting the lead. (A sample recording sheet is included in Appendix B of this book.) Confer with the various research teams throughout the search.

Once students have completed their research, assemble the class and allow time for each team to share their findings. Again, it is up to you to decide how many examples will be shared with the entire class. The format should be the same as your initial read-alouds, wherein the selected students will read the excerpt aloud and share their thoughts about the technique the author used to craft the lead. You should record the findings on chart paper or on an interactive whiteboard.

The final step in this exploration phase is to organize and consolidate the students' findings into an Effective Lead Resource Chart that students can refer to time and again when crafting their own leads. The chart should highlight the different techniques discovered, along with a lead that exemplifies the craft.

Give It a Try

Instruct students to go back through their writer's notebook entries and find a piece whose lead is weak or ordinary. Encourage students to experiment with this craft by using the Effective Lead Resource Chart. Each student should rewrite three leads using three different techniques. Students should then meet with their writing partners to decide which lead works best. Take a look at Figure 2 to see how some of Lisa Mozian's and Kathy DeBono's fourth graders jazzed up their leads during writing workshop.

Celebration

Gather students to share their work. Each student should read his or her original lead and then the newly crafted lead. This should be done across multiple sessions. Students should be encouraged to evaluate one another's writing as a part of this process.

Remind students to use what they have learned as they craft new pieces of writing. The Effective Lead Resource Chart should remain visible as a reference so that students are mindful of the importance of this craft. Consider the chart a work in progress, allowing students to add to it throughout the year.

Adaptations for Writers New to This Craft

This study can be simplified and easily adapted for students at younger grade levels. For instance, select a few very distinct leads to read aloud, such as a question, an exclamation, onomatopoeia, an elliptical sentence. Young students should be given the same opportunity to notice and name what the author is doing and why it is effective. Decide how many leads you want to introduce based upon the makeup of your class. If your students are very young and inexperienced, you may choose to introduce only one or possibly two types of leads. Once again, you should chart the example leads.

The goal remains for students to work on crafting their own effective leads. Second-grade students may be capable of going back into a piece of writing they have done to try out a new lead or even a few different leads. If your students are not ready for this, make this an interactive writing experience. Select a few pieces of students' writing and put them on an overhead projector or interactive whiteboard. (Be sure to ask the students for permission to share their work.) Work as a class to craft a new lead or a few different leads according to the techniques you have discussed. Determine which

FIGURE 2. Fourth Graders' Effective Lead Revisions

	Original lead	3 Rewrites	And the winner is....
Jillian	My favorite part of playing basketball is sprinting down the court with the wind in my face, Shoot! Score!	1. Have you ever played basketball in a newly waxed gym? 2. "I'm open," I call to my teammates as I sprint down the court. 3. Sprinting down the court. My hair whipping me in the face. My favorite sport...basketball!	#3
Mikayla	My mom and I slowly got out of the car because my wrist hurt too much to jump.	1. Vroom, vroom, the engine was on. I was going somewhere but I didn't know where. 2. "Mom, I can't get up!" I was lying on the sand beside the slide. My wrist hurt so much. 3. It all began at the beach. My brother Trevor, my sister Brenna, and I were playing tag and then it happened... The fall!	#3
Max	It was a sunny Monday and my third grade teacher was so hot that she had to open all the windows and the back door.	1. It was the hottest day on Earth. It felt like I was standing on the sun but instead I was trapped in my classroom! 2. It was a really hot day and everyone was talking which just made it worse. 3. It all began one day at school....	#1

ones are most effective. Encourage students to try out this craft as they write new pieces during writing workshop. Be sure to celebrate the students who take a chance and give it a try!

ONOMATOPOEIA

Suggested Grade Levels: 1–3

MENTOR TEXTS FOR ALL YOUNG WRITERS

If You Were Onomatopoeia by Trisha Speed Shaskan

The Listening Walk by Paul Showers

Vroomaloom Zoom by John Coy

Listen, Listen by Phyllis Gershator

Water Hole Waiting by Jane and Christopher Kurtz

Max Found Two Sticks by Brian Pinkney

Onomatopoeia and alliteration are typically the first two crafts that students learn because both are so plentiful in children's literature and easily identified. Onomatopoeia is typically a favorite craft of young writers because it is within their reach and, moreover, it's fun to use. Students at St. James Elementary enjoy crafting onomatopoeia within their writing pieces. Lauren, a first grader in Mrs. Petruzzelli's class, wrote, "Oink, oink, oinkety oink! The pig fell in the mud!" Nicole, a first grader in Louise Mahler's class, wrote, "Jingle, Jingle, went the bells when my dad took down the wreath." Luke, a fourth grader in Mrs. DeBono's class, combined onomatopoeia with personification for this descriptive sentence: "Crash! The waves dance onto the damp, smooth sand." Another fourth grader, John, combined onomatopoeia with a simile to create this effective image: "Boom! There it went. I hit the ball so far up it looked like an airplane flying by."

Notice and Name for Writers New to This Craft

There are *many* books that contain onomatopoeia. We have listed just a few suggestions in the Mentor Texts box. Use the Craft Study Charts in Part 3 to direct you to additional books in the Annotated Bibliography that contain this craft. Select the books you will use as mentor texts for this craft. You may want to read a book in its entirety or select excerpts from several books that exemplify this craft. Read your selections aloud to the students. Invite them to share what they notice. You will find that some books are *filled* with onomatopoeia and others contain just one or two choice examples. Encourage the students to notice these differences and think about the authors' choices. Many already will have been introduced to this craft, but it is important to ascertain that they know that these sound words have a name: onomatopoeia!

Explore

During your next read-aloud session, read *If You Were Onomatopoeia* by Trisha Speed Shaskan to the class. The technical explanations, along with the many examples of onomatopoeic use, will guide your students through an exploration of this craft. Discuss the many different kinds of onomatopoeia as you enjoy this book together. Guide your students to ensure that they recognize the distinctions. Chart their findings: Animal Sounds, Indoor Sounds, Nature Sounds, Action Sounds, and so forth.

Give It a Try

Gather your class in your meeting area. Read *The Listening Walk* by Paul Showers. The book ends with an invitation to listen for the many different sounds all around. Ask the students to close their eyes and listen very carefully for 30 seconds. The students should then share the sounds they heard. Chart the sound each student volunteers and then, as a class, come up with an onomatopoeic word that captures that sound. For example, a student might say, "I heard someone moving his feet." The class might then come up with, "Shuffle-Shuffle" or "Scritch-Scratch" or even "Tap, Tap, Tap."

Tell your students that you are going to go on a Listening Walk. Decide whether you want to walk through the hallways of your school or venture outside for a stroll. Pair each student with a partner for the walk. They should have a clipboard or notebook to record the sounds they hear. Explain that they can add an onomatopoeic word that captures the sound if one immediately comes to mind. If one doesn't come to mind, assure them that there will be time later to craft the onomatopoeia.

When you return from the Listening Walk, allow students time to craft onomatopoeia. Then gather together as a class to share their sounds. If some students are having difficulty crafting an onomatopoeic word for their sounds, encourage the others to offer suggestions.

Celebration

There are several options for the celebration. The finished product should be a whole-class descriptive writing piece called *Our Listening Walk*. Use the book *The Listening Walk* as your model for this writing. Decide which one of the following options best suits your students and your time constraints:

- Create a shared writing experience, in which you as the teacher compose the framework on chart paper or an interactive whiteboard. Students should be invited to insert their onomatopoeic sentences.

- Create an *Our Listening Walk* book. This can be a class book, in which each student or partnership creates a page(s). If students have enough examples, allow them to create individual *My Listening Walk* books.

Adaptations

For Writers New to This Craft

Kindergartners would enjoy a simplified version of this study. Take your little ones on a Listening Walk with you as the tour guide. Instead of the students recording sounds they hear, you will guide their listening. Stop as you hear new sounds and encourage the students to listen and share what they hear. When you return to the classroom, ask the students to remember some of the sounds. As a class, think of onomatopoeic words to match the sounds. Chart the sounds with simple illustrations to serve as a reference. Students then will return to their seats. Each should select one sound and illustrate it. Encourage the students to add an onomatopoeic speech bubble. Provide time for students to share their work.

A kindergartner returning from a Listening Walk was distinctly aware of the sounds of the students shoes as they walked through the hall. If you try this lesson with your beginning writers, a finished product might look something like the student work in Figure 3.

For Writers Familiar With This Craft

You might find that even your intermediate grade students would enjoy taking a Listening Walk. A suggestion might be to buddy up an older class with a younger class and have the students work together to create an onomatopoeic mural with speech bubbles or work together to create a class book as mentioned above. Of course, the goal of any craft study is for students to employ the craft effectively in their own writing. After a study of onomatopoeia, encourage your more experienced writers to go back into their writing notebooks and find places where inclusion of onomatopoeia would improve the piece. Ultimately, the goal should be for our young writers to add onomatopoeia to their craft toolboxes, as well, to be used again and again with purpose and for effect.

FIGURE 3. Kindergartner's Onomatopoeic Illustration

POINT OF VIEW

Suggested Grade Levels: 3–6

MENTOR TEXTS

For Writers New to This Craft
Dirty Laundry Pile: Poems in Different Voices by Paul B. Janeczko
Doodle Dandies: Poems That Take Shape by J. Patrick Lewis

For Writers Familiar With This Craft
Atlantic by G. Brian Karas

This is a craft study that students are bound to enjoy! Young writers have good imaginations. Their natural inclination toward make believe will serve them well in learning to work with point of view.

In addition, much of the writing that students do in grades K through 6 is in first-person narration. This craft study will allow your students to experiment with first-person narration by giving voice to an unlikely subject.

Notice and Name for Writers Familiar With This Craft

Gather your class for a read-aloud of *Atlantic* by G. Brian Karas. Before reading the book, explain that the author uses a very specific craft to impart information about the Atlantic Ocean. Challenge the students to determine the craft after listening to only the opening line. Once it is established that the book is written from the ocean's point of view, read the book aloud. After reading the book, invite your students to talk about the style of writing. Why would Karas have chosen to write from the ocean's perspective? What effect does this have on the reader? What effect does this have on the story itself?

Once these general observations have been discussed, you will want to direct your students to a more detailed analysis of the text. Type the book in poem format, one stanza for each page. Make an overhead transparency or display the poem on an interactive whiteboard. As a class, you will use this touchstone text to dissect how the author uses point of view to tell the story or give information throughout the book. Although the ideas should be student generated, you will have to prompt and guide the discussion and then restate what has been said in clear and concise language.

Explore

Ask your students what they think Karas had to do to prepare for writing *Atlantic*. Ascertain that they understand the in-depth research that went into this project. Tell the class that they will each be publishing a piece of writing modeled after *Atlantic*.

You should decide the broad topic you want your students to research and provide guidance. Marianne Marquart's third-grade class, for example, wrote their poems about animals of New York State. During the Explore phase of this study, your students will research their selected topics. Start with a simple outline that will provide them with the information needed to create their poems. To use the example above, if you were to choose animals as your broad topic, students might need to research the following information:

- Physical appearance
- Natural habitat
- Food
- Unusual facts about the animal

Give It a Try

In this lesson, where you expect the final product to have a certain level of sophistication, modeling is especially important. We suggest that you guide your students through a class-created parallel poem that directly mirrors what Karas did in *Atlantic*. As you're writing, keep in mind what you would like to see reflected in your student poems. Share the poem on an overhead transparency or interactive whiteboard. Just as you dissected Karas's writing in *Atlantic*, analyze your class-created parallel poem. Your poem and *Atlantic* will serve as your students' mentor texts throughout their writing. Students will need touchstone copies of both poems.

Figure 4 shows a portion of the parallel poem Mrs. Marquart wrote and the analysis her third-grade class performed. As the third graders in our school analyzed Mrs. Marquart's poem, they noticed a number of things about its content, structure, and craft, including an opening line that serves as the topic of the poem, facts and imagery about the animal and its habitat, animal actions using strong verbs, people's feelings about the animal, feelings and thoughts that might be expressed from the animal's point of view, use of onomatopoeia and personification, and an ending that repeats the first line.

Students are now ready to write! Using their research and the two mentor touchstone texts, students should work on writing and illustrating their own poems. You should decide how many writing workshop sessions it will take to complete this project. Decide how you want the final published piece to look. Our third graders, with the help of our computer teacher put together an

---

FIGURE 4. Analysis of Point of View Craft

Class Poem: Sea Horse

topic
I am a sea horse.

personality, looks like
I am the shyest in the sea
with a head like a horse
a tail like a monkey
and a pouch like a kangaroo

facts + imagery
In my underwater gallery
my black eyes peer out
at my sea life surroundings
Dangerous predators are
all around me

location imagery
In such a big sea
a small creature like me sits
As a baby I curl my tail
and sink to the safety of my home
Huge walls of water, monstrous storms
and swirling whirlpools
carry me on a never ending journey
My holdfast is my home sweet home

animals in same family
I am not alone
My brothers and sisters
are dwarf sea horses, short snouted sea horses,
lemur tail sea horses and spotted sea horses

how animal adapts or special fact
On the day I am born
I am as tiny as the tiniest eyelash
but I am an exact replica of
Mom and Dad
I instinctively know to camouflage
as powerful predators pass
I am the artist's palette of the sea
I sit on the easel

personification
I curl my tail
Sinking to where I want to be
I shop for food in a fresh fish market
of tasty treats
I whisper a sweet song to my mate

actions strong verbs
I wait shyly in my ocean paradise
gracefully falling
to the bottom
of the deep dark depths of the ocean
I twist and turn
as my babies dart
from the warmth of my pouch

how people feel
People are amazed by me
I am thought of as a majestic wonder
Others will think of me as a souvenir

color
Children draw pictures of me
with violet red,
coral pink
and sea green

point of view
I am a living creature
I don't belong in the shop
I need to be in the sea
Please don't take away
my friends and family
I have feelings just like you

onomatopoeia
Swish, swish, swish
I gallop through the water

topic
I am a sea horse

interactive whiteboard presentation of their finished poems for their parents. Figure 5 shows a strong example—Michaela's poem from the point of view of a turtle.

Adaptations for Writers New to This Craft

Point-of-view writing is not a craft that kindergartners would be expected to generate; however, most kindergartners will be able to recognize when something is written from a unique point of view. We encourage you to expose your kindergartners to this craft through read-alouds and discussion.

There are several poems in *Dirty Laundry Pile* by Paul B. Janeczko and *Doodle Dandies* by J. Patrick Lewis that work well when introducing this craft to primary-grade students. Both of these books lend themselves well to a guessing-game format, wherein students have to guess the animal or object that is speaking. Read through each of the books and pick out the poems that you feel will be accessible to your students. Read these poems aloud, having students make their guesses. Be sure to leave off any line that specifically names the subject.

Students who are ready to begin experimenting with this craft can begin by using speech bubbles and illustrations. After reading several poems aloud and engaging your students in the guessing game, encourage them to give it a try. Students should select an animal or object to draw. While

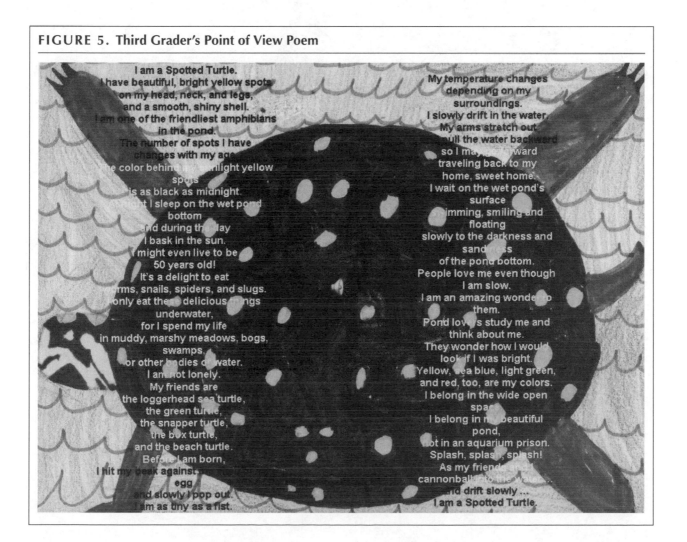

FIGURE 5. Third Grader's Point of View Poem

they're illustrating they should be thinking about what that animal or object might say if given a voice. Students should then insert appropriate speech bubbles.

Second graders (and some first graders) will be able to mimic some of the simple poems found in Janeczko's *Dirty Laundry Pile* and Lewis's *Doodle Dandies*. We even had a kindergartner try it successfully! Riley shows what life would be like as a chair in her illustration for Figure 6.

FIGURE 6. Kindergartner's Point of View Illustration

Suggested Grade Levels: 2–6

Print Features and Print Layout go hand in hand. These two crafts are almost always taught at the same time and, for that reason, we have written this craft study to incorporate both. When selecting the books you want to use as mentor texts for this craft, take care to select examples where the reasons for the print features or print layout are obvious. There are many picture books that have colorful varied fonts with unique print placement, but there seems to be no rhyme or reason behind these stylistic choices. In the Annotated Bibliography in Part 3 we have included picture books in which the print features and print layout are meaningful within the context. When teaching these crafts to students, we want them to make purposeful stylistic choices. It is especially important that the purpose be obvious for students who are just beginning to discover this craft. If you choose to add books of your own to the suggestions we have provided, please keep this in mind.

Notice and Name for Writers Familiar With This Craft

Gather your students in your classroom meeting area. Explain that instead of being asked to listen with their writers' ears, this time they're going to be asked to observe with the eyes of an author or illustrator.

All of the books listed as Mentor Texts provide examples that will work well for a study of these crafts. Select a few from the list (there is no need to use all the books on the list) and then pick the pages that you feel best exemplify these crafts. Because the exemplars for these two crafts are visual rather than aural, your students will have to have a clear view of the pages of the books. If your group is large or if the print is small, we suggest that you make overhead transparencies or scan the pages for display on an interactive whiteboard.

Ask the students to discuss what they notice about the way the print appears. Be sure to focus on both print features and print layout. Name the crafts for the students and help them to understand the distinctions between the two. Discuss reasons why the author, illustrator, or publisher may have chosen to present the text in this way. Be sure to touch on as many varied purposes as possible. List your class findings on chart paper or the interactive whiteboard.

Explore

Children should work in pairs or small groups, depending on the structure of your writing workshop and on the number of mentor texts available for this exercise. First assemble baskets of books that contain a variety of print features and unique print layout. In addition to the Mentor Texts listed above, you can use the Craft Study Chart and the Annotated Bibliography in Part 3 locate good books that incorporate these crafts. You also may have some favorites of your own.

Ask students to analyze the different ways that authors present the text in their books and decide which ones are especially effective. Many of these will be techniques you have discussed during the Notice and Name portion of this study. The goal is to have students find examples of these techniques and expand upon the list. They can record their findings in their writing notebooks. Remind students that they do not have to chart *every* example they find. It is more important to find a few good samples where authors use the techniques for different purposes. You may want to assign each student or research team to find a specific number of examples. Instruct students to mark the pages with sticky notes so they will be readily available during the share time. Students should chart the title, the author, the technique the author used in presenting the text, and what they feel was the author's purpose in using the particular print feature or print layout. (A reproducible recording sheet is included in Appendix B of this book.) Confer with the various research teams throughout the search.

Once students have completed their research, assemble the class and allow time for them to share their findings. Again, it is up to you to decide how many examples will be shared with the entire class. Students should have the book(s) available to share with the class in order for the other students to see the visual effects. You should record the class's findings on chart paper or on the interactive whiteboard.

Give It a Try

This craft links well to your technology curriculum. If you have a computer lab or computer teacher at your school, work together to help students craft pieces of writing that make effective use of print features and print placement. If children have pieces of writing in their notebooks that would work well with revisions to the print, by all means encourage that venue. More likely, this will be a new piece of writing written with these crafts in mind. Students at our school typically complete this process across several revisions leading up to the final published piece, which is crafted on the computer.

Poetry seems to work well for this craft study, but any type of writing genre can be transformed through the use of interesting print features and print layout. Some of the teachers in our school who have studied these crafts with their students have given students the option of finding a poem or selection in a children's book and reworking it to incorporate more stylistic print features and print layout. This is an option you may want to consider depending on the age, experience, and make-up of your class.

Have fun with this study! Students typically love experimenting with these crafts and the results can be impressive. Take a look at Figure 7 to see the creative use of print features and print layout by one of the young writers in our building.

Adaptations for Writers New to This Craft

This study can be simplified and easily adapted for kindergarten and first grade. *Freight Train* by Donald Crews and *Colors! ¡Colores!* by Jorge Luján are perfect choices for introducing this craft to our youngest writers. Young students should be given the same opportunity to notice and name what the author is doing and why it is effective.

Begin by reading one or both of these books, pointing to the words as you read. After reading, ask the students whether they notice something special about the way the author has written the words. Provide as much prompting as needed. For instance, talk about why the author has used colored font instead of black.

Convey to the students that they can write like Donald Crews and Jorge Luján. Using a black marker, write two sentences that include color words on chart paper or an interactive whiteboard. Ask for volunteers to come up and change the sentences using the craft that the authors used. Once

FIGURE 7. Fourth Grader's Poem with Creative Print Features and Layout

Based on the poem "Dog" by Valerie Worth

Under the covers,

THE CAT LIES DOWN
rests her sharp teeth,
yawns,
rests her LONG TAIL
carefully next to
her body,
looks up,
alert,
runs with *amazing speed*
from a **chasing sister**
stretches on the chair
rolls,
on her side,
closes her eyes:
sleeps
all afternoon
in her

loose skin

Adam, Grade 4

students understand this craft, it is time for independent follow-up. Depending on the level of your students, have them write either a sentence or a few sentences that contain color words. Provide them with the necessary markers, crayons, or colored pencils needed to convert their sentences into color. If you are doing this lesson in first grade, you may find that your students can write simple color poems like some of the ones found in *Colors! ¡Colores!*

REPETITION

Suggested Grade Levels: 1–6

The craft of repetition can be simple and obvious or it can be subtle and sophisticated. When students are in the early stages of exploring this craft, it is best to use mentor texts wherein the repetition is easily identified and mimicked. There are countless books that employ this craft in a variety of ways. For the purposes of *this* lesson, we have chosen books that use a repeating phrase or line as a thread to carry the story. We encourage you to use the Annotated Bibliography in Part 3 to find other options that may work well within your curriculum.

Notice and Name for All Writers

Begin with a reading of *In November* by Cynthia Rylant. Teachers in our school have found that this book works especially well as a mentor text to introduce this craft because the use of repetition is obvious and the subject is one to which all students can relate. Because this book is rich in many crafts, you will want to focus your students' attention on the pattern of the book rather than asking the usual broad question of "What do you notice that the author is doing?"

Students will readily recognize the repeating phrase "In November," which serves as the thread that carries the story. Discuss why Rylant may have chosen to repeat the phrase over and over throughout the book.

Explore

Over the next several days read some or all of the books listed in the Mentor Texts at the start of this lesson. You will note that although each book uses the same type of repetition, some are more appropriate for primary grade students, while others will work well with the intermediate grades. After each read-aloud, discuss the repetitious pattern and talk about the rationale behind the author's use of this craft.

Give It a Try

Your students should now be ready to try out this craft. Keep the mentor texts available for the students to use as models as they set to writing. You may want to restrict your students to a specific mentor text, such as *In November*, having all students write about months of the year. Another option would be to give them the flexibility of creating any poem or piece of prose that includes a repeating line. A third alternative with intermediate students would be to encourage them to go back into their writing notebooks and recraft a piece they already have written. Sara Long Harte, a third-grade teacher in our school, used *In November* as her mentor text, and her student, Drew, chose to write about January, as you can read in Figure 8.

Louise Mahler's first graders took what they learned from the mentor texts to craft original pieces with repeating lines. Check out Figure 9 to see how the use of this craft turns Nicole's piece from the

MENTOR TEXTS

For All Young Writers
In November by Cynthia Rylant

For Writers New to This Craft
Birthday Presents by Cynthia Rylant
In My New Yellow Shirt by Eileen Spinelli
Just Like Daddy by Frank Asch
The Moon Was the Best by Charlotte Zolotow
Where Once There Was a Wood by Denise Fleming

For Writers Familiar With This Craft
Grandad Bill's Song by Jane Yolen
The Important Book by Margaret Wise Brown
On the Same Day in March: A Tour of the World's Weather by Marilyn Singer
Saturdays and Teacakes by Lester Laminack

FIGURE 8. Third Grader's Repetition Poem

In January

In January
I sample steamy, chocolaty hot cocoa
I taste cold snow melting in my mouth
I nearly attack a tray of gingerbread and other pastries

In January
I listen to the snow ruffle under my dark black boots
I hear Christmas carolers singing to the groovy beat of "Jingle Bell Rock"
I take in the sound of Santa's bells heading back to the North

In January
I notice birds flying south for migration
I spot my friend making a round snowman
I see people sledding down a long bumpy hill

In January
I stuff my gloved hand in the freezing snow
I pet my dog Reggie's soft fluffy fur by the fire
As I click my remote looking for a good movie.

FIGURE 9. First Grader's Repetition Story

Watching the Birds Go By

One day I saw a big bird fly over my house while my dog Bella was outside. But then it flew away. So I went downstairs to have some breakfast with toast and eggs. I saw more birds.

I had fun watching the birds go by.

In the afternoon I asked my mom if I could ride my bike. She said yes. When I rode my bike I saw more birds.

I had fun watching the birds go by.

Then I had lunch. It was delicious. I watched the birds again. The birds were very colorful. They had colors like blue, brown and orange. At night I saw another bird, but not a regular bird. It was an owl. I like the way owls make the whooing sound. It went whooooo-whoooo-whooo. The owl was all brown. When it made its sound it got closer and closer so the sound got really loud. It was this loud...

WHOOO WHOOO WHOOO!!!

It was fun watching the owl go by.

standard "bed-to-bed" story that is typically so popular with first graders into a well-crafted piece of writing.

Adaptations

Because most grade levels were targeted in this study lesson, the adaptations described below are suggestions of ways to explore the many other uses of repetition rather than ways to adapt the study to various grade levels. Spend some time reviewing the many ways that authors use the craft of repetition by using the Craft Study Chart to direct you into the Annotated Bibliography. You need to decide how much time you want to devote to studying the many uses of repetition and then decide which of these titles are within your students' reach.

For Writers New to This Craft

As early as kindergarten, students can be taught the craft of repetition in its most basic form. Instead of simply, "I have a big dog," show the young writer that the size of the dog can be emphasized: "I have a big, big dog." Instead of "I love to dance," show the child that writing "I love, love, love to dance" lets the reader know that dancing is something *really* special.

For Writers Familiar With This Craft

Intermediate grade students are capable of spending time doing independent in-depth exploration and analysis of the craft. Confer with your students and guide them throughout this process. Writers' Workshop time should then be allotted to give your students the opportunity to put what they've learned to use, whether it be creating a new piece or recrafting a piece from their notebooks.

SEE-SAW PATTERN

Suggested Grade Levels: 1–3

In addition to making stylistic choices about word choice and presentation to create a desired effect, authors also make choices about *structures* with which to format a book. The crafts highlighted in this book that fall within this category are Circular Ending, Cumulative Text, Interesting Format, Repetition (in some instances), See-Saw Pattern, and Sequencing. Each of these craft elements looks at the big picture. Whereas most of the other crafts are stylistic choices that a writer may make during the revision process, the structural crafts are choices that a writer makes in the planning stage before putting pencil to paper.

And so it is with this study of the See-Saw Pattern. This is a very specific and focused study in which students will have the structure in mind even before formulating ideas for the subject of the writing piece.

MENTOR TEXTS
For Writers New to This Craft
Someday by Eileen Spinelli
When I Was Little: A Four-Year-Old's Memoir of Her Youth by Jamie Lee Curtis
For Writers Familiar With This Craft
Farmer's Garden: Rhymes for Two Voices by David L. Harrison
Grandad Bill's Song by Jane Yolen
I Am the Dog, I Am the Cat by Donald Hall
Loki & Alex: Adventures of a Dog and His Best Friend by Charles R. Smith, Jr.
Rosie and Michael by Judith Viorst

Notice and Name for Writers New to This Craft

Gather your students for a read-aloud of *When I Was Little: A Four-Year-Old's Memoir of Her Youth* by Jamie Lee Curtis. Explain that the author has set up this book in a special way. Encourage them to listen with their writers' ears as they enjoy the story so that they will be prepared to talk about the way Curtis wrote the book. Typically, we would encourage you to read the book aloud once for enjoyment and then again to analyze a particular craft; however, the see-saw structure of this book is so obvious that this may not be necessary. If you would prefer to read it twice, by all means do so.

After you have finished the book, invite students to share what they notice. Record student comments on chart paper or on the interactive whiteboard. Students should recognize the pattern fairly readily. Sum up their findings and explain that the author has written a See-Saw book. Ask students how this structure is like a see-saw. Guide them toward making the connection of taking turns or back and forth.

Explore

The primary goal of the Explore phase of a craft study is to allow students to discover other examples of a particular craft. For the purposes of this study, giving your young writers the opportunity to hear a second read-aloud written in a See-Saw Pattern will strengthen the awareness that there are many books written in this style. Tell your students that you are going to read *Someday* by Eileen Spinelli. Explain that they should be listening for the See-Saw Pattern, and tell them they are going to have the opportunity to do some writing that is just like Eileen Spinelli's.

After reading the book aloud, spend some time discussing what students noticed. Be sure they understand not only the structure, but also that the little girl narrator's dreams for *someday* are very grand, but for *today* she's just a kid! Discuss how the See-Saw Pattern helps to tell the story.

Give It a Try

It is now time for the students to apply this technique. Explain to the students that they will each be completing two pages of a class book in a See-Saw Pattern like that in *Someday*. Model two pages on chart paper or on the interactive whiteboard so that students will have a reference. An example might look something like this:

> Someday
> I will be a famous author and I will write wonderful books. People will ask me for my autograph.
> Someday...
> But today...
> I'm a first-grade teacher teaching students how to be good writers.

Send the students back to their writing stations and have them begin work. Confer with them as they write. Some students may need guidance for ideas, particularly in first grade. Remind them that their writing is going to be put together into a book so their final copy should have their best writing and best illustrations.

Celebration

When all the students are finished, invite each one to come up before the group to share his or her writing. Applaud each author's use of craft.

Design a cover, laminate and bind the book, and add it to your classroom library. This would be a guaranteed hit with parents if you have the opportunity to invite them in for a year-end celebration of your authors' work! The pages of your book might look something like those in Figure 10 by Anna Grace, a first grader in Mrs. Petruzzelli's class.

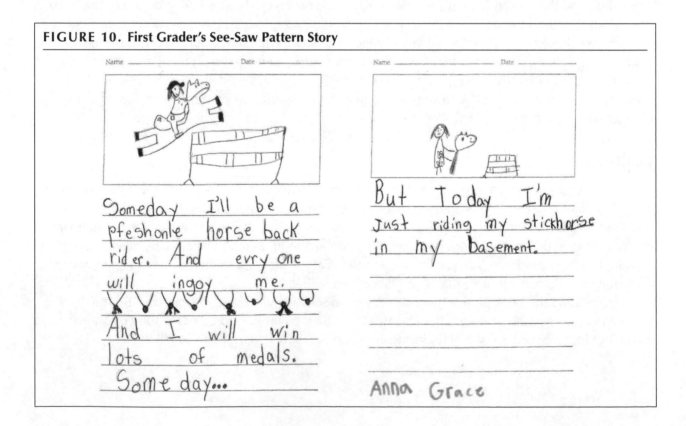

FIGURE 10. First Grader's See-Saw Pattern Story

Adaptations for Writers Familiar With This Craft

Older students can be taught the varied ways that authors use See-Saw Patterns in their writing. The *Someday* lesson described above can be adapted for intermediate grade students, and you may want to broaden the study of this craft for your fourth, fifth, or sixth graders.

Select one book from the Mentor Texts list found at the beginning of this craft study. After reading the book aloud, invite the students to share what they notice about the structure. When it is clear that they recognize the format, name the craft and discuss why it might be termed a See-Saw Pattern.

Over the next few days during your read-aloud time, select books that follow this structure. After reading each book, encourage students to identify the author's unique use of the See-Saw Pattern.

Using these books as mentors, instruct your students to craft a piece of writing modeled after one of the See-Saw Patterns they have studied. Based on the make-up of your class, determine how many writing workshop sessions it will take to complete this study.

SIMILE

Suggested Grade Levels: 1–2

MENTOR TEXTS

For Writers New to This Craft

All the Colors of the Earth by Sheila Hamanaka

Fishing in the Air by Sharon Creech

Gentle Giant Octopus by Karen Wallace

Leaf Jumpers by Carole Gerber

My Dog Is as Smelly as Dirty Socks: And Other Funny Family Portraits by Hanoch Piven

For Writers Familiar With This Craft

Hello, Harvest Moon by Ralph Fletcher

Night Rabbits by Lee Posey

Owl Moon by Jane Yolen

Puddles by Jonathan London

The Storm Book by Charlotte Zolotow

Sun Dance Water Dance by Jonathan London

Tigress by Nick Dowson

Up North at the Cabin by Marsha Wilson Chall

Know where your students are in their understanding of simile and its use. In choosing the appropriate mentor texts for your study, it is important to determine whether your students are at the introductory stage or are ready to take their exploration of this craft to the next level. For writers new to this craft, it is important to choose similes that are obvious and contain simple language. More experienced writers will require mentor texts that use similes to make unexpected comparisons. They need mentor authors who will stretch their knowledge of when and where a simile will create the desired impact on the reader.

Similes abound at St. James Elementary School. Bobby, a second grader, writes, "Sometimes I chew on my fingers like a Twizzler." J.P., a third grader, paints an even more detailed picture when he writes, "The trees stand still like scarecrows silently awaiting the crow's arrival." Antonio, a fifth grader, captures an emotion when he writes, "Winning is like a sugar rush, just ten times more powerful and not powered by sugar, but by excitement."

Notice and Name for Writers New to This Craft

Gather your students on the carpet and explain that you are going to read some authors' writing. Go on to explain that you will not be reading the books in their entirety, but only parts. Ask them to listen carefully with their writers' ears.

Listed below are some excerpts that would serve as effective models. For more options, you can use the Craft Study Charts and the Annotated Bibliography found in Part 3 to locate additional books that include similes. You also may have some favorites of your own.

Copy each simile example onto chart paper or the interactive whiteboard prior to starting this lesson so that they will be available afterward for the students to analyze. Then, read the excerpts slowly, with careful enunciation and emphasis on the simile. The following is a list of great similes you can find in the Mentor Texts provided:

In *Gentle Giant Octopus*, Karen Wallace describes the octopus, *She's huge like a spaceship*. She also writes, *Her body stretches like taffy over the stones.*

In *All the Colors of the Earth*, Sheila Hamanaka writes about children's hair as *Children come with hair like bouncy baby lambs, Or hair that flows like water, Or hair that curls like sleeping cats….*

In *Fishing in the Air*, Sharon Creech describes the streetlamps *glowing like tiny moons all in a row*. She describes the trees *like tall green soldiers standing at attention*. And she writes about the *birds singing their songs like little angels*.

In *Leaf Jumpers*, Carole Gerber describes different leaves this way: *The sugar maple's leaves are orange, like pumpkins in a pumpkin patch*. She also writes *The ginkgo's wavy golden leaf is shaped just like a little fan.*

In *My Dog Is as Smelly as Dirty Socks*, Hanoch Piven writes *My daddy is as jumpy as a SPRING*. He also writes *My baby brother is as sweet as candy*. But he saves the best for describing his dog Schmutz: *Schmutz is as stinky as an onion...as icky as pepperoni, and as smelly as dirty socks.*

After you've read the examples aloud, allow students to tell what they've noticed. Students zero in on this technique quite readily when they've been exposed to multiple examples. At this point, hang the chart paper or bring up the excerpts on interactive whiteboard. Analyze each comparison. Discuss the mental imagery each creates. If they don't pick up on it at first, direct students' attention to the use of the words *like* and *as* typically found in similes. Name the craft for the students.

Explore

For several days, during the daily read-aloud, select books from the Mentor Texts list that contain a few similes, or use the Craft Study Chart to direct you to the Annotated Bibliography for books you think will work well for your students. Each day read one book in its entirety, allowing students the opportunity to enjoy the book and familiarize themselves with the story. During your next writers' workshop, reread the book, inviting students to listen with their writers' ears, picking out the similes used within.

Record the findings on chart paper or on an interactive whiteboard that has been divided into two columns:

1. Person, place, or thing being described
2. Simile

As your list builds with your daily readings be sure to analyze the similes, discussing the image that each evokes in the students' minds.

Give It a Try

It is now time for the students to apply this technique. Before incorporating it as part of their own writing, students need plenty of opportunity to practice this craft in isolation. Choose a familiar subject that lends itself to simile writing, such as the sun or stars, physical characteristics such as someone's hair or eyes, fire, the ocean, mountains, buildings, animals. Encourage students to use their five senses when creating effective similes.

A favorite annual lesson of the second-grade classes in our school is the Snowflake Similes project. Ask students to work independently to create a simile that describes some element of winter. Encourage them to write three such similes.

Celebration

Have each student select one favorite example from his or her list. Create a Snowflake Similes bulletin board display in the hallway. Ask each student to record his or her simile on a snowflake that he or she cuts out independently, or on one that you have precut. Allow students the opportunity to share their creations with their classmates. Finally, hang all the snowflakes on the bulletin board to create a winter wonderland of similes.

Here is a sampling of Snowflake Similes created by the second-grade students at St. James Elementary School:

Snow falls as quiet as a whisper
Icicles sparkling like new glass
Snow sits like a white blanket on the ground
Glistening snow like silver glitter in the sky
Snow as soft and white as a baby's quilt

Adaptations for Writers Familiar With This Craft

Students who understand the craft and are able to write similes need to take their use of this craft to the next level. For students who have heretofore experimented with writing similes in isolation, the next level would mean effectively incorporating the craft to improve their written pieces. For students who have mastered the appropriate use of simile in their written work, the next step might be to increase the level of sophistication or subtlety in the comparisons they craft. All of this is accomplished, of course, by using mentor texts that allow the students to discover how authors use similes to their greatest effect.

Read the following excerpt from *Night Rabbits* by Lee Posey wherein the author writes about a girl who is watching rabbits in her back yard: *Their leaps are soft as shyness*. Elicit explanations as to what makes this simile more sophisticated. If students are unable to do this, prompt them with discussion such as, "If you wanted to describe *soft* what words might you use for comparison? When I think of soft things, I think of a kitten's fur or a pillow or a bunny's tail or a baby's skin. I would never think of shyness, yet this simile works so well. It definitely creates a mental picture. What do you think? Is Posey successful with her choice of words?"

Read another excerpt, this time from *The Storm Book* by Charlotte Zolotow, in which the author describes a little boy's feelings during a thunderstorm. He makes two distinct comparisons as he thinks about the light from the lightning outside and the light from the lamp in his room: *The lightning was like a wild white wolf running free in the woods and the lamp like the gentle white terrier who came when the little boy called*. Once again, ask the students to determine how the author has taken the use of simile to an advanced level.

Below is a list of similes that may be used for this exercise. Keep in mind the age of your students and their experience in identifying and using similes when selecting appropriate excerpts for this lesson.

Jonathan London (*Puddles*) describes the end of a rainstorm in this way: *like a curtain rising on a shiny new day*.

Ralph Fletcher (*Hello, Harvest Moon*) describes moonset as *sprinkling silver coins like a careless millionaire over ponds, lakes, and seas, till all the money is spent*.

Jane Yolen (*Owl Moon*) uses a beautifully crafted simile when she describes the owl's flight: *Then the owl pumped its great wings and lifted off the branch like a shadow without sound*.

Marsha Wilson Chall (*Up North at the Cabin*) uses two effective similes to describe a bull moose: *Like a house on stilts, a bull moose stands in the shallows. His chest heaves and rumbles, mighty as a diesel engine*.

Patricia MacLachlan (*All the Places to Love*) makes a unique comparison when she writes: *I will show her my favorite place, the marsh, / Where ducklings follow their mother / Like tiny tumbles of leaves*.

Encourage students to be on the lookout for examples as they read independently. Students should record their findings on a class chart titled Sophisticated Similes. Be sure to spend a few minutes each day highlighting and discussing any additions to the chart. This is a means for you to assess your students' deeper understanding of the nuances of simile use.

Instruct students to go back through their writer's notebook entries and find places to insert similes. Encourage them to experiment with sophisticated use of this craft by using the mentor authors as models. While conferring with your students, focus on the use of simile, helping them to hone this craft. At the end of each writer's workshop, highlight a few students who are employing this technique successfully. Have each student select one favorite example from his or her writing notebook. Encourage students to share and evaluate one another's writing as a part of this process.

Explain to the students that you will be making a class book of Sophisticated Similes. Each simile should be highlighted on a separate page of the book. You may choose to have your students write out the simile or publish them on a computer. Students should then illustrate their similes. Bind the book. Laminate the cover. Add it to your library for your future students! In this way, your students will serve as mentor authors to one another and to future generations of writers. Students welcome the chance to serve as models and take this role very seriously. Celebrations such as these help your students view themselves as real authors.

Mentor Texts to Demonstrate Craft Elements

So, here it is—the heart of our book! We have explored with you 27 different craft elements and the important role that they play in teaching students to write well. We have suggested the framework for 10 different craft studies that may be adapted and incorporated into your writers' workshop. So now it's time to take a look at the foundation upon which all of your writing instruction will be built—the books that will serve as models for your aspiring young writers. In *First Grade Writers*, Parsons (2005) stresses the importance of having a collection of quality books for this purpose, writing, "Of course, I may refer to other books, but I need a core set of books to which I can return again and again as I teach the skills and qualities of good writing" (p. 8). We believe you will find Part 3 to be a valuable resource as you build your library of quality mentor texts.

Part 3 includes the following:

- Craft Elements Matrix—Mentor Texts Sorted by Title
- Craft Elements Matrix—Mentor Texts Sorted by Author
- Annotated Bibliography

The two quick-reference matrixes will serve as handy tools to cross-check book titles or authors with the craft elements found within each book. The annotated bibliography that follows provides you with a wide-ranging list of picture books from which you can select your "core set of books." We hope we have saved you time and effort by compiling for you this treasure trove of wonderful books and highlighting the many teaching possibilities found within each gem. Wherever copyright permission allowed, we have included excerpts to serve as exemplars of craft use.

Parsons (2005) sums up our goal in this one simple sentence: "Having a good understanding of what mentor texts have to offer gives me a greater vision of what my students can do" (p. 8). It is our hope that you will come to know and love these books as we do—and, more important, that you often will hear your students say, "I can write like that!"

Craft Elements Matrix—Mentor Texts Sorted by Title

Column key (Book Title — Author):

1. A Is for Amos — Chandra, Deborah
2. All the Colors of the Earth — Hamanaka, Sheila
3. All the Places to Love — MacLachlan, Patricia
4. All You Need for a Snowman — Schertle, Alice
5. Atlantic — Karas, G. Brian
6. Aunt Flossie's Hats (and Crab Cakes Later) — Howard, Elizabeth Fitzgerald
7. Autumnblings — Florian, Douglas
8. Bat Loves the Night — Davies, Nicola
9. Bats at the Beach — Lies, Brian
10. Bats at the Library — Lies, Brian
11. Beach Day — Roosa, Karen
12. Bigmama's — Crews, Donald
13. Birthday Presents — Rylant, Cynthia
14. Busy Toes — Bowie, C.W.
15. Butternut Hollow Pond — Heinz, Brian J.
16. Candy Corn — Stevenson, James
17. Clara Caterpillar — Edwards, Pamela Duncan
18. Cloud Dance — Locker, Thomas
19. Colors! ¡Colores! — Luján, Jorge
20. Come On, Rain! — Hesse, Karen
21. Come to the Ocean's Edge — Pringle, Laurence
22. Creatures of Earth, Sea, and Sky — Heard, Georgia
23. Crocodile Listens — Sayre, April Pulley
24. Dear Mrs. LaRue — Teague, Mark

Craft Element	1	2	3	4	5	6	7	8	9	10	11	12	13	14	15	16	17	18	19	20	21	22	23	24
Wordplay							✓	✓	✓	✓	✓												✓	
Voice						✓							✓				✓							✓
Verbs and Verb Forms					✓			✓			✓				✓					✓		✓	✓	✓
Text Features					✓	✓	✓	✓										✓	✓			✓	✓	✓
Simile		✓	✓			✓	✓	✓							✓	✓				✓	✓	✓	✓	
Sequencing													✓								✓	✓		✓
See-Saw Pattern																								
Rhyme	✓	✓		✓			✓		✓	✓	✓									✓				
Repetition	✓	✓	✓	✓	✓	✓				✓			✓						✓	✓				
Punctuation	✓		✓		✓			✓	✓		✓	✓	✓		✓					✓			✓	✓
Print Layout	✓	✓	✓		✓			✓	✓		✓						✓	✓		✓	✓	✓	✓	
Print Features	✓		✓	✓	✓	✓		✓	✓		✓	✓			✓		✓					✓	✓	
Point of View					✓																		✓	
Personification		✓			✓			✓	✓		✓				✓			✓	✓	✓		✓	✓	
Onomatopoeia	✓							✓	✓				✓		✓	✓				✓	✓	✓	✓	
Metaphor		✓						✓	✓		✓				✓				✓	✓	✓	✓	✓	
Lists		✓		✓	✓	✓			✓					✓		✓					✓	✓		
Lead					✓							✓			✓						✓			
Interesting Format																								✓
Hyperbole						✓													✓					✓
Flashback						✓						✓												
Effective Ending	✓			✓							✓	✓												
Descriptive Language		✓	✓		✓	✓	✓	✓	✓		✓	✓	✓		✓		✓	✓	✓	✓	✓			
Cumulative Text																								
Circular Ending																					✓			
Breaking the Rules		✓		✓		✓			✓	✓		✓	✓		✓								✓	✓
Alliteration	✓		✓			✓	✓	✓	✓	✓							✓		✓	✓	✓	✓	✓	✓

Book Title	Author	Wordplay	Voice	Verbs and Verb Forms	Text Features	Simile	Sequencing	See-Saw Pattern	Rhyme	Repetition	Punctuation	Print Layout	Print Features	Point of View	Personification	Onomatopoeia	Metaphor	Lists	Lead	Interesting Format	Hyperbole	Flashback	Effective Ending	Descriptive Language	Cumulative Text	Circular Ending	Breaking the Rules	Alliteration
Dear Tooth Fairy	Edwards, Pamela Duncan		✓								✓		✓							✓								
Dear Willie Rudd,	Gray, Libba Moore									✓	✓		✓									✓	✓	✓				
Diamond Life	Smith Jr., Charles R.	✓	✓		✓				✓	✓	✓	✓	✓			✓	✓	✓			✓	✓					✓	
Diary of a Worm	Cronin, Doreen		✓		✓		✓						✓	✓		✓				✓								
Dirty Laundry Pile	Janeczko, Paul B.	✓	✓		✓	✓			✓	✓	✓	✓	✓	✓	✓	✓	✓							✓				✓
Dogs Rule!	Kirk, Daniel		✓		✓	✓			✓		✓		✓	✓			✓				✓						✓	✓
Doodle Dandies	Lewis, J. Patrick	✓				✓			✓			✓	✓	✓														✓
Dream Weaver	London, Jonathan		✓	✓	✓	✓				✓	✓		✓		✓	✓	✓		✓				✓	✓			✓	
Earrings!	Viorst, Judith									✓	✓			✓					✓		✓						✓	
Earthdance	Ryder, Joanne							✓	✓			✓			✓		✓		✓				✓	✓				
Ellsworth's Extraordinary Electric Ears	Fisher, Valorie	✓			✓					✓	✓	✓	✓							✓								✓
Farmer's Garden	Harrison, David L.									✓			✓															✓
Fireflies	Brinckloe, Julie														✓		✓				✓		✓	✓			✓	
Fishing in the Air	Creech, Sharon									✓	✓	✓					✓					✓	✓	✓	✓		✓	✓
Four Famished Foxes and Fosdyke	Edwards, Pamela Duncan										✓	✓	✓				✓											✓
Freight Train	Crews, Donald				✓		✓				✓																✓	
Gentle Giant Octopus	Wallace, Karen		✓	✓	✓	✓	✓			✓	✓	✓		✓								✓	✓				✓
The Gift of the Tree	Tresselt, Alvin		✓	✓		✓		✓						✓		✓		✓				✓	✓			✓	✓
Gila Monsters Meet You at the Airport	Sharmat, Marjorie Weinman		✓							✓		✓		✓	✓			✓	✓			✓	✓			✓	
Gilberto and the Wind	Ets, Marie Hall						✓				✓												✓					
Grandad Bill's Song	Yolen, Jane									✓	✓		✓						✓									
Grandpa Loved	Nobisso, Josephine	✓		✓	✓	✓	✓		✓	✓	✓			✓	✓	✓		✓					✓	✓				✓
Grandpa Never Lies	Fletcher, Ralph		✓		✓	✓				✓		✓			✓		✓						✓	✓			✓	
Grandparents' Song	Hamanaka, Sheila		✓			✓	✓		✓	✓	✓				✓		✓											
Green Eyes	Birnbaum, Abe					✓	✓					✓		✓			✓							✓				

(continued)

Craft Elements Matrix—Mentor Texts Sorted by Title (continued)

Books (columns):

1. H Is for Home Run — Herzog, Brad
2. Hair Dance! — Johnson, Dinah
3. Hairs/Pelitos — Cisneros, Sandra
4. Hello Harvest Moon — Fletcher, Ralph
5. Hello Ocean — Ryan, Pam Muñoz
6. Hide and Seek Fog — Tresselt, Alvin
7. Hot City — Joosse, Barbara
8. I Am the Dog, I Am the Cat — Hall, Donald
9. If You Were Alliteration — Shaskan, Trisha Speed
10. If You Were Onomatopoeia — Shaskan, Trisha Speed
11. The Important Book — Brown, Margaret Wise
12. In My New Yellow Shirt — Spinelli, Eileen
13. In November — Rylant, Cynthia
14. Journey Around Chicago From A to Z — Zschock, Martha Day
15. Just Like Daddy — Asch, Frank
16. A Kitten's Year — Day, Nancy Raines
17. Last Night at the Zoo — Garland, Michael
18. Leaf Jumpers — Gerber, Carole
19. Listen, Listen — Gershator, Phyllis
20. The Listening Walk — Showers, Paul
21. The Little House — Burton, Virginia Lee
22. The Little Yellow Leaf — Berger, Carin
23. Loki & Alex — Smith Jr., Charles R.
24. The Lonely Scarecrow — Preston, Tim

Craft Element	1	2	3	4	5	6	7	8	9	10	11	12	13	14	15	16	17	18	19	20	21	22	23	24
Wordplay					✓	✓						✓										✓		
Voice							✓	✓															✓	
Verbs and Verb Forms					✓	✓						✓									✓	✓		
Text Features	✓	✓	✓			✓			✓	✓			✓			✓						✓		
Simile			✓	✓	✓		✓		✓	✓							✓					✓		✓
Sequencing																		✓		✓				
See-Saw Pattern										✓												✓		
Rhyme	✓	✓			✓														✓	✓				
Repetition	✓	✓			✓		✓				✓	✓	✓		✓		✓	✓	✓	✓		✓		
Punctuation	✓	✓		✓	✓	✓	✓	✓	✓						✓	✓	✓	✓	✓	✓	✓	✓		
Print Layout	✓	✓	✓	✓	✓				✓	✓	✓		✓			✓	✓	✓	✓	✓	✓	✓		
Print Features	✓	✓	✓	✓		✓	✓		✓	✓	✓						✓	✓	✓	✓	✓	✓		
Point of View								✓		✓							✓	✓	✓	✓			✓	
Personification				✓	✓	✓					✓	✓					✓	✓	✓	✓	✓	✓		✓
Onomatopoeia									✓	✓							✓			✓				
Metaphor		✓		✓	✓		✓				✓	✓			✓		✓					✓		✓
Lists								✓								✓								
Lead					✓									✓										
Interesting Format	✓													✓										
Hyperbole				✓			✓																	
Flashback																								
Effective Ending		✓		✓	✓						✓				✓			✓	✓	✓				
Descriptive Language		✓	✓	✓	✓	✓	✓					✓	✓				✓	✓		✓	✓	✓		✓
Cumulative Text																								
Circular Ending																✓		✓					✓	
Breaking the Rules			✓			✓	✓				✓	✓	✓		✓				✓	✓	✓		✓	✓
Alliteration	✓	✓		✓	✓	✓			✓			✓		✓							✓	✓	✓	✓

Book Title	Author	Wordplay	Voice	Verbs and Verb Forms	Text Features	Simile	Sequencing	See-Saw Pattern	Rhyme	Repetition	Punctuation	Print Layout	Print Features	Point of View	Personification	Onomatopoeia	Metaphor	Lists	Lead	Interesting Format	Hyperbole	Flashback	Effective Ending	Descriptive Language	Cumulative Text	Circular Ending	Breaking the Rules	Alliteration
Icng night moon	Rylant, Cynthia					✓	✓			✓		✓	✓		✓		✓							✓			✓	
Max Found Two Sticks	Pinkney, Brian										✓		✓			✓			✓								✓	
Mojave	Siebert, Diane						✓		✓					✓	✓				✓					✓		✓		
The Moon Was the Best	Zolotow, Charlotte				✓	✓				✓		✓	✓		✓				✓				✓	✓			✓	✓
Mud	Ray, May Lyn	✓				✓				✓			✓		✓	✓			✓				✓	✓			✓	✓
My Dog Is as Smelly as Dirty Socks	Piven, Hanoch		✓		✓	✓					✓		✓			✓		✓									✓	
My Little Island	Lessac, Frané					✓					✓		✓								✓		✓	✓			✓	✓
My Mama Had a Dancing Heart	Gray, Libba Moore	✓			✓	✓				✓	✓	✓	✓		✓	✓	✓		✓				✓	✓			✓	
My Map Book	Fanelli, Sara		✓		✓							✓	✓							✓								
Night in the Country	Rylant, Cynthia						✓		✓	✓	✓	✓	✓		✓	✓	✓		✓		✓		✓	✓		✓	✓	✓
Night Rabbits	Posey, Lee					✓					✓				✓	✓	✓		✓					✓			✓	
On the Same Day in March	Singer, Marilyn	✓		✓	✓	✓	✓		✓	✓	✓	✓	✓		✓	✓	✓	✓	✓		✓		✓	✓			✓	✓
The Other Way to Listen	Baylor, Byrd							✓			✓	✓	✓		✓			✓	✓					✓			✓	
Out of the Ocean	Frasier, Debra				✓						✓	✓				✓		✓									✓	
Over and Over	Zolotow, Charlotte						✓			✓						✓		✓	✓					✓		✓	✓	
Owl Moon	Yolen, Jane		✓	✓		✓			✓	✓	✓	✓	✓		✓	✓	✓	✓	✓		✓		✓				✓	✓
Parade	Crews, Donald										✓	✓	✓													✓	✓
Pot Luck	Shelby, Anne										✓		✓						✓									✓
Pssst! It's Me...the Bogeyman	Park, Barbara	✓	✓		✓		✓			✓	✓	✓	✓			✓	✓		✓		✓			✓		✓	✓	✓
Puddles	London, Jonathan	✓		✓		✓			✓	✓	✓	✓	✓		✓	✓		✓					✓	✓		✓		
The Pumpkin Book	Gibbons, Gail				✓					✓	✓																✓	
A Quiet Place	Wood, Douglas	✓				✓				✓	✓	✓	✓		✓	✓	✓						✓	✓		✓	✓	
Rain	Stojic, Manya			✓			✓			✓	✓		✓			✓							✓	✓	✓				
Roller Coaster	Frazee, Marla			✓	✓						✓	✓	✓			✓			✓				✓				✓	
Rosie and Michael	Viorst, Judith		✓					✓		✓			✓															
Saturdays and Teacakes	Laminack, Lester	✓	✓	✓		✓				✓	✓		✓		✓	✓	✓	✓					✓	✓			✓	✓

(continued)

Book Title	Author	Wordplay	Voice	Verbs and Verb Forms	Text Features	Simile	Sequencing	See-Saw Pattern	Rhyme	Repetition	Punctuation	Print Layout	Print Features	Point of View	Personification	Onomatopoeia	Metaphor	Lists	Lead	Interesting Format	Hyperbole	Flashback	Effective Ending	Descriptive Language	Cumulative Text	Circular Ending	Breaking the Rules	Alliteration
Scarecrow	Rylant, Cynthia	✓		✓		✓				✓	✓				✓						✓			✓			✓	
Scoot!	Falwell, Cathryn			✓	✓	✓			✓	✓	✓	✓	✓															✓
Shortcut	Crews, Donald			✓						✓		✓	✓			✓			✓					✓			✓	
Sky Tree: Seeing Science Through Art	Locker, Thomas			✓	✓		✓																	✓		✓		
Small Green Snake	Gray, Libba Moore					✓			✓	✓	✓	✓	✓			✓	✓						✓					✓
Snow	Rylant, Cynthia					✓				✓	✓				✓								✓	✓			✓	
Snow Is Falling	Branley, Franklyn M.				✓	✓				✓								✓										
Snow Music	Perkins, Lynne Rae			✓		✓			✓	✓	✓	✓	✓		✓	✓			✓				✓	✓				✓
Snow Sounds	Johnson, David A.										✓	✓	✓			✓												✓
The Snow Speaks	Carlstrom, Nancy White			✓	✓	✓				✓		✓			✓									✓			✓	✓
The Snowy Day	Keats, Ezra Jack								✓	✓	✓					✓								✓		✓		
Some Smug Slug	Edwards, Pamela Duncan					✓											✓						✓	✓				✓
Someday	Spinelli, Eileen							✓		✓	✓						✓				✓			✓			✓	
Spots (Counting Creatures From Sky to Sea)	Lesser, Carolyn		✓						✓			✓	✓							✓								✓
The Squiggle	Schaefer, Carole Lexa	✓		✓							✓	✓	✓			✓											✓	✓
The Storm Book	Zolotow, Charlotte	✓			✓	✓				✓		✓	✓		✓	✓	✓						✓	✓			✓	✓
Storm in the Night	Stolz, Mary	✓		✓	✓	✓			✓		✓	✓	✓		✓	✓	✓		✓			✓	✓	✓			✓	✓
Summersaults	Florian, Douglas	✓	✓							✓	✓	✓	✓			✓											✓	✓
Sun Dance, Water Dance	London, Jonathan	✓	✓	✓		✓				✓					✓						✓			✓				
A Swim Through the Sea	Pratt, Kristin Joy				✓						✓	✓	✓						✓	✓								✓
This Place in the Snow	Bond, Rebecca	✓				✓						✓	✓				✓		✓					✓				✓
Tigress	Dowson, Nick	✓	✓	✓	✓	✓			✓		✓	✓	✓		✓									✓				✓
Treasures of the Heart	Miller, Alice Ann		✓															✓					✓					
Turtle Splash! Countdown at the Pond	Falwell, Cathryn	✓		✓	✓	✓			✓	✓	✓	✓	✓		✓	✓	✓											✓
Twilight Comes Twice	Fletcher, Ralph					✓									✓		✓							✓				✓

Craft Elements Matrix — Mentor Texts Sorted by Title (rows = craft elements, columns = book titles)

Craft Element	Twister (Beard, Darleen Bailey)	Up North at the Cabin (Chall, Marsha Wilson)	Uptown (Collier, Bryan)	Very Last First Time (Andrews, Jan)	Vroomaloom Zoom (Coy, John)	The Wacky Wedding (Edwards, Pamela Duncan)	Walk On! A Guide for Babies of All Ages (Frazee, Marla)	Walter Was Worried (Seeger, Laura Vaccaro)	Watch William Walk (Jonas, Ann)	Water Hole Waiting (Kurtz, Jane and Christopher)	Water Music: Poems for Children (Yolen, Jane)	Welcome to the Green House (Yolen, Jane)	What's Up, What's Down? (Schaefer, Lola M.)	When I Was Little (Curtis, Jamie Lee)	When Marcus Moore Moved In (Bond, Rebecca)	When the Fireflies Come (London, Jonathan)	When the Moon Is Full: A Lunar Year (Pollock, Penny)	When the Sky Is Like Lace (Horwitz, Elinor Lander)	Where Once There Was a Wood (Fleming, Denise)	White Snow, Bright Snow (Tresselt, Alvin)	Whoosh Went the Wind (Derby, Sally)	Winter: An Alphabet Acrostic (Schnur, Steven)	Winter Is the Warmest Season (Stringer, Lauren)	the wonderful happens (Rylant, Cynthia)	The World That We Want (Toft, Kim Michelle)	The Worrywarts (Edwards, Pamela Duncan)
Wordplay	✓	✓		✓	✓						✓	✓					✓		✓				✓			
Voice			✓				✓							✓		✓					✓					
Verbs and Verb Forms	✓	✓		✓					✓	✓		✓	✓							✓	✓					✓
Text Features		✓					✓			✓	✓	✓					✓		✓	✓				✓	✓	
Simile	✓	✓	✓							✓	✓	✓			✓	✓	✓	✓		✓	✓	✓		✓		
Sequencing								✓							✓		✓					✓				
See-Saw Pattern														✓												
Rhyme	✓									✓		✓					✓		✓	✓						
Repetition	✓	✓	✓		✓					✓		✓	✓			✓	✓	✓	✓	✓				✓	✓	✓
Punctuation	✓	✓	✓	✓					✓	✓		✓			✓	✓	✓	✓		✓	✓					
Print Layout			✓		✓		✓	✓	✓	✓	✓				✓		✓	✓		✓	✓		✓	✓		
Print Features	✓		✓		✓	✓		✓		✓		✓	✓		✓		✓		✓		✓			✓	✓	✓
Point of View						✓	✓																			
Personification	✓	✓	✓	✓						✓	✓	✓			✓	✓	✓		✓		✓			✓		
Onomatopoeia	✓	✓		✓	✓	✓				✓		✓			✓	✓								✓		
Metaphor	✓	✓	✓							✓	✓	✓			✓		✓	✓		✓						
Lists		✓								✓		✓		✓		✓	✓					✓				
Lead							✓					✓	✓		✓			✓	✓	✓		✓				
Interesting Format								✓																		
Hyperbole					✓															✓						
Flashback																										
Effective Ending		✓	✓	✓	✓										✓	✓		✓		✓		✓				
Descriptive Language	✓	✓	✓	✓						✓		✓	✓		✓	✓	✓	✓		✓		✓	✓			
Cumulative Text														✓												
Circular Ending																										✓
Breaking the Rules					✓							✓	✓		✓	✓	✓	✓	✓	✓		✓	✓			
Alliteration		✓				✓			✓	✓		✓	✓		✓	✓	✓	✓	✓	✓	✓		✓			✓

Craft Elements Matrix—Mentor Texts Sorted by Author

Craft Element	Very Last First Time	Just Like Daddy	The Other Way to Listen	Twister	The Little Yellow Leaf	Green Eyes	This Place in the Snow	When Marcus Moore Moved In	Busy Toes	Snow Is Falling	Fireflies	The Important Book	The Little House	The Snow Speaks	Up North at the Cabin	A Is for Amos	Hairs/Pelitos	Uptown	Vroomaloom Zoom	Fishing in the Air	Bigmama's	Freight Train	Parade	Shortcut	Diary of a Worm
Wordplay	✓			✓			✓								✓				✓						
Voice											✓							✓		✓	✓				✓
Verbs and Verb Forms	✓			✓							✓				✓										
Text Features										✓							✓								✓
Simile				✓		✓	✓	✓			✓			✓		✓	✓			✓					
Sequencing						✓		✓					✓												✓
See-Saw Pattern			✓																						
Rhyme				✓													✓								
Repetition		✓	✓	✓	✓		✓	✓		✓	✓	✓		✓	✓	✓		✓	✓	✓		✓		✓	
Punctuation	✓	✓	✓	✓	✓				✓		✓		✓		✓	✓		✓			✓	✓	✓		
Print Layout			✓		✓	✓	✓	✓	✓		✓	✓	✓		✓		✓	✓			✓	✓	✓	✓	
Print Features			✓	✓	✓		✓	✓	✓			✓	✓			✓	✓	✓			✓		✓	✓	✓
Point of View						✓								✓										✓	
Personification	✓		✓	✓	✓						✓		✓	✓	✓			✓							
Onomatopoeia	✓			✓			✓		✓						✓	✓			✓		✓			✓	✓
Metaphor				✓		✓	✓				✓				✓	✓		✓		✓					
Lists			✓						✓	✓					✓		✓								
Lead						✓	✓						✓					✓							
Interesting Format																								✓	
Hyperbole											✓														
Flashback													✓												
Effective Ending	✓	✓			✓		✓	✓			✓	✓	✓		✓	✓		✓	✓	✓					
Descriptive Language	✓		✓	✓	✓	✓	✓				✓		✓	✓	✓		✓	✓	✓	✓	✓		✓		
Cumulative Text																			✓		✓				
Circular Ending																✓									
Breaking the Rules		✓	✓		✓		✓	✓			✓	✓	✓	✓		✓		✓	✓	✓	✓	✓	✓	✓	
Alliteration			✓				✓	✓						✓	✓	✓						✓	✓		

Author	Book Title
Andrews, Jan	Very Last First Time
Asch, Frank	Just Like Daddy
Baylor, Byrd	The Other Way to Listen
Beard, Darleen Bailey	Twister
Berger, Carin	The Little Yellow Leaf
Birnbaum, Abe	Green Eyes
Bond, Rebecca	This Place in the Snow
Bond, Rebecca	When Marcus Moore Moved In
Bowie, C.W.	Busy Toes
Branley, Franklyn M.	Snow Is Falling
Brinckloe, Julie	Fireflies
Brown, Margaret Wise	The Important Book
Burton, Virginia Lee	The Little House
Carlstrom, Nancy White	The Snow Speaks
Chall, Marsha Wilson	Up North at the Cabin
Chandra, Deborah	A Is for Amos
Cisneros, Sandra	Hairs/Pelitos
Collier, Bryan	Uptown
Coy, John	Vroomaloom Zoom
Creech, Sharon	Fishing in the Air
Crews, Donald	Bigmama's
Crews, Donald	Freight Train
Crews, Donald	Parade
Crews, Donald	Shortcut
Cronin, Doreen	Diary of a Worm

Author	Book Title	Alliteration	Breaking the Rules	Circular Ending	Cumulative Text	Descriptive Language	Effective Ending	Flashback	Hyperbole	Interesting Format	Lead	Lists	Metaphor	Onomatopoeia	Personification	Point of View	Print Features	Print Layout	Punctuation	Repetition	Rhyme	See-Saw Pattern	Sequencing	Simile	Text Features	Verbs and Verb Forms	Voice	Wordplay
Curtis, Jamie Lee	When I Was Little										✓	✓					✓			✓		✓					✓	
Davies, Nicola	Bat Loves the Night	✓				✓	✓						✓		✓		✓		✓					✓	✓	✓		✓
Day, Nancy Raines	A Kitten's Year											✓						✓	✓							✓		
Derby, Sally	Whoosh Went the Wind	✓	✓			✓	✓		✓		✓		✓		✓		✓	✓	✓					✓		✓	✓	
Dowson, Nick	Tigress	✓	✓			✓					✓		✓		✓		✓	✓						✓	✓	✓		✓
Edwards, Pamela Duncan	Clara Caterpillar	✓				✓											✓	✓						✓		✓	✓	
Edwards, Pamela Duncan	Dear Tooth Fairy									✓							✓		✓								✓	
Edwards, Pamela Duncan	Four Famished Foxes and Fosdyke	✓											✓				✓						✓	✓	✓	✓	✓	
Edwards, Pamela Duncan	Some Smug Slug	✓				✓	✓																	✓	✓	✓		
Edwards, Pamela Duncan	The Wacky Wedding	✓							✓					✓			✓								✓			
Edwards, Pamela Duncan	The Worrywarts	✓		✓										✓	✓		✓			✓						✓		
Ets, Marie Hall	Gilberto and the Wind		✓				✓							✓	✓		✓		✓	✓							✓	
Falwell, Cathryn	Scoot!	✓															✓	✓	✓	✓	✓			✓	✓	✓		
Falwell, Cathryn	Turtle Splash! Countdown at the Pond	✓												✓			✓	✓	✓		✓				✓	✓		
Fanelli, Sara	My Map Book									✓							✓	✓							✓		✓	
Fisher, Valorie	Ellsworth's Extraordinary Electric Ears	✓															✓								✓			
Fleming, Denise	Where Once There Was a Wood	✓	✓			✓	✓				✓									✓	✓				✓			
Fletcher, Ralph	Grandpa Never Lies		✓			✓	✓					✓	✓		✓			✓		✓			✓					
Fletcher, Ralph	Hello, Harvest Moon	✓				✓	✓		✓				✓		✓		✓	✓	✓					✓				
Fletcher, Ralph	Twilight Comes Twice	✓				✓							✓		✓			✓		✓				✓				
Florian, Douglas	Autumnblings	✓				✓							✓	✓	✓		✓	✓			✓			✓	✓			✓
Florian, Douglas	Summersaults	✓											✓	✓				✓		✓	✓			✓	✓			✓
Frasier, Debra	Out of the Ocean		✓									✓					✓		✓						✓			
Frazee, Marla	Roller Coaster		✓	✓		✓					✓			✓			✓	✓	✓							✓		
Frazee, Marla	Walk On! A Guide for Babies of All Ages										✓					✓	✓	✓									✓	
Garland, Michael	Last Night at the Zoo			✓							✓								✓	✓	✓			✓		✓		

(continued)

Craft Elements Matrix—Mentor Texts Sorted by Author (continued)

Author	Book Title	Alliteration	Breaking the Rules	Circular Ending	Cumulative Text	Descriptive Language	Effective Ending	Flashback	Hyperbole	Interesting Format	Lead	Lists	Metaphor	Onomatopoeia	Personification	Point of View	Print Features	Print Layout	Punctuation	Repetition	Rhyme	See-Saw Pattern	Sequencing	Simile	Text Features	Verbs and Verb Forms	Voice	Wordplay
Gerber, Carole	Leaf Jumpers					✓							✓					✓			✓			✓	✓			✓
Gershator, Phyllis	Listen, Listen	✓		✓		✓								✓	✓			✓	✓	✓	✓		✓		✓			
Gibbons, Gail	The Pumpkin Book		✓																✓	✓					✓			
Gray, Libba Moore	Dear Willie Rudd,					✓	✓	✓									✓		✓	✓								
Gray, Libba Moore	My Mama Had a Dancing Heart		✓			✓	✓	✓			✓						✓	✓	✓	✓			✓	✓				✓
Gray, Libba Moore	Small Green Snake	✓											✓	✓			✓	✓	✓	✓	✓			✓				
Hall, Donald	I Am the Dog, I Am the Cat											✓				✓	✓	✓	✓			✓					✓	
Hamanaka, Sheila	All the Colors of the Earth		✓			✓						✓	✓		✓			✓		✓	✓			✓				
Hamanaka, Sheila	Grandparents' Song												✓		✓				✓	✓	✓			✓				
Harrison, David L.	Farmer's Garden	✓								✓							✓			✓	✓	✓						✓
Heard, Georgia	Creatures of Earth, Sea, and Sky	✓				✓							✓	✓	✓			✓		✓	✓			✓	✓			
Heinz, Brian J.	Butternut Hollow Pond		✓			✓							✓	✓	✓				✓					✓		✓		
Herzog, Brad	H Is for Home Run	✓								✓							✓	✓	✓	✓	✓				✓			
Hesse, Karen	Come On, Rain!	✓				✓			✓		✓		✓		✓		✓	✓	✓	✓				✓		✓		
Horwitz, Elinor Lander	When the Sky Is Like Lace	✓	✓			✓						✓		✓	✓		✓	✓	✓	✓				✓				✓
Howard, Elizabeth Fitzgerald	Aunt Flossie's Hats (and Crab Cakes Later)	✓	✓			✓		✓	✓			✓					✓		✓	✓				✓	✓		✓	
Janeczko, Paul B.	Dirty Laundry Pile	✓				✓							✓	✓	✓	✓	✓	✓	✓	✓	✓			✓	✓		✓	✓
Johnson, David A.	Snow Sounds	✓												✓			✓	✓	✓									
Johnson, Dinah	Hair Dance!	✓				✓	✓						✓				✓	✓	✓	✓	✓			✓	✓			
Jonas, Ann	Watch William Walk	✓																✓	✓							✓		
Joosse, Barbara	Hot City		✓			✓			✓				✓				✓		✓	✓				✓			✓	
Karas, G. Brian	Atlantic					✓					✓	✓			✓	✓	✓	✓	✓	✓					✓	✓		
Keats, Ezra Jack	The Snowy Day			✓		✓								✓					✓	✓								
Kirk, Daniel	Dogs Rule!	✓	✓						✓				✓			✓	✓				✓			✓	✓		✓	
Kurtz, Jane and Christopher	Water Hole Waiting	✓	✓			✓						✓	✓	✓	✓		✓	✓	✓	✓	✓			✓	✓	✓		

Author	Book Title	Alliteration	Breaking the Rules	Circular Ending	Cumulative Text	Descriptive Language	Effective Ending	Flashback	Hyperbole	Interesting Format	Lead	Lists	Metaphor	Onomatopoeia	Personification	Point of View	Print Features	Print Layout	Punctuation	Repetition	Rhyme	See-Saw Pattern	Sequencing	Simile	Text Features	Verbs and Verb Forms	Voice	Wordplay
Laminack, Lester	Saturdays and Teacakes	✓	✓			✓	✓						✓	✓	✓		✓		✓	✓				✓		✓	✓	✓
Lessac, Frané	My Little Island	✓	✓			✓						✓		✓	✓		✓	✓	✓					✓				
Lesser, Carolyn	Spots (Counting Creatures From Sky to Sea)	✓																✓			✓					✓		
Lewis, J. Patrick	Doodle Dandies	✓														✓	✓	✓			✓			✓				✓
Lies, Brian	Bats at the Beach	✓	✓			✓						✓	✓		✓		✓	✓	✓		✓							✓
Lies, Brian	Bats at the Library	✓	✓			✓											✓	✓	✓	✓	✓							✓
Locker, Thomas	Cloud Dance					✓									✓			✓							✓			
Locker, Thomas	Sky Tree: Seeing Science Through Art			✓		✓																	✓		✓	✓		
London, Jonathan	Dream Weaver		✓			✓	✓				✓		✓	✓	✓		✓		✓					✓	✓	✓		
London, Jonathan	Puddles			✓		✓			✓		✓		✓	✓	✓		✓	✓	✓	✓	✓			✓		✓		✓
London, Jonathan	Sun Dance, Water Dance					✓			✓				✓		✓		✓	✓	✓					✓		✓		✓
London, Jonathan	When the Fireflies Come	✓	✓			✓	✓				✓	✓	✓	✓	✓		✓		✓	✓				✓			✓	
Luján, Jorge	Colors! ¡Colores!					✓							✓		✓		✓			✓				✓	✓			
MacLachlan, Patricia	All the Places to Love	✓				✓											✓	✓	✓	✓				✓				
Miller, Alice Ann	Treasures of the Heart						✓					✓					✓	✓			✓						✓	
Nobisso, Josephine	Grandpa Loved	✓				✓		✓							✓				✓	✓						✓		
Park, Barbara	Psssst! It's Me…the Bogeyman	✓	✓	✓							✓		✓				✓	✓	✓						✓		✓	✓
Perkins, Lynne Rae	Snow Music	✓				✓	✓				✓			✓	✓		✓	✓	✓		✓			✓				
Pinkney, Brian	Max Found Two Sticks		✓											✓			✓		✓									
Piven, Hanoch	My Dog Is as Smelly as Dirty Socks		✓														✓		✓					✓	✓		✓	
Pollock, Penny	When the Moon Is Full: A Lunar Year	✓				✓							✓		✓						✓		✓	✓	✓			
Posey, Lee	Night Rabbits					✓					✓		✓	✓			✓							✓				
Pratt, Kristin Joy	A Swim Through the Sea	✓								✓							✓	✓							✓			
Preston, Tim	The Lonely Scarecrow	✓	✓			✓							✓		✓		✓		✓					✓				
Pringle, Laurence	Come to the Ocean's Edge	✓		✓		✓							✓		✓		✓		✓				✓	✓	✓	✓		
Ray, May Lyn	Mud	✓	✓			✓					✓			✓	✓		✓	✓		✓				✓				✓

(continued)

Craft Element	Beach Day	Hello Ocean	Earthdance	Birthday Presents	In November	long night moon	Night in the Country	Scarecrow	Snow	the wonderful happens	Crocodile Listens	The Squiggle	What's Up, What's Down?	All You Need for a Snowman	Winter: An Alphabet Acrostic	Walter Was Worried	Gila Monsters Meet You at the Airport	If You Were Alliteration	If You Were Onomatopoeia	Pot Luck	The Listening Walk	Mojave	On the Same Day in March	Loki & Alex
Wordplay	✓	✓								✓								✓				✓	✓	
Voice																					✓			✓
Verbs and Verb Forms	✓	✓								✓								✓				✓		✓
Text Features																✓		✓	✓					✓
Simile					✓	✓			✓	✓						✓			✓	✓		✓	✓	✓
Sequencing				✓			✓										✓						✓	✓
See-Saw Pattern																								✓
Rhyme	✓	✓												✓								✓	✓	✓
Repetition			✓	✓	✓	✓	✓	✓			✓	✓		✓			✓		✓			✓	✓	
Punctuation	✓	✓		✓				✓	✓		✓	✓	✓		✓		✓		✓	✓		✓		
Print Layout	✓	✓	✓			✓	✓				✓		✓	✓	✓		✓	✓		✓		✓	✓	
Print Features						✓	✓				✓		✓	✓	✓		✓	✓		✓		✓	✓	
Point of View			✓											✓					✓		✓		✓	✓
Personification	✓	✓	✓			✓	✓		✓	✓			✓		✓		✓				✓	✓	✓	
Onomatopoeia							✓				✓		✓				✓		✓		✓			
Metaphor	✓	✓	✓			✓	✓	✓					✓									✓		
Lists											✓				✓									
Lead		✓	✓			✓					✓			✓				✓						
Interesting Format													✓											
Hyperbole							✓										✓							
Flashback																								
Effective Ending		✓	✓	✓			✓		✓								✓			✓	✓			
Descriptive Language	✓	✓	✓	✓	✓	✓	✓	✓	✓						✓							✓	✓	
Cumulative Text													✓											
Circular Ending																						✓		
Breaking the Rules				✓	✓	✓	✓	✓	✓	✓	✓		✓	✓			✓					✓	✓	
Alliteration		✓									✓	✓	✓			✓		✓		✓		✓		

Author	Book Title
Roosa, Karen	Beach Day
Ryan, Pam Muñoz	Hello Ocean
Ryder, Joanne	Earthdance
Rylant, Cynthia	Birthday Presents
Rylant, Cynthia	In November
Rylant, Cynthia	long night moon
Rylant, Cynthia	Night in the Country
Rylant, Cynthia	Scarecrow
Rylant, Cynthia	Snow
Rylant, Cynthia	the wonderful happens
Sayre, April Pulley	Crocodile Listens
Schaefer, Carole Lexa	The Squiggle
Schaefer, Lola M.	What's Up, What's Down?
Schertle, Alice	All You Need for a Snowman
Schnur, Steven	Winter: An Alphabet Acrostic
Seeger, Laura Vaccaro	Walter Was Worried
Sharmat, Marjorie Weinman	Gila Monsters Meet You at the Airport
Shaskan, Trisha Speed	If You Were Alliteration
Shaskan, Trisha Speed	If You Were Onomatopoeia
Shelby, Anne	Pot Luck
Showers, Paul	The Listening Walk
Siebert, Diane	Mojave
Singer, Marilyn	On the Same Day in March
Smith Jr., Charles R.	Loki & Alex

Column key (Author — Book Title):

1. Smith Jr., Charles R. — Diamond Life
2. Spinelli, Eileen — In My New Yellow Shirt
3. Spinelli, Eileen — Someday
4. Stevenson, James — Candy Corn
5. Stojic, Manya — Rain
6. Stolz, Mary — Storm in the Night
7. Stringer, Lauren — Winter Is the Warmest Season
8. Teague, Mark — Dear Mrs. LaRue
9. Toft, Kim Michelle — The World That We Want
10. Tresselt, Alvin — Hide and Seek Fog
11. Tresselt, Alvin — The Gift of the Tree
12. Tresselt, Alvin — White Snow, Bright Snow
13. Viorst, Judith — Earrings!
14. Viorst, Judith — Rosie and Michael
15. Wallace, Karen — Gentle Giant Octopus
16. Wood, Douglas — A Quiet Place
17. Yolen, Jane — Grandad Bill's Song
18. Yolen, Jane — Owl Moon
19. Yolen, Jane — Water Music: Poems for Children
20. Yolen, Jane — Welcome to the Green House
21. Zolotow, Charlotte — Over and Over
22. Zolotow, Charlotte — The Moon Was the Best
23. Zolotow, Charlotte — The Storm Book
24. Zschock, Martha Day — Journey Around Chicago From A to Z

Craft Element	1	2	3	4	5	6	7	8	9	10	11	12	13	14	15	16	17	18	19	20	21	22	23	24
Wordplay	✓	✓				✓	✓			✓		✓			✓	✓				✓			✓	
Voice	✓		✓			✓		✓						✓	✓				✓					
Verbs and Verb Forms		✓				✓	✓				✓	✓	✓			✓	✓		✓		✓		✓	
Text Features	✓							✓	✓			✓			✓		✓				✓	✓		✓
Simile				✓	✓	✓					✓	✓			✓	✓				✓	✓		✓	
Sequencing								✓			✓											✓		
See-Saw Pattern			✓											✓		✓								
Rhyme	✓	✓										✓			✓			✓						
Repetition	✓	✓	✓		✓			✓	✓		✓	✓	✓	✓	✓	✓	✓			✓	✓	✓	✓	
Punctuation	✓	✓	✓			✓	✓	✓			✓	✓	✓		✓	✓	✓	✓					✓	
Print Layout	✓		✓			✓			✓			✓			✓	✓		✓	✓				✓	
Print Features	✓	✓	✓	✓		✓	✓		✓		✓				✓	✓	✓						✓	✓
Point of View				✓				✓																
Personification		✓		✓		✓	✓			✓	✓	✓					✓		✓	✓			✓	
Onomatopoeia	✓	✓		✓		✓										✓	✓		✓	✓			✓	
Metaphor	✓	✓		✓			✓				✓	✓				✓	✓		✓	✓				
Lists	✓			✓								✓					✓	✓						
Lead						✓	✓				✓	✓	✓			✓	✓					✓		
Interesting Format								✓												✓				
Hyperbole	✓		✓					✓			✓	✓			✓	✓								
Flashback	✓					✓																		
Effective Ending					✓		✓				✓				✓	✓	✓	✓						
Descriptive Language		✓	✓		✓	✓				✓	✓	✓			✓	✓	✓		✓	✓	✓	✓	✓	
Cumulative Text					✓				✓															
Circular Ending					✓																✓			
Breaking the Rules	✓	✓	✓			✓	✓	✓		✓	✓	✓	✓			✓	✓		✓		✓		✓	
Alliteration		✓				✓	✓			✓	✓	✓			✓			✓	✓			✓	✓	✓

Annotated Bibliography

A Is for Amos, written by Deborah Chandra and illustrated by Keiko Narahashi. 1999. New York: Farrar, Straus and Giroux. Fiction. (32 pp.)

Summary: A young girl imagines an alphabetical journey around the farm on her rocking horse, Amos.

- **Alliteration**—Each letter of the alphabet is highlighted. For example, *B for the bumpity bridge we cross; W for wild wind whirling.*
- **Effective ending**—The reader discovers that the eventful horseback ride was in the narrator's imagination as she rides on her wooden hobby horse.
- **Onomatopoeia**—Examples include *Clippety clap clippety clap; Sloppity cloppety thumpety thud.*
- **Print features**—The letter highlighted in each alliterative phrase is written in large bold font; onomatopoeic words that represent the sounds of the horse's hooves are written in italics; some pages have black type, others white.
- **Print layout**—Onomatopoeic phrases are written in an undulating font that supports the rhythmic movement of the horse's hooves; there is some purposeful layout of lines of print to support the meaning such as *J for going to jump this time,* which arcs up and then down to simulate the jump over a fence; and purposeful placement of letters within a word emphasize the meaning, such as *bumpity,* which is written in letters that appear to bump up and down.
- **Punctuation**—Hyphens are used throughout to slow down onomatopoeic words (*clop-pet-y lop-pet-y clip-pet-y clops*). Dashes are used to slow the reader's pace as Amos comes to a stop (*And Z—for lazy Amos—stops.*), and as a lead-in (*G for gallop—off we go!*).
- **Repetition**—The alphabet pattern (*A is for…*) repeats as the story progresses through the letters of the alphabet.
- **Rhyme**—Most of the book is cleverly written in soothing rhyming verse.

All the Colors of the Earth, written and illustrated by Sheila Hamanaka. 1994. New York: Morrow Junior, HarperCollins. Fiction. (32 pp.)

Summary: Children are celebrated for their physical diversity and the shared laughter and spirit for which they all are loved.

- **Breaking the rules**—Uppercase letters are sometimes used mid-sentence to support the poetic print layout.
- **Descriptive language**—This craft is used throughout to capture the varying ethnicities of children: *The tinkling pinks of tiny seashells by the rumbling sea.*
- **Lists**—The book contains only five sentences, three of which are lists.
- **Metaphor**—Good examples include *Love is amber and ivory and ginger and sweet,* and *The roaring browns of bears.*
- **Personification**—A good example of personification is this line: *laughter that kisses our land.*
- **Print layout**—Each page contains just one line of text; the unique and meaningful placement of the text prompts a rhythmic, lyrical read.
- **Repetition**—The title phrase, *All the Colors of the Earth*, is repeated on the opening page and the final page.
- **Rhyme**—Portions of the text are written in rhyming verse.
- **Simile**—Examples include *hair like bouncy baby lambs; Dark as leopard spots, light as sand; sunlight like butterflies happy and free.*

All the Places to Love, written by Patricia MacLachlan and illustrated by Mike Wimmer. 1994. New York: HarperCollins. Fiction. (32 pp.)

Summary: Life on an American farm is lovingly depicted through MacLachlan's tender words about a young boy who vows to continue the cross-generational tradition of telling his new sister about "all the places to love" that can be found in and around their rural home.

- **Alliteration**—Examples include *sly smiles, marsh marigolds, blueberry buckets, tiny tumbles.*
- **Descriptive language**—A child's first-person reminiscing captures the simple wonders of the American farm, such as in this line: *My grandfather's barn is sweet-smelling and dark and cool.*
- **Print features**—The first letter of the first word on each page is in a large font, varying in color; italics are used for dialogue; the names of the narrator and his sister are in a unique font to display how their names looked when carved in wood by Grandfather.

- **Print layout**—The poetic flow is encouraged by the placement of the text; uppercase letters are used mid-sentence to support the print layout.

- **Punctuation**—Colons introduce lists, as in the following example: *What I saw first were all the places to love: The valley, The river falling down over the rocks, The hilltop where the blueberries grew.* Dashes are used in place of commas to direct the reader to pause: *And the old turtle—his shell all worn.* Semicolons are used throughout.

- **Repetition**—Words repeat for emphasis: *We jumped from rock to rock to rock*; the word *and* repeats to create a list: *the names of Grandfather and Grandmother, And my mama and papa, And me*; a phrase repeats in several sentences: *Someday I might live in the city. Someday I might live by the sea.*

- **Simile**—We love this book for its beautiful similes, such as: *Crows in the dirt that swaggered like pirates. Trout flashed like jewels in the sunlight. Cattails stood like guards. And wild turkeys left footprints for us to find, like messages.*

All You Need for a Snowman, written by Alice Schertle and illustrated by Barbara LaVallee. 2002. New York: Scholastic. Fiction. (32 pp.)

Summary: All the wonder and work required when building a snowman are captured as the children delight from the very first fluttering snowflake. Please note there is a companion book, as well, titled *All You Need for a Beach*.

- **Breaking the rules**—The author uses fragments throughout.

- **Lists**—Examples include *Walnut buttons, five in a row, belts in the middle, boots below, big wool scarf, broom to hold, mittens (in case his hands get cold), earmuffs, fanny pack, something to read....*

- **Print features**—The first letter of the first word is in a red font; italics and uppercase letters are used for emphasis.

- **Print layout**—Unique and meaningful placement of the print complements the text and illustrations and directs the flow of the text; there are words found at the bottom right-hand corner of several pages which instruct the reader to pause, creating anticipation just before the page is turned.

- **Punctuation**—Ellipses build anticipation of the snowfall (*two more snowflakes...three flakes... four...five...six...seven thousand...eight million more...*), and instruct the reader to pause (*Uh-oh...Look in the sky again. One small snowflake falling then...*). Dashes are used in place of colons, as in *One small snowflake fluttering down—that's all you need for a snowman.* Parentheses are used to show an aside: *mittens (in case his hands get cold).*

- **Repetition**—Words repeat for emphasis: *pat them and pack them and roll them around.* The phrase *that's all you need for a snowman* is repeated throughout.

- **Rhyme**—Although most of the text does not rhyme, there are some lines of rhyming text that enhance the lyrical quality of this book.

Atlantic, written and illustrated by G. Brian Karas. 2002. New York: Putnam. Fiction, with factual information about the Atlantic Ocean. (32 pp.)

Summary: The grandeur and beauty as well as the trials and tribulations of the Atlantic Ocean are told through the ocean's own words, providing extensive factual information along the way.

- **Descriptive language**—Through the voice of the Atlantic Ocean, the reader experiences the natural wonder of one of earth's great bodies of water: *I am the blue water at the beach, the waves, mist and storms.*

- **Lead**—The opening line is powerful in its simplicity: *I am the Atlantic Ocean.*

- **Lists**—Examples include: *Gulfs, seas, sounds, and channels lead to me; at the end of yards and streets and hills; I've been crossed and probed, charted, studied, dirtied.*

- **Personification**—The entire book personifies the ocean. In addition, there are individual examples, such as the following: *The dancing shadow of your airplane skips over wave.*

- **Point of view**—The book is a first-person narration from the Atlantic Ocean's point of view.

- **Print features**—The first word of the book, *I*, appears in large boldface font; font color alternates between black and white; and one line of smaller font exhorts the reader, *Don't forget I am here.*

- **Print layout**—Paragraph alignment prompts a lyrical reading; two pages contain curving lines that mimic the ocean's undulating movement; and two pages incorporate (into the illustrations) poetic lines about the sea from famous literary works.

- **Punctuation**—There are no periods or ending punctuation marks, though the author uses commas to create a list: *I've been crossed and probed, charted, studied, dirtied.* He also uses parentheses to add an aside and provide voice: *First I was discovered (even though I was here first).*

- **Repetition**—Words repeat for emphasis: *lead to me / and into me / They are me.* The word *and* is used instead of commas to group words: *with skates and whales and fish that fly.* Phrases repeat to create a sense of endlessness: *skips over wave over wave.*

- **Text features**—*Some Things About Me*, a factual addendum, is located at the end of the book.

- **Verbs and verb forms**—This book employs interesting verbs such as the following: *slosh, lapping, heaving, raging, rattle, clatter.*

Aunt Flossie's Hats (and Crab Cakes Later),
written by Elizabeth Fitzgerald Howard and illustrated by James Ransome. 1991. New York: Clarion, Houghton Mifflin. Fiction. (40 pp.)

Summary: Two young girls spend Sunday afternoons visiting their aunt whose extensive collection of hats prompts Aunt Flossie to regale the girls with colorful stories from the past.

- **Alliteration**—Examples include *Buglers bugling. Drummers drumming. Flags flying.*

- **Breaking the rules**—Author uses fragments throughout, such as *A stiff black one with bright red ribbons.* Many sentences begin with *and*, such as *And Daddy tried to reach it...* or with *but*, as in *But I thought I could smell some, just a little.*

- **Descriptive language**—A detailed description of Aunt Flossie's house, creates a strong sense of setting and imagery is used throughout to create mental pictures of Aunt Flossie's hats.

- **Flashback**—The author moves the action back and forth between the present and the past.

- **Hyperbole**—A good example is the following: *but here's one with a trillion flowers!*

- **Lists**—The description of the setting is enhanced with lists, such as *Books and pictures and lamps and pillows...,* as are the descriptions of Aunt Flossie's hats, *Green or blue or pink or purple.*

- **Print features**—Uppercase letters add emphasis, as in *and boxes of HATS!*

- **Punctuation**—Ellipses slow down a moment, for example, *but it dried just fine...almost like new.* Dashes interject a clarification: *The boys—soldiers, you know—back from France.*

- **Repetition**—Words repeat for emphasis (*My favorite favorite best Sunday hat*) and to imply a large quantity (*And boxes and boxes and boxes of HATS!*). The words *and* or *or* repeat in lists. Phrases repeat to echo within the dialogue between Aunt Flossie and the girls (*"Just a little smoky smell now," she said..."Smoky smell, Aunt Flossie?"*), and phrases repeat to add nostalgic voice as Aunt Flossie reminisces. *Big fire* appears four times on a two-page spread, and a variation on a sentence repeats to serve as a thread and to establish a sense of time *On Sunday afternoons; One Sunday afternoon.*

- **Simile**—A favorite example is *And your favorite best Sunday hat just floated by like a boat!*

- **Text features**—Elizabeth Howard includes an Afterword in which she provides family photos and history, including the fact that Aunt Flossie was her godmother and had many hats for young Elizabeth to try on during her visits.

- **Voice**—First-person narration and dialogue lends voice to Aunt Flossie and the girls.

Autumnblings, written and illustrated by
Douglas Florian. 2003. New York: Greenwillow, HarperCollins. Poetry. (48 pp.)

Summary: This collection of poems, some playful and some lovely, captures the spirit and beauty of autumn.

- **Alliteration**—Examples include *Frisbee flicking, Bracing breeze, First frost, First flake.*

- **Descriptive language**—Florian shows us how even the simplest words can capture precisely an image.

- **Metaphor**—This craft is used effectively to describe the autumn leaves: *A palette falls / To forest floor.* A series of metaphors are used to describe the wind in the poem titled "The Wind."

- **Onomatopoeia**—Good examples include *gulp, buzz, chirp, Brrrrrrr.*

- **Personification**—Autumn and leaf are given human characteristics.

- **Print features**—Italics emphasize clever wordplay, boldface and uppercase letters add emphasis and increase volume, purposeful selection of font size complements the meaning of the words.

- **Print layout**—Some poems have unique and meaningful placement of print.
- **Rhyme**—Some poems contain rhyme schemes.
- **Simile**—A playful simile example is *all fall down—like fallicopters to the ground.*
- **Text features**—A table of contents helps the reader locate favorite poems.
- **Wordplay**—Clever wordplay is employed throughout, as in *industree, hi-bear-nate, leaf-dancer, seed-prancer, Decembrrrrrr, owlphabet.*

Bat Loves the Night, written by Nicola Davies and illustrated by Sarah Fox-Davies. 2001. Cambridge, MA: Candlewick. Fiction. (32 pp.)

Summary: Through lyrical language interspersed with factual information, the reader glides through the night with this book's nocturnal heroine as she awakens at dusk, hunts for food, and returns to her hungry babies at dawn's blush. (This is a Bank Street College of Education Best Children's Book of the Year.)

- **Alliteration**—An example is *batlings hang in a huddle, hooked to a rafter.*
- **Descriptive language**—Davies creates vivid images that bring beauty to even a typically detested creature: *Her beady eyes open. Her pixie ears twitch. She shakes her thistledown fur. She unfurls her wings, made of skin so fine the finger bones inside show through.*
- **Effective ending**—The last line of the book echoes the title.
- **Metaphor**—*She shouts her torch of sound among the trees* is a fine example of metaphor.
- **Personification**—*The flowers turn their faces to the sun* provides a good example of this craft.
- **Print features**—One word—*Out!*—is in a large bold font and signifies the start of Bat's evening excursion; small italicized font is used to incorporate factual information about bats.
- **Punctuation**—The author uses hyphens to combine words (*coat-hanger feet*) and dashes to provide clarification, as in *She doesn't need to see—she can hear where she is going.*
- **Simile**—Good examples include the following: *She beams her voice around her like a flashlight; Its wings fall away like the wrapper from a candy; Bat is at home in the darkness as a fish is in water.*
- **Text features**—A two-page spread, found before the title page, includes pencil sketches and factual information about bats. It includes an introduction to the main character of the book, a pipistrelle bat. Interesting facts about bats are interwoven throughout the story and set apart in a smaller italicized font; an index appears at the end of the book.
- **Verbs and verb forms**—Examples include verbs such as *unfurls, beams, fluttering,* and *plunges.*
- **Wordplay**—The author combines words to create playful, descriptive language such as *moon-dust slippery* and *coat-hanger feet.*

Bats at the Beach, written by and illustrated by Brian Lies. 2006. Boston: Houghton Mifflin. Fiction. (32 pp.)

Summary: What happens at the beach when all the sunbathers have gone home for the night? Why, the bats pack up their towels, pails, and shovels and head for the shore for a frolicking night of moonlit fun, of course!

- **Alliteration**—Good examples include *salty sea spray, salted 'skeeters, slender sticks, tired and teary, leathery lap,* and *now back to crack and crevice creep.*
- **Breaking the rules**—Sentences often begin with *And;* the author uses fragments throughout.
- **Descriptive language**—Lies creates imagery that captures the setting and escapades of the bats' night at the beach: *Sun slips down and all is still, and soon we can't tell sky from hill.*
- **Lists**—Playful lists add to the rhythm and imagery of the bats' visit to the beach: *Soon we've got our buckets, trowels, banjoes, blankets, books, and towels; Beetles, ants, and milkweed bugs, crickets, moths, and pickled slugs.*
- **Metaphor**—The bats' antics turn them into kites in the sky—*taking turns at being kites*—and the waves become musical instruments—*At last we hear the deep bass thump, as waves on seashore crash and bump.*
- **Personification**—Examples include *bats pour out with shrieks of laughter* and *the old bats are singing.*
- **Print features**—Italics are used to create a sense of urgency when the bats are calling out to one another: *Quick, let's go, let's fly away—we've got to be home before it's day!*
- **Print layout**—Rather than indented paragraphs, the text is set up to resemble stanzas of poetry, with purposeful line breaks that prompt a lyrical reading.

- **Punctuation**—Use of hyphens to create wordplay and use of dashes to pace the reader.
- **Rhyme**—The text is rhythmic and contains a rhyme scheme that adds to the playful mood of the story.
- **Wordplay**—Playful images are created with imaginative words, like *moon-tan lotion, wing-boat races, munchtime,* and *bug-mallows.*

Bats at the Library, written and illustrated by Brian Lies. 2008. Boston: Houghton Mifflin. Fiction. (32 pp.)

Summary: The bats are at it again! Looking for adventure, they discover an open library window and through a hilarious nocturnal romp manage to impart a valuable lesson about the wonder of books.

- **Alliteration**—Great examples include *Cool and calm and clear; feasted, fluttered, swooped, and soared.*
- **Breaking the rules**—Sentences begin with *And* or *But.*
- **Descriptive language**—Lies creates imagery that captures the escapades of the bats' night at the library: *Breathless, lost within a tale, no one sees the sky grow pale.*
- **Print features**—Italics are used to create a sense of excitement and urgency when the bats are calling out to one another and for emphasis.
- **Print layout**—Rather than indented paragraphs, the text is set up to resemble stanzas of poetry, with purposeful line breaks that prompt a lyrical reading.
- **Punctuation**—Ellipses instruct the reader to pause (*We've feasted, fluttered, swooped, and soared, and yet…we're still a little bored*) and to build suspense before turning the page (*they coax and pull us in, until…*). Dashes are used throughout to pace the reader.
- **Repetition**—The line *Can it be true? Oh, can it be? Yes!—Bat Night at the library!* begins the adventure and then is repeated again at the end of the book as the bats return home. Words are also repeated for emphasis, as in *louder, louder, louder still.*
- **Rhyme**—The text is rhythmic and contains a rhyme scheme that adds to the playful mood of the story.
- **Wordplay**—Whimsical words include the following examples: *wingtip-tag, play-exhausted.*

Beach Day, written by Karen Roosa and illustrated by Maggie Smith. 2001. New York: Clarion, Houghton Mifflin. Fiction. (40 pp.)

Summary: Short lines of rhyming text rhythmically enchant the reader with all that a day at the beach has to offer.

- **Descriptive language**—Lively rhyming text transports the reader to a childhood day at the beach: *A freckled nose, Sandy toes. Ocean's salty Sea breeze blows.*
- **Metaphor**—The author compares the water spray to sparkling gems (*jeweled array*).
- **Personification**—*Waves roar* and *Insects dancing* are good examples of this craft.
- **Print layout**—Purposeful placement of print complements the text and the illustrations.
- **Punctuation**—Commas throughout create a list of beach day descriptions; dashes and ellipses instruct the reader to pause.
- **Rhyme**—The book is made up of a series of quatrains that follow a consistent rhyming pattern.
- **Verbs and verb forms**—Playful verbs such as *chatter, clatter, scatter, flurry, scurry,* and *lapping* add to the frolicking tone.
- **Wordplay**—*Sun-warmed skin* and *Lickety-split* are just two examples of imaginative words that enhance the whimsy of the story.

Bigmama's, written and illustrated by Donald Crews. 1991. New York: Scholastic. Memoir. (40 pp.)

Summary: The author fondly remembers his childhood summer trips with his family to visit his maternal grandmother in rural Cottondale.

- **Breaking the rules**—The author uses fragments throughout and uses the word *now* instead of *then* in past-tense sentences to allow the reader to relive the moment with him: *Now we were nearly there.*
- **Descriptive language**—By zooming in and using extensive details, the author vividly recreates time and place.
- **Effective ending**—The reflective ending poignantly and powerfully brings the reader back to the present with a tone of wistfulness.
- **Flashback**—The story is told in flashback as the author recalls childhood memories, and ends in the present when he is an adult.

- **Lead**—The use of dialogue in question form immediately sets the mood: *"Did you see her? Did you see Bigmama?"*

- **Onomatopoeia**—The sound of the train whistle: *WHOO…WHOO…*acts as the dinnertime signal for the children.

- **Print features**—The first letter of the first word of the book is boldface and larger font; use of uppercase letters to show excitement: *A FISH! A FISH! I GOT ONE, I GOT ONE!*

- **Print layout**—Text is placed in various places on the page to complement the illustration; the first page has two columns of print; unique and purposeful alignment of text in some paragraphs.

- **Punctuation**—The author uses dashes in place of commas to direct the reader to pause a second longer (*where we washed our hands, faces—and feet.*). Ellipses instruct the reader to pause: *"How tall you are…is this you?"* and stretch out onomatopoeic phrases.

- **Voice**—Through the use of first person narration and dialogue, the author captures both the excitement he felt as a child and the nostalgia the memories evoke in him as a man.

Birthday Presents, written by Cynthia Rylant and illustrated by Suçie Stevenson. 1987. New York: Orchard. Fiction. (n.p.)

Summary: As a little girl approaches her sixth birthday her parents lovingly reminisce with her about each of her previous birthdays beginning with the day she was born, assuring her that she is the best present of all.

- **Breaking the rules**—The author uses fragments throughout, such as *Your real birthday.*

- **Descriptive language**—Rylant has a way of capturing a moment and making it real: *You sat with your friends and everyone giggled and all of you had chocolate faces, but you most of all.*

- **Effective ending**—The final sentence echoes the title.

- **Punctuation**—Ellipses instruct the reader to pause in anticipation: *We promised you more….*

- **Repetition**—The phrase *Happy Birthday* repeats to mark the passing years; the phrase *We told you we loved you* repeats as a thread to show that love remains a constant throughout the years; and certain words repeat for emphasis and to suggest a large quantity, such as *but you ignored everybody and wanted only presents, presents, presents.*

- **Sequencing**—Text moves clearly through a chronology from the moment of the young girl's birth until she is six by focusing on just one day each year.

Busy Toes, written by C.W. Bowie and illustrated by Fred Willingham. 1988. Watertown, MA: Charlesbridge. Fiction. (32 pp.)

Summary: Who ever knew that toes could do so many things? Herein lies a lighthearted list of all the feats that your 10 little digits can perform.

- **Lists**—The entire book is made up of one continuous, playful list of different kinds of toes.

- **Print features**—Font choice, as well as font size, style, and case complement the text and print layout.

- **Print layout**—The minimal print is thoughtfully laid out to complement the wording and illustrations.

- **Punctuation**—Other than two commas and one ellipsis, the only punctuation used in this book is an exclamation point after the final word; the ellipsis is used to instruct the reader to pause in anticipation.

Butternut Hollow Pond, written by Brian J. Heinz and illustrated by Bob Marstall. 2000. Brookfield, CT: Millbrook, Lerner. Nonfiction. (32 pp.)

Summary: The flora and fauna of a North American pond are lyrically, but factually, described through five vignettes that begin with daybreak and conclude with night and the promise that it all will repeat as dawn creeps back into the morning sky.

- **Breaking the rules**—Many sentences begin with *And* or *But.*

- **Descriptive language**—Heinz creates imagery throughout that brings to life the sights and sounds of a day at Butternut Hollow Pond such as in the opening paragraph: *Sunbeams fall in slender shafts through a canopy of swamp maples. The water is dappled in a confetti of pale light. Dewdrops sparkle on the reeds.*

- **Metaphor**—Lovely metaphors include the following: *wildflowers sway in a crazy quilt of colors, Young bluegills hover under a blanket of duckweed.*

- **Onomatopoeia**—Effective examples of this craft capture the sounds of hunters finding their prey all around the pond: *Snap! Snap! Swoosh! Splash! Crack! Kerploosh!*

- **Personification**—The author gives nature personality with phrases such as *wisps of fog dance over the pond, The sky is blushed....*
- **Punctuation**—Ellipses are used to instruct the reader to pause in anticipation: *His sticky tongue flies out and...slurp!*
- **Simile**—Creative comparisons include *whirligig beetles tumble and dive in the shallows like a troupe of acrobats; wisps of fog dance over the pond like ghosts;* and *weaving behind their parents like floats in a parade.*
- **Verbs and verb forms**—The author uses interesting verbs to move the action, such as *hover, dart, plummet, bursts, sway, clambers,* and *flutter.*

Candy Corn, written and illustrated by James Stevenson. 1999. New York: Greenwillow, William Morrow. Poetry. (56 pp.)

Summary: This collection of short poems offers some lighthearted and some thought-provoking images of everyday sights, sounds, and activities.

- **Lists**—One poem, "Main Street" is a listing of different things that people carry when walking on the sidewalk.
- **Metaphor**—This craft is used to describe a paving machine: *Part tank, part spaghetti*; to describe the branches of a big oak tree: *Waving banners of green*; and to describe the arrival of dawn: *A grand parade is coming With white clouds marching.*
- **Onomatopoeia**—The poem "Early Morning Conversation" consists almost entirely of onomatopoeic descriptions, such as *Twitter-twitter, Chaychit-chaychit,* and *Gulp.*
- **Personification**—Good examples of this craft include the following: *Even the beech tree has sent a branch to pay a visit to my porch; the dumpsters start to dance, and rock and roll till dawn.*
- **Point of view**—The poem, "Night" is written from the point of view of several school buses after a long day of driving noisy, restless children.
- **Print features**—Each poem has a distinct font with variations in color; bold print adds force to some poems, while italics softens others; and enlarged font and uppercase letters are used to add emphasis.

- **Simile**—This craft is used to describe dawn as *Scattered through the trees, / Fallen like confetti.* Another good example is the following: *The dogwoods are blooming / Like white surf tumbling / From a light green sea.*

Clara Caterpillar, written by Pamela Duncan Edwards and illustrated by Henry Cole. 2001. New York: HarperCollins. Fiction. (40 pp.)

Summary: Clara, a common cabbage caterpillar, is destined to become an ordinary cream-colored butterfly and to be spurned by the more colorful butterflies, especially the conceited Catisha—until the moment when Clara's courage and lack of color save the day.

- **Alliteration**—The intentional exaggerated use of words beginning with the letter *C* throughout the book creates a playful, almost tongue-twister effect.
- **Descriptive language**—This book is filled with sophisticated vocabulary such as *conceited, catty, colossal,* and *crestfallen.*
- **Print features**—Bold print and varied font size on the two-page spreads correspond with the sentiments expressed by the caterpillars in their chrysalises.
- **Print layout**—Each two-page spread includes unique and meaningful placement of print that captures the trials and tribulations of a chrysalis.
- **Simile**—A great example provides mental imagery: *I'm coiled like a corkscrew.*
- **Verbs and verb forms**—Interesting verbs such as *scoffed, clustered, clambered,* and *capered* move the action.
- **Voice**—Through the use of dialogue, the author captures the personalities of the caterpillar characters.

Cloud Dance, written and illustrated by Thomas Locker. 2000. New York: Harcourt. Nonfiction. (32 pp.)

Summary: No one can paint a sky like Locker! In this paean to clouds of every kind, Locker paints images with his words as well as his brush. The book concludes with factual information about clouds.

- **Descriptive language**—Locker uses lush language to create imagery that supports the beautiful oil illustrations.

- **Personification**—Clouds are given human traits throughout.
- **Print layout**—Each page contains only one sentence except for the last page, which has two; unique and meaningful placement of text on the page gives a poetic feel.
- **Text features**—A page at the end includes facts about clouds and identifies the different types of clouds; the inside of the back cover offers the reader directions on how to "Make Your Own Clouds" and how to "Write a Cloud Autobiography."

Colors! ¡Colores!, written by Jorge Luján and illustrated by Piet Grobler. 2008. Toronto: House of Anansi, Groundwood. Poetry. (36 pp.)

Summary: Through the use of simple language that is rich with imagery, this bilingual picture book pays tribute to the colors of nature with which our planet is harmoniously infused.

- **Descriptive language**—The playful, beautiful language is highly descriptive in its simplicity, capturing the essence of each color.
- **Metaphor**—This craft is used beautifully to describe colors, as in *Orange, little sun of the orchard*, and to describe a bird, as in *Burning spark lands on the elm*.
- **Personification**—Colors are given human traits, such as in the following lines: *beige fell asleep on the sand*; *Who's singing? Red*; *Night has put on her black gown*; *The moon opens and closes her fan*.
- **Print features**—The color word that is the subject of each poem appears in a corresponding colored font.
- **Repetition**—Words repeat for emphasis, as in *fits clover, fits a tree, fits the whole jungle…fits green*. Parts of phrases also repeat for emphasis: *I saw a lake. I saw a flower. I saw the twilight*.
- **Simile**—Luján creates lovely similes, such as *bright as a little girl's nose*, *makes everything smell like a rose* and *Yellow rolls through the sky like a warm gold coin*.
- **Text features**—Each poem is first presented in English, followed by the Spanish translation.

Come On, Rain!, written by Karen Hesse and illustrated by Jon J. Muth. 1999. New York: Scholastic. Fiction. (32 pp.)

Summary: On a sweltering summer's day, a young girl and her neighbors anticipate the coming rain and then savor its exhilarating arrival.

- **Alliteration**—Good examples of this craft are found throughout the book, including phrases such as *lifts a listless vine* and *Trees sway under a swollen sky*.
- **Descriptive language**—From the anticipation of the rain to the quenching relief of the summer storm, the exquisite imagery slows down the action, allowing the reader to experience it all.
- **Hyperbole**—The phrase *the endless heat* conveys the relentlessness of the summer heat as the narrator awaits the cooling rain.
- **Lead**—The first line of the text echoes the title.
- **Metaphor**—There are many fine examples of this craft throughout, including this sentence that creates a vivid image at the end of the downpour: *Everywhere, everyone, everything is misty limbs, springing back to life*.
- **Personification**—Smells of tar and garbage are referred to as bullies, and dust is said to dance.
- **Print features**—The first line is in a larger red font, mimicking the title.
- **Print layout**—Unique and meaningful placement of the print evokes a lyrical read and directs the flow of the text.
- **Punctuation**—Ellipses zoom in, slowing down a moment, and are used to instruct the reader to pause.
- **Repetition**—The title is repeated several times throughout the text; words repeat for emphasis, and phrases repeat to stretch out the action, as in *Jackie-Joyce chases Rosemary who chases Liz who chases me*. The word *and* repeats instead of commas to group words, such as *shimmies and sparkles and streaks*.
- **Simile**—The author uses similes throughout, including this great example: *Her long legs, like two brown string beans*.
- **Verbs and verb forms**—Effective verbs include *tromping, freckles, shimmies*, and *whooping*.

Come to the Ocean's Edge: A Nature Cycle Book, written by Laurence Pringle and illustrated by Michael Chesworth. 2003. Honesdale, PA: Boyds Mills. Nonfiction. (32 pp.)

Summary: In this work of literary nonfiction, the reader is transported to the seashore one misty dawn to experience the setting as morning turns to day, and day turns to the night with its promise of a new day, *vast, wild, and mysterious.*

- **Alliteration**—Examples include *wind and waves* and *pockets and pails.*

- **Circular ending**—The book ends as it began, with the dawn of a new day.

- **Descriptive language**—Imagery brings the setting to life: *The sky brightens. Golden sunbeams pierce the fog. A breeze stirs the grasses at the tops of the dunes.*

- **Metaphor**—Imagery is also presented through interesting metaphors, such as *The next wave erases their claw prints from the sandy page;* and *a calico crab wriggles out of its old shell and swims away in a new suit of armor.*

- **Personification**—Fog, kelp, and waves are given human traits: *fog's wet breath; kelp holds fast to the rocky sea bottom and sways to the rhythm of the waves and currents;* and the waves *roar and growl.*

- **Print features**—The first letter of the first word on each page is in a large, bold font.

- **Punctuation**—Colons introduce examples, as in *for what the waves have left behind: scattered pebbles, shining like jewels in a long necklace, and pieces of glass worn smooth from being tumbled over the sand by endless waves.* Dashes instruct the reader to pause, such as in this example: *Look—there's a crab's claw, and some shells that were once the homes of sea animals.*

- **Sequencing**—The reader encounters the cycle of life at the ocean's edge from early morning, when the sun *pierces the misty fog* to when the *moon sets beyond the dunes* and then finally to a new day.

- **Simile**—Examples are used to describe seagulls, *their shadowy forms like ghosts in the mist;* barnacles, *shaped like tiny volcanoes;* and pebbles, *shining like jewels in a long necklace.*

- **Text features**—A page titled "More About the Ocean's Edge" is located at the back of the book where the reader can find more about the creatures, plants, and happenings at the ocean's edge.

- **Verbs and verb forms**—*Recedes, pierce, patrol, retreat, burst,* and *prowl* are just a few examples of effective verbs.

Creatures of Earth, Sea, and Sky, written by Georgia Heard and illustrated by Jennifer Owings Dewey. 1992. Honesdale, PA: Boyds Mills. Poetry. (32 pp.)

Summary: Through this book of short poems, Heard has crafted an homage to the animals with whom we share our planet.

- **Alliteration**—This craft occurs throughout the book, as in the following example: *wind is whistling through your wings.*

- **Descriptive language**—Imagery is used effectively as the poems pay tribute to the natural beauty of the animal world.

- **Metaphor**—The author compares wings to stained glass, as in *Wings flicker and still: stained-glass windows with sun shining through;* speaks to the eagle: *You're a graceful kite with no string;* and describes migrating birds as *the feathered compasses of the sky.*

- **Onomatopoeia**—This is demonstrated in words such as *Clank,* as a raccoon overturns a garbage can, and *Ga-lunk Ga-lunk Ga-lunk* to capture the frog serenade.

- **Personification**—Wind, a snake, and hummingbirds are given human traits: *wind is whistling, A snake changes its clothes,* and *Ruby-throated hummingbird zig-zags from morning glories to honeysuckle sipping honey from a straw.*

- **Print layout**—The collection contains two poems for two voices, "Fishes" and "Frog Serenade"; many of the poems incorporate unique and meaningful placement of print.

- **Repetition**—Words repeat to slow down the moment, as in *Weaving and weaving and weaving its web…it weaves and weaves, round and round.* There are occasional series of questions. Lines repeat at the beginning and ending of a poem, such as *Walk carefully, elephants, through the grass,* and lines repeat at the end of each stanza: *Try and catch me—you won't, you won't!*

- **Rhyme**—Several poems contain varying rhyme schemes.

- **Simile**—The bat's sonar is compared to *an invisible song / Echoing like ripples on a pond.*

- **Text features**—A table of contents, index of titles, and index of first lines help the reader navigate.

Crocodile Listens, written by April Pulley Sayre and illustrated by JoEllen McAlister Stammen. 2001. New York: Greenwillow, William Morrow. Fiction. (24 pp.)

Summary: The sounds of the Nile come to life as all the animals but the crocodile satisfy their hunger. Why does the hungry crocodile just lie and listen? Maternal instinct brings out a very different side to this otherwise fearsome creature. This tender story concludes with factual information about Nile crocodiles.

- **Alliteration**—Examples of this craft include the following: *A thunder of thumps, The sand seems to sing*, and *They squirm and squeak in the sand*.

- **Breaking the rules**—Sentences often begin with *And* or *But*, and the author uses fragments.

- **Lead**—The book opens with a simile: *Like an ancient dinosaur with scraggly teeth, Crocodile lies in the sand*.

- **Onomatopoeia**—This is used throughout in describing the animals' movements: *Thump, thump, thump; Tromp, tromp, tromp; Croak, croak, croak!*

- **Print features**—The first letter of the first word of the book is in large boldfaced font; *Crocodile* always begins with an uppercase letter, giving it the importance of a proper name; each instance of onomatopoeia has variations of font, font size, boldface print, uppercase letters, or italics.

- **Punctuation**—Ellipses indicate the continuation of a sound, such as *Thump, thump, thump…*; instruct the reader to pause in anticipation, as in *Crocodile's mouth is open. She has not eaten in weeks…*; separate and draw out onomatopoeic words such as *Eeeeep…eeeeep…eeeeep, Kaak…kaak…kaak…*; and indicate there is more to come, as in the book's final sentence: *Crocodile has babies to tend, and they have the whole Nile to explore…*.

- **Repetition**—The title is echoed in various sentences, providing a thread that links the passages until the key moment when Crocodile hears her babies' cries: *Now, at last, Crocodile hears them.*

- **Text features**—More About the Nile Crocodile, a factual addendum, is included with the book.

- **Verbs and verb forms**—Purposeful verb choices link the animals to their actions: *A herd of giraffes gallops, Warthog toes trot, Baboons file past, Weaverbirds chatter, Elephants trumpet*.

- **Wordplay**—The author uses wordplay to create imagery, as in the following examples: *egg-eating lizards*, and *sun-warmed crocodile*.

Dear Mrs. LaRue: Letters From Obedience School, written and illustrated by Mark Teague. 2002. New York: Scholastic. Fiction. (32 pp.)

Summary: Through newspaper clippings and a series of pleading letters to his owner, Gertrude LaRue, Ike's plight at obedience school and his harrowing return home are related humorously. (This book is a winner of the Christopher Award.)

- **Breaking the rules**—Many sentences begin with *And* or *But*.

- **Hyperbole**—Ike's melodramatic nature leads to exaggeration as he bemoans his life at obedience school and later, his life on the road as a stray.

- **Interesting format**—The book uses letters and newspaper clippings to tell of Ike's ordeal.

- **Point of view**—Life at the Brotweiler Canine Academy (pictured in vivid colored illustrations) is interpreted through Ike's words and thought bubbles (in black and white): school becomes a prison, his teachers become wardens, his luxury suite becomes a prison cell block, and a gourmet dining experience becomes a Dickensian scene.

- **Print features**—Ike's letters switch from a typed font to paw-written after his typewriter is confiscated, and newspaper headlines and environmental print appear in varied fonts. Uppercase letters are used to emphasize words, as in the following examples: *Of course I was SEVERELY punished; The way my teach—I mean WARDEN, Miss Klondike, barks orders is shocking.*

- **Punctuation**—Ellipses cause the reader to pause in anticipation, and indicate that there is more to come.

- **Sequencing**—The passing of time is indicated by the date, beginning with the newspaper article about Ike's incarceration on September 30th, moving through his series of dated letters, and ending with the newspaper headline of October 13th, hailing Ike's return home as a hero.

- **Text features**—The story is laid out in a series of letters, newspaper clippings, and headlines; further humor is shown in the illustrations through environmental print.

- **Voice**—Through his increasingly pleading letters, Ike's voice rings with humor, a tinge of sarcasm, desperation, and a good dose of melodrama; on a much smaller scale, Mrs. LaRue's voice comes through in several newspaper interviews.

Dear Tooth Fairy, written by Pamela Duncan Edwards and illustrated by Marie-Louise Fitzpatrick. 2003. New York: Katherine Tegen, HarperCollins. Fiction. (32 pp.)

Summary: Claire is worried. She is 6 years old and does not yet have a wobbly tooth. Through an exchange of letters with the Tooth Fairy, the reader becomes privy to the anticipation and thrill of losing a first tooth.

- **Interesting format**—The book uses letters back and forth between Claire and the Tooth Fairy to carry the book's story.

- **Print features**—The author uses uppercase letters for emphasis; the letters from the Tooth Fairy are in a typewriter font.

- **Punctuation**—Dashes are used to instruct the reader where to pause.

- **Voice**—The letter format lends voice to the Tooth Fairy, who imparts her knowledge about teeth but gives particular strength to Claire's 6-year-old excitement about losing her first tooth.

Dear Willie Rudd, written by Libba Moore Gray and illustrated Peter M. Fiore. 1993. New York: Aladdin, Simon & Schuster. Fiction. (40 pp.)

Summary: Miss Elizabeth reminisces about her childhood relationship with her African American housekeeper and, through a letter she composes to the long-deceased Willie Rudd, Miss Elizabeth thanks her for all she did and apologizes for the racial injustices of the past.

- **Descriptive language**—Sensory details are used to create imagery in both the present and in the character's childhood memories.

- **Effective ending**—The story ends just as it began, with Miss Elizabeth on the front porch rocking in her grandmother's wicker chair.

- **Flashback**—The main character, Miss Elizabeth, remembers Willie Rudd, the housekeeper who raised her when she was a little girl, over 50 years ago.

- **Print features**—The first letter of the first word in the book is in a large blue font, and italics are used for the letter that Miss Elizabeth writes to Willie Rudd.

- **Punctuation**—The author uses ellipses to interject a clarification and to slow down a moment.

- **Repetition**—Phrases repeat for emphasis. For instance, the same phrase begins several consecutive sentences as Miss Elizabeth flashes back to her childhood memories. The strong sense of setting is established at the beginning and then repeated with similar language at the end.

Diamond Life: Baseball Sights, Sounds, and Swings, written and illustrated by Charles R. Smith Jr. 2004. New York: Orchard, Scholastic. Poetry and vignettes. (32 pp.)

Summary: Through photographs, poetry, and vignettes, the author celebrates the sights, sounds, and spirit of our nation's favorite pastime.

- **Breaking the rules**—"Stealing Second" consists entirely of phrases and fragments. Sentences begin with *And* or *But*. There are instances of incorrect grammar and lazy pronunciation to capture the quick-fire baseball banter and add to the voice of the players.

- **Flashback**—The first poem, "I Remember," serves as a flashback as the author remembers all things baseball.

- **Hyperbole**—Examples of this craft appear a few times, such as in one instance when the narrator states daisies grew around his cleats because he had been out in the field so long, and in another when the narrator says home plate was three miles wide. The poem "To the Moon" exemplifies hyperbole as a few baseball buddies brag about their homers.

- **Lists**—"EXCUSES, EXCUSES" is a list of excuses players use to cover their errors; "Listen, kid..." is a list of well-known baseball expressions.

- **Metaphor**—The ball is compared to a rocket.

- **Onomatopoeia**—Baseball lends itself nicely to onomatopoeic words such as *ping, CRACK,* and *BAM BAM BAM!!* The poem "Hear That Sound?" consists entirely of sounds heard during the game of baseball.

- **Print features**—A variety of print features are used throughout for effect: italics, boldface, enlarged print, uppercase letters, and varied font size and color.

- **Print layout**—Each poem employs unique and meaningful placements of print which complement the photographs and meaning of the text.

- **Punctuation**—Hyphens are used for clever wordplay. Ellipses instruct the reader to pause, stretch out a moment, and bring voice to the writing. Parentheses are used for an aside.

- **Repetition**—Words repeat throughout for emphasis.
- **Rhyme**—Some poems contain a rhyme scheme.
- **Text features**—A table of contents helps the reader find what he or she is looking for. On the final page of the book the author tells about the shared baseball moments between him and his dad and the moments he looks forward to sharing with his own children.
- **Voice**—Through the use of monologue, dialogue, and first-person narration, the distinct voices and emotions of baseball players and fans come to life.
- **Wordplay**—Smith creates fun, baseball-specific words such as *batta-batta-batta-batta-battaaaaaaa!, Fireball-flinging Flame-throwing Fascinator*, and *The Super-Split-Finger*.

Diary of a Worm, written by Doreen Cronin and illustrated by Harry Bliss. 2003. New York: HarperCollins. Fiction. (40 pp.)

Summary: Using diary format, a young worm resplendent in a red baseball cap gives the reader a hilarious worm's-eye-view of the world. There are several other "Diary" titles by Cronin that offer point-of-view writing.

- **Interesting format**—The book is written in diary format.
- **Onomatopoeia**—Examples include the following: *CHOMP* and *THUD*.
- **Point of view**—The diary format in the first person allows the reader a worm's-eye-view of the world.
- **Print features**—Unique font gives the book a playful feel, the dates are in different colored fonts, and word bubbles are in tiny fonts. Uppercase letters are used for emphasis, as in *I wiggled up right between them and they SCREAMED*, onomatopoeic words are in uppercase letters incorporated into the illustrations.
- **Sequencing**—The diary format uses dates to move the story through four months in the life of a worm.
- **Text features**—The characters us speech bubbles, the inside covers contain illustrated photo spreads, each diary entry is labeled with the date, and numerals are used to bullet items.

- **Voice**—Humor and humanlike qualities bring voice to the worm-narrator.

Dirty Laundry Pile: Poems in Different Voices, selected by Paul B. Janeczko and illustrated by Melissa Sweet. 2001. New York: HarperCollins. Poetry. (40 pp.)

Summary: This collection of poems, written in the voices of animals and inanimate objects, allows the reader to see the world through different eyes.

- **Alliteration**—Examples of this craft include *trim track, sledded slope, sip soup*, and *my white wings lift into warm starlight*.
- **Descriptive language**—Janeczko creates vivid images as he brings ordinary everyday objects to life, such as when he gives voice to a snowflake: *I hope for my swirling journey to end instantly on the hot tongue of some shivering child out reveling in the return of my tribe*.
- **Metaphor**—This is used to describe clouds: *seas of cloud*; sunsets: *our sunset red and gold igniting autumn's blaze*; a broom: *I am blunt whisker*; a pair of gloves: *Without your hands, we are five-room houses waiting for our inhabitants to come home*; and a bear's dreams: *And they will be your winter meat*.
- **Onomatopoeia**—Words like *Glubita glubita, GLUB*, and *Babba-da-swaba* give voice to a washing machine.
- **Personification**—The subject of each poem, whether it be an object or animal, is given human characteristics. Examples include a horse pleading with its owners to bring it a warm blanket: *Dampness climbs into my ears*; a tortoise describing the wonders of nature when one slows down to listen: *Their leaves are softly singing*; and a bullying wind looking for someone to harass: *I'm winter wind shaking the door with both my fists*.
- **Point of view**—Each poem is written from the point of view of an object or an animal, allowing the reader to hear its voice.
- **Print features**—Enlarged print, bold print, and uppercase letters enhance the text.
- **Print layout**—Unique and meaningful placement of the print complements the text and illustrations.
- **Punctuation**—Hyphens are used to create wordplay and onomatopoeic words, such as *lippety-blop-blippety-blop*.

- **Repetition**—Words and phrases repeat for emphasis, such as *Heavy / Heavy hot / Heavy hot hands, loop and climb loop and climb*, and *gazelle, gazelle*.
- **Rhyme**—Many of the poems contain a rhyme scheme.
- **Simile**—A well-crafted example of simile is this line: *My rippling paper skin would rustle like applause*. Other good examples include: *Roots like ours, coarse and strong as a grandmother's fingers; A tangled weave, rough and aged like wooden lace; like puppies who warm each other all night*.
- **Text features**—The book includes an introduction by Janeczko, the selector of the poems, in which he explains his rationale for compiling the collection and encourages the reader to *Let that new voice sing!*
- **Voice**—The poems' unique points of view create humor and give each object or animal a distinct voice.
- **Wordplay**—Fun words such as *giddy-quick, ghost-voiced, shadow-sweeper*, and *keeper-of-the-uncherished* add to the poems' whimsy. Another good example is this word created from words strung together to convey a sense of urgency: *Pickmepickmepickme*.

Dogs Rule!, written and illustrated by Daniel Kirk. 2003. New York: Hyperion. Poetry. (56 pp.)

Summary: Kirk, a self-admitted dog lover, has written a highly amusing and insightful collection of 22 poems from a canine perspective that establishes once and for all that dogs rule and cats drool!

- **Alliteration**—Alliteration abounds in this collection: *You beg and you bargain, you rave and you rant; I'm perfumed and powdered, and pampered all day; fine feathered friends; the wind's in my whiskers; chipmunks chirp... Schnauzers snicker...Scotties smirk.*
- **Breaking the rules**—Incorrect grammar and use of vernacular brings voice to the dogs' words: *There ain't nothin' I can do: and if she thinks it suits me, brother, she don't have a clue!*
- **Hyperbole**—There are great examples of this craft, such as *My head's too big. It weighs a ton; I'll drown in all the tears I'm gonna cry!; I'm gonna wake up everyone from Maine to Tennessee....*
- **Metaphor**—A cat's claws become *daggers*.

- **Point of view**—Each of the poems is written in the first person with a different dog as narrator, showing a distinctly canine view of the world.
- **Print features**—The titles of the poems are written in extra-large colorful fonts; colored font is used for the repeating phrase *DOGS RULE!* in the poem of the same name; italics and uppercase letters are used in several poems for varying effects.
- **Rhyme**—All of the poems have rhyming patterns which lend themselves to song.
- **Simile**—The dog narrators compare themselves to a jet, a hawk, a hot dog bun, and milk. In addition, they compare certain characteristics to items such as jellyfish and a hot-air balloon.
- **Text features**—The 22 poems that make up this book are put to music and included on a CD; a table of contents lists the poems for easy navigation.
- **Voice**—Through the first-person narration and some very amusing (and some touching) poems, the voices of the various dogs are distinct and clear.

Doodle Dandies: Poems That Take Shape, written by J. Patrick Lewis and illustrated by Lisa Desimini. 1998. New York: Aladdin Paperbacks, Simon & Schuster. Poetry. (40 pp.)

Summary: In this unique poetry collection, each poem is written in the shape of its subject and then creatively interwoven with the illustration.

- **Alliteration**—There are examples of this craft in several poems, including *Weeping Willow, The butterfly is,* and *Creep and Slither*.
- **Point of view**—Several of the poems are written in the first person, giving the reader insight on the way an animal or inanimate object might view the world.
- **Print features**—Text is printed in various fonts of different size, color, and case, complementing the subject and shape of the poem; one poem about basketball substitutes a picture of a basketball for the letter *O* in each line of poetry.
- **Print layout**—Each poem in this collection is written so that it takes the shape of its subject. This necessitates unusual line breaks, word separations, and, in two poems, words written in mirror image.
- **Rhyme**—Most of the poems contain (often playful) rhyme schemes.

- **Simile**—The author creates fitting similes, comparing a dog on a leash to *a sausage on a string*; a swimming pool to a *blue quilt*; scurrying ants to people walking far below.
- **Wordplay**—In one example, the mysteries of the winter sky become *mist-eries* and many other poems contain playfully constructed words.

Dream Weaver, written by Jonathan London and illustrated by Rocco Baviera. 1998. San Diego: Silver Whistle, Harcourt. Fiction with factual information about spiders. (32 pp.)

Summary: While walking near his valley home, a young boy comes upon a yellow spider weaving a sparkling web. As he quietly watches her, he sees the world from a different perspective.

- **Breaking the rules**—The authors uses sentence fragments throughout that work perfectly to convey the young boy's thoughts as he gazes in wonder at the yellow spider.
- **Descriptive language**—Lyrical prose written in the second person combines with purposeful print layout and punctuation to slow down the reader's pace while extending an invitation to share in a little boy's wondrous journey into a spider's life.
- **Effective ending**—The final line of text echoes the title of the book.
- **Lead**—The opening sentence creates a strong sense of setting and invites the reader to come along.
- **Metaphor**—This craft, in one instance, conveys the smallness of the spider: *A raindrop on a fallen leaf is a forest pool.*
- **Onomatopoeia**—A good onomatopoeic phrase is the following: *crash, thrash, crash.*
- **Personification**—Trees take on human traits: *the trees hum.*
- **Print features**—All text is imprinted directly on the illustrations is in yellow font; the first letter of the first word of the book is in a large distinct font.
- **Punctuation**—Ellipses and dashes are used to make the reader pause.
- **Simile**—This craft is used in describing the spider: *her legs like threads; as still and silent as Yellow Spider; Yellow Spider glows like the evening star....*

- **Text features**—Some Facts about Spiders, a factual addendum written from a young boy's point of view, has been included.
- **Verbs and verb forms**—Descriptive verbs like *gleaming, oozes,* and *nestled* enhance the story's lyricism.

Earrings!, written by Judith Viorst and illustrated by Nola Langner Malone. 1990. New York: Aladdin Paperbacks, Simon & Schuster. Fiction. (32 pp.)

Summary: The quintessential "drama queen" employs every trick in the book while trying to convince her parents to allow her to have her ears pierced.

- **Breaking the rules**—Extensive use of run-on sentences coupled with the use of fragments develop the narrator's voice. Some sentences begin with *And* or *But.*
- **Hyperbole**—This craft is used throughout and adds to the humor.
- **Lead**—Four short but effective sentences immediately set the tone of the book.
- **Print features**—Italics and uppercase letters are used for emphasis.
- **Punctuation**—Dashes and ellipses instruct the reader to pause while parentheses are employed to indicate an aside.
- **Repetition**—This craft is used in a variety of ways including the repetition of a single word, of a phrase, and of a sentence pattern.
- **Voice**—The character's use of sophisticated language and her spunky attitude humorously capture the voice of a persistent young girl.

Earthdance, written by Joanne Ryder and illustrated by Norman Gorbaty. 1996. New York: Henry Holt. Fiction. (32 pp.)

Summary: Ryder invites the reader to imagine becoming the earth and experiencing all its glory. The book ends with the hope that all the inhabitants of this planet we call home will understand its needs and treasure it.

- **Descriptive language**—Ryder creates imagery through her simple vocabulary and soothing tone: *wrapped in a quilt of bright colors—blue flowing seas, dark green woods, and deserts of golden sand.*

- **Effective ending**—The book ends with a powerful entreaty to the earth's inhabitants to take care of our planet.
- **Lead**—The dramatic opening line immediately draws the reader in and introduces the premise of the book: *Imagine you are standing tall in an empty space.*
- **Metaphor**—The author asks the reader to imagine what it would be like to be the earth through a series of metaphors that mirror the earth's appearance and movements.
- **Personification**—Cities are given human traits, as in *cities wake up, yawning to morning.*
- **Point of view**—The reader sees everything through the earth's eyes.
- **Print layout**—Unique and meaningful placement of the print complements the text and illustrations and evokes a lyrical read.
- **Repetition**—Words repeat for emphasis: *taller than the trees, taller than the hills.*

Ellsworth's Extraordinary Electric Ears: And Other Amazing Alphabet Anecdotes, written and photographed by Valorie Fisher. 2003. New York: Atheneum, Simon & Schuster. Fiction. (40 pp.)

Summary: Fisher uses photographs and lines of alliterative text to create 26 imaginative miniature scenes, one for each letter of the alphabet.

- **Alliteration**—Each letter of the alphabet is featured on a separate page with a character whose name begins with that letter and an alliterative description. Even the author's acknowledgements are written using alliteration.
- **Print features**—The first letter of each name appears in large and colorful font to make the featured letter stand out.
- **Text features**—Alliterative environmental print is featured in several of the photographs; the book ends with a two-page spread that is set up with alphabetical lists of words challenging the reader to find the objects in the pictures throughout the book.

Farmer's Garden: Rhymes for Two Voices, written by David L. Harrison and illustrated by Arden Johnson-Petrov. 2000. Honesdale, PA: Wordsong, Boyds Mills. Poetry. (32 pp.)

Summary: A farmer's inquisitive dog goes about the garden asking questions and receiving responses from the various creatures, fruits, and vegetables encountered.

- **Alliteration**—Alliterative examples throughout, including *squiggle and squirm* and *Beetles and bugs are hard to beat,* add to the playful and rhythmic air of the poems.
- **Interesting format**—Each of the poems in this collection is written in two voices—the dog's and the interviewee's—allowing for a shared recitation between two readers.
- **Print features**—The title of each poem is written in large playful boldface font; the text of each poem alternates between regular and italicized font as the voice shifts.
- **Repetition**—Each poem begins with a question posed to a creature, fruit, or vegetable whose name repeats, as in *Redbird, Redbird, why do you sing?* and *Corn, Corn, why do you grow?*; the word *garden* repeats through most poems acting as a connecting thread; the question/answer rhythm repeats throughout each poem.
- **Rhyme**—Most verses have a rhyming pattern.
- **See-saw pattern**—Although not a typical see-saw book, each poem follows a see-saw pattern of question and response.
- **Wordplay**—Fun words include *hippity-hop* and *Lickey-split*, and when the cow speaks she says, *"I'll go to the barn and chew some hay and moooove on out of the garden."*

Fireflies, written and illustrated by Julie Brinckloe. 1985. New York: Aladdin Paperbacks, Simon & Schuster. Fiction. (32 pp.)

Summary: A childhood summer ritual—catching fireflies—is perfectly captured in this poignant tale with the larger message that we sometimes have to let go of the things we love.

- **Breaking the rules**—Many sentences begin with *And* or *But.*
- **Descriptive language**—Brinckloe floods the reader's mind with heart-warming images, capturing the sights and sounds of a summer evening filled with fireflies.
- **Effective ending**—The mixed emotions of joy and sadness intermingle to create a powerful ending.
- **Hyperbole**—The word *hundreds* is repeated in several places to allow the reader to share the boy's perception of a night filled with fireflies.

- **Metaphor**—The boy compares the glow of the captive fireflies to moonlight as he peers into the jar.
- **Personification**—Moonlight, stars, and fireflies are given human abilities such as swimming and dancing.
- **Print layout**—Meaningful placement of print slows down the moment.
- **Punctuation**—The author uses dashes throughout to cause the reader to pause or to indicate an unfinished sentence.
- **Repetition**—The title is repeated throughout to create a sense of wonder and excitement.
- **Simile**—The boy realizes that the fireflies are dying when he sees their light dim and turn green, the way that moonlight changes color underwater. Then he exults as they brighten like moonlight when he sets them free.
- **Verbs and verb forms**—The author uses interesting verbs such as *dipping, soaring, thrusting,* and *grasping* to convey the movement of the fireflies and the action of the children chasing and catching them.
- **Voice**—Through the use of monologue, dialogue, and first-person narration, the voice and emotions of the character ring true to the story and evoke the wonder of a childhood summer night.

Fishing in the Air, written by Sharon Creech and illustrated by Chris Raschka. 2000. New York: HarperCollins. Fiction. (n.p.)

Summary: In this tribute to father–son relationships, the narrator reminisces about the magic of his first fishing trip with his father who, in turn, relates to his son his memories of fishing with his own dad.

- **Alliteration**—Nice examples of this craft include *clear, cool river; bubbles of breeze; sack of sandwiches; sliver of sky.*
- **Breaking the rules**—Sentences begin with *And,* as in *And what was beyond the trees?*; the author uses fragments and run-on sentences to create a whimsical rhythm. Lines such as *"And," I asked, "who taught you how to fish in that clear, cool river beyond the trees around the green fields around the gray house you lived in when you were a boy?"* force the reader to quicken the reading to mirror the pace of the exchange between the boy and his father.
- **Cumulative text**—As the father answers each of the boy's questions, the boy adds the new information, steadily building the details into his subsequent questions.
- **Descriptive language**—The opening line effectively captures the setting: *One Saturday, when I was young, my father and I left the house early in the morning, when it was still blue-black outside.* Creech's language brings the father's imaginative tale to life and creates vivid images of a day spent fishing, as in this sentence: *My line had no hook, only a blue feather midway down the line and a red and white bobber near the end.*
- **Effective ending**—The fishing metaphor is applied again at the end to describe a special moment and a special bond between a father and son: *And we caught a father, and we caught a boy, who learned to fish.*
- **Metaphor**—The title is a metaphor for using one's imagination, and the fishing metaphor is woven throughout the story, as in *We'd catch the air! We'd catch the breeze!*
- **Repetition**—Single words repeat to slow down the action: *We bumped along, along, along the winding lane;* to add emphasis: *White white white clouds;* or to create rhythm: *What was it like in your house, the house you lived in when you were a boy?* Also, phrases repeat stylistically. For instance, throughout the story the father's words are echoed in the boy's questions.
- **Simile**—Some examples of powerful similes include *those streetlamps…glowing like tiny moons all in a row; birds singing their songs like little angels;* and *bright red flowers here and there like floating rubies.*
- **Voice**—Through the use of dialogue and first-person narration, each character's voice is evident: the father's nostalgic, the boy's inquisitive.

Four Famished Foxes and Fosdyke, written by Pamela Duncan Edwards and illustrated by Henry Cole. 1995. New York: HarperCollins. Fiction. (32 pp.)

Summary: Fosdyke, the vegetarian gourmet fox, has no interest in hunting in the farmyard with his four famished siblings. In this cleverly humorous alliterative tale, Fosdyke's ingenuity and epicurean talents save the day.

- **Alliteration**—All of the foxes' names and much of the other playful but sophisticated vocabulary in the story begin with the letter F: *"We'll filch* fowl from the farmyard" But oh, what a fracas faced the flabbergasted felons.

- **Metaphor**—The moon's rays become *Fingers of moonlight*.

- **Print features**—The author uses uppercase letters to emphasize size, and the print on each page that chronicles the date and time is larger than the print throughout the rest of the story.

- **Sequencing**—The foxes' gastronomic adventure, which covers roughly a 25-hour period, is chronicled for the reader with headings of date and time.

- **Simile**—*The moon shone like a floodlight* as the famished foxes set forth for a night of foraging.

- **Text features**—The page preceding the start of the story challenges the reader to a game of finding pictures that begin with the letter *F*.

- **Verbs and verb forms**—Even the verbs carry on the alliterative effect: *filch, flambéed, fussed, famished, forged, flinch*, and *fathom*.

- **Voice**—Through the use of dialogue and clever language, the personalities of Fosdyke, the vegetarian gourmet, and his four carnivorous siblings emerge.

Freight Train, written and illustrated by Donald Crews. 1978. New York: HarperCollins. Fiction. (24 pp.)

Summary: Through simple text and vivid illustrations, this short book tracks the long journey of a colorful freight train, from its black steam engine to its red caboose. (This is a Caldecott Honor Book.)

- **Breaking the rules**—The author uses sentence fragments that mimic the rhythmic movement of the train and underscore the simplicity of the book: *Freight train. Moving.*

- **Print features**—The font is large with each line in a new color: font colors correspond to the color word used to describe the particular train car.

- **Print layout**—Short simple lines of text run across the tops of the pages and correspond to the car of the freight train depicted below it, giving a train-like illusion.

- **Punctuation**—There is very little punctuation: some lines have a final period, others have no end punctuation; ellipses direct the reader to pause in anticipation of the book's ending: *Going, going…gone.*

- **Repetition**—Phrases follow a repetetive pattern that mimics the chugging of the train as it moves on and on along its journey: *Moving. Going through tunnels Going by cities Crossing trestles. Moving in darkness. Moving in daylight.*

Gentle Giant Octopus, written by Karen Wallace and illustrated by Mike Bostock. 1998. Cambridge, MA: Candlewick. Fiction. (32 pp.)

Summary: This tender and highly descriptive book traces the final journey of a female giant octopus as she sets out to lay her eggs and protect them. It reminds us of the common bond shared by mothers of all species, and provides factual information about octopi. (This book was selected by the National Science Teachers Association and the Children's Books Council as an Outstanding Science Trade Book for Children.)

- **Alliteration**—Phrases such as *Shrinks in the shadows*; *scuttles sideways and escapes in the sand*; *slides over the seabed*; and *gentle Giant octopus* add to the aural as well as visual effect of this beautifully written book.

- **Descriptive language**—Wallace creates imagery throughout, especially through the use of similes.

- **Effective ending**—A poetic bittersweet ending reminds us that mothers make sacrifices for their children no matter what the species.

- **Print features**—Interesting facts about octopi, and more specifically the Giant Octopus, are interwoven throughout the story and set apart in a smaller italicized font that ripples across the pages.

- **Print layout**—Unique and meaningful placement of print directs the flow of the text.

- **Punctuation**—An ellipsis combined with an undulating word builds suspense: *It stretches and touches….*

- **Repetition**—The words *Giant octopus* repeat throughout, each time with a new adjective describing the octopus as she continues on her quest: *gentle Giant octopus*, *mother Giant octopus, frightened Giant octopus, quivering Giant octopus*.

- **Simile**—Beautiful similes add to the imagery. Examples include the following: *huge like a spaceship*; *Long tentacles fly like ribbons behind her*; *Her skin ripples like seaweed*; *Then sinks like a nightmare into his den*; and *sinks like a huge rubber flower.*

- **Text features**—A brief introduction, found before the title page, provides background information about octopi and the Giant Octopus. An index in the back of the book helps the reader find information.

- **Verbs and verb forms**—The book employs verbs highly appropriate to undersea life: *jets*, *muddies*, *scuttles*, and *squirm*.

- **Wordplay**—The author playfully combines words to create imagery, as in *Silver-backed fish*, or *goggle-eyed octopus*.

The Gift of the Tree, written by Alvin Tresselt and illustrated by Henri Sorensen. 2003. New York: Lothrpp, Lee & Shepard, William Morrow. Fiction. (32 pp.)

Summary: With elegance and grace, this book portrays the life cycle of an old oak tree and its role in the forest in which it has lived for more than a century.

- **Alliteration**—Tresselt is known for his beautifully crafted language, including these examples of alliteration that add to the lyrical effect: *Waited out the winter weather; rich rain of acorns; scrambling scurrying legs; clusters of giant clamshells.*

- **Breaking the rules**—Sentences begin with *And* or *But*, as in *And a rot spread inside the healthy bark.*

- **Descriptive language**—Eloquent language throughout the book describes the oak's life cycle: *Slowly, slowly, over the years the forest soil increased as the brown, leathery leaves, shaken down by the autumn winds, moldered under the snow.*

- **Effective ending**—The final sentence serves as an epitaph for the tree: *On the ground there remained only a brown ghost of richer loam where the proud tree had come to rest.*

- **Lead**—A simple sentence with an unidentified subject draws the reader in: *It stood tall in the forest.*

- **Metaphor**—The moss that grows on the fallen trunk becomes *a green carpet softer than the softest wool.*

- **Personification**—Elements of nature are given human characteristics, such as *the proud trunk, holding its broken arms up to the sky; But even as the tree grew, life gnawed at its heart;* and *the fierce wind shrieked through the forest.*

- **Print features**—The first letter of the first word of the book is in large boldface font.

- **Sequencing**—Through the descriptive passage of seasons and references to the passing of years we witness the life of a tree, for example, *Slowly, slowly, over the years; Year by year the tree grew weaker; The years passed....*

- **Verbs and verb forms**—Examples of interesting verbs include *peppered*, *pierced*, and *waddling*.

Gila Monsters Meet You at the Airport, written by Marjorie Weinman Sharmat and illustrated by Byron Barton. 1980. New York: Aladdin, Simon & Schuster. Fiction. (32 pp.)

Summary: This humorous picture book chronicles the move of a young boy from New York City. Along the way, there is a chance meeting with a boy from "Out West," and the boys trade preconceived notions about their new homes as each boy's family moves across the country. This funny story captures the fear and trepidation of moving to a new place.

- **Breaking the rules**—Many sentences begin with *And* or *But*, and the author uses fragments and run-on sentences to convey the voices of the young narrators.

- **Effective ending**—A surprise ending reveals a change in the character's point of view.

- **Hyperbole**—The boys' exaggerated views of their new homes add humor to the story.

- **Lead**—An interesting opening sentence engages the reader.

- **Point of view**—Two opposing points of view are defined through voice and hyperbole.

- **Repetition**—The phrase *Out West* is repeated throughout the story and serves as a thread.

- **Sequencing**—The stages of the boy's trip "Out West" serve as the thread through which the story is sequenced, and these stages are divided into numbered chapters.

- **Voice**—First-person narration in the present tense humorously brings voice to the two young boys facing an unwanted move.

Gilberto and the Wind, written and illustrated by Marie Hall Ets. 1963. New York: Puffin, Penguin. Fiction. (n.p.)

Summary: A young boy interacts with the wind, which comes to life through his eyes.

- **Breaking the rules**—Many sentences begin with *And* or *But*.

- **Effective ending**—The final sentence changes the fast pace of the book as Wind's antics cease and the boy and Wind tire out and all is still: *So I lie down beside him and we both go to sleep—under the willow tree.*

- **Onomatopoeia**—This craft is used when the Wind speaks: *You-ou-ou-ou! Sh-sh-sh-sh.*

- **Personification**—The wind is brought to life throughout, and even has a proper name. One great example is the following: *Wind loves to play with the wash on the line. He blows the pillow slips into balloons and shakes the sheets and twists the apron strings. And he pulls out all the clothespins that he can. Then he tries on the clothes—though he knows they're too small.*

- **Print features**—The first letter of the first word is in large bold font; italics used throughout to emphasize individual words.

- **Punctuation**—Hyphens are used throughout to create and stretch onomatopoeic words, as in *You-ou-ou-ou!* Dashes are used to add an aside, such as *Then he tries on the clothes—though he knows they're too small*; to cause the reader to pause, as in *And when I have a boat with a paper sail Wind comes and sails it for me—just as he sails the big sailboats for sailors on the sea*; and to link two independent clauses, such as *He can't make the bubbles—I have to do that.*

- **Repetition**—The boy's pleas to the wind begin with slight variations on the repeating line *"Wind! Oh, Wind!" I say.*

- **Voice**—The child's voice comes through, particularly when he is unhappy with something Wind has done: *"I don't like you today!"*

Grandad Bill's Song, written by Jane Yolen and illustrated by Melissa Bay Mathis. 1994. New York: Paperstar, Putnam. Fiction. (32 pp.)

Summary: A young boy asks family members and friends of his grandfather what they did on the day that his granddad died, and struggles to come to grips with his own feelings.

- **Effective ending**—The boy begins to understand and come to terms with his feelings about his grandfather's death.

- **Lead**—The use of a poignant question immediately engages the reader.

- **Print features**—The author uses italics for dialogue and cursive for photograph captions.

Each line begins with an uppercase letter even if it is mid-sentence, which further adds to the poetic tone.

- **Punctuation**—Ellipses indicate the reader should pause as the boy searches for words. Dashes also show the reader where to pause: *And deep in your heart, you are doing that—still*; and create wonder and surprise in the boy's questions: *Grandad Bill—young?* or *Grandad Bill—strong?*

- **Repetition**—The question, *What did you do on the day Grandad died?*, is repeated throughout and serves as a thread that ties the story together.

- **Rhyme**—The text is rhythmic and contains a rhyme scheme.

- **See-saw pattern**—A question and answer format makes up the see-saw pattern as the boy asks others about what they did on the day Grandad died.

Grandpa Loved, written by Josephine Nobisso and illustrated by Maureen Hyde. 1989. Westhampton Beach, NY: Gingerbread House. Fiction. (32 pp.)

Summary: A young boy remembers the things his Grandpa loved and the special times they shared, knowing that even though Grandpa has died, Grandpa is still with him and with all those who loved him.

- **Alliteration**—Some examples include the following: *moist moss; drifts of dry leaves; We let any lost and lonely person tell us a life's story.*

- **Descriptive language**—Nobisso creates imagery that appeals to the reader's senses: *We let the dusty warm scent in museums carry us away, and the quiet buzz of the library lull us to doze.*

- **Flashback**—The story is told from the point of view of an older boy, as he reminisces about his grandfather.

- **Personification**—Air is personified in a creative role reversal: *We let the sea air breathe us—in and out, in and out—very deeply, very friendly.*

- **Punctuation**—Dashes are used in place of colons, as in *That's what Grandpa loved most about the beach—catching all that wind*; to include a parenthetical remark; and to zoom in and stretch out a thought, for example: *That must be what Grandpa loves most now—being with us everywhere, all the time—on the beach, in the country, and in the city—in the lives of all who loved him.*

- **Repetition**—Single words repeat for emphasis, as in *very deeply, very friendly*. The word *and* repeats to create lists, such as *where deer and raccoons and birds came to eat our bread and corn and garden greens*. The title repeats throughout in order to name the people and places that Grandpa loved.
- **Verbs and verb forms**—Interesting verbs describe the action, including *hurtling, tunneled, lull,* and *doze*.

Grandpa Never Lies, written by Ralph Fletcher and illustrated by Harvey Stevenson. 2000. New York: Clarion, Houghton Mifflin. Fiction. (32 pp.)

Summary: Fletcher has written a lyrical and realistic tribute to the special relationship between a young girl and her grandfather.

- **Breaking the rules**—Sentences often begin with *And*. Also, the author uses one powerful sentence fragment to describe Grandma's death: *Suddenly*.
- **Descriptive language**—A young girl's visits to her grandparents' house in the woods come to life through Fletcher's use of imagery: *I see on the windows the blooming frost and ask about those delicate lines. Grandpa tells me about the winter elves who come at dusk with magical brushes to sketch on glass their silvery hues.*
- **Effective ending**—The final sentence is a twist on the title and the line that has been repeating throughout the book.
- **Lists**—The list of activities described at the beginning: *We eat Grandma's blueberry pancakes, track wild deer, hunt trilobite fossils, swim, play cards, but mostly just talk* is replaced with a slightly altered version, touchingly missing Grandma's pancakes after her passing: *We'll dig for crystals, sleep under the stars, swim, play cards, but mostly just talk.*
- **Metaphor**—This craft is used to describe the morning dew, as in *diamonds dance all over the lawn* and a spider's web, which becomes a necklace as *spiders work, stringing water beads on the finest thread*.
- **Personification**—Ice, diamonds, and the wind all have human characteristics in the following examples: *We could hear the ice settle and moan; diamonds dance; the wind works at night, sharpening icicles as they grow.*
- **Print layout**—Rather than through indented paragraphs, the text is set up as stanzas of poetry

with purposeful line breaks that prompt a lyrical reading.
- **Repetition**—The title is incorporated into a single line that repeats throughout the book, lending a lyrical quality.
- **Sequencing**—The author uses the changing seasons to move the young girl's description of her time spent with her grandfather from summer to fall to winter to spring and coming full circle with plans for the summer.

Grandparents' Song, written and illustrated by Sheila Hamanaka. 2003. New York: HarperCollins. Fiction. (32 pp.)

Summary: This short, poetic book celebrates ancestry and the melding of ethnicities that has made all of us unique.

- **Metaphor**—Great examples of metaphor include the following: *my roots run deep; Freedom was water and she had a great thirst; Freedom was music and her heart was a drum; Their lives are a river that flows through my veins.*
- **Personification**—Phrases such as *the trees talk to heaven* add lyricism and whimsy.
- **Punctuation**—Following poetic form, there is no end-of-sentence punctuation.
- **Repetition**—This craft is used throughout to create a rhythmic pattern, as in *My eyes are green like the sea, like the sea and my hair is dark and blows free, blows free*; the last line of the book echoes the first.
- **Rhyme**—The book is written in rhyme that adds to the rhythmic read.
- **Simile**—Through the following comparison, the narrator alludes to the theme of the book, a history of her family "tree": *I reach for the sky like a tree*. She then describes her green eyes, which she inherited from her grandfather: *My eyes are green like the sea.*

Green Eyes, written and illustrated by Abe Birnbaum. 1953. New York: Golden Book, Random House. Fiction. (n.p.)

Summary: This first-person narration chronicles the first year of a cat's life through the changing seasons. (This is a Caldecott Honor Book.)

- **Descriptive language**—This book's use of simple adjectives makes it an excellent choice for teaching imagery to our youngest writers.
- **Metaphor**—The sky is compared to a ceiling.

- **Point of view**—The kitten's first year of life is narrated in first person from the kitten's point of view.
- **Print layout**—One two-page spread uses print layout to complement the text.
- **Sequencing**—Transitional words and phrases are used to sequence the seasons as a means of moving through the kitten's memories of its first year of life, as well as its imaginings of what the coming seasons will hold in store.
- **Simile**—The cat compares itself to a lion in the jungle.

H Is for Home Run: A Baseball Alphabet, written by Brad Herzog and illustrated by Melanie Rose. 2004. Chelsea, MA: Sleeping Bear, Gale. Nonfiction. (40 pp.)

Summary: This baseball alphabet book is a home run for fans of all ages. It provides a simple alliterative rhyme along with a column of factual information for each letter of the alphabet. This book is part of a series of similar alphabet books by the same author.

- **Alliteration**—Each letter of the alphabet is represented in verses that include alliterative facts about America's favorite pastime: *D is for the diamond, a delightful design that gives us daring double plays and doubles down the line.*
- **Interesting format**—The book uses an alphabet book format to impart factual information about baseball.
- **Print features**—The letter that starts each alphabetic verse is written in large boldface font.
- **Print layout**—Each page or two-page spread contains an alphabetic quatrain within the illustration, as well as a column of factual text on a background of coordinating color.
- **Punctuation**—The author uses dashes extensively for several purposes: as a break in a sentence or to introduce an idea, as in *B is for the best—Babe Ruth*; to cause the reader to pause, as in *G is for a grand slam, a bases-loaded clout that clears the big Green Monster—over, up, and out*; or to show a parenthetical statement *E is for an error, a fielder's—oops!—mistake, and games in extra innings that keep us wide-awake.* He also uses hyphens to combine words to form new words, such as *wide-awake, all-stars,* and *bases-loaded.*
- **Repetition**—Repeating a single word emphasizes a large number, as in *who won and won and won—511 victories.*

- **Rhyme**—Each of the alphabetic quatrains follow the same rhyme pattern.
- **Text features**—In addition to the literary verse, each page contains a column that includes baseball facts, as well as historical notes on players, teams, and the game itself.

Hair Dance!, written by Dinah Johnson and illustrated with photographs by Kelly Johnson. 2007. New York: Henry Holt. Fiction. (32 pp.)

Summary: Through a combination of photographs and lyrical text, this book celebrates and glorifies African American hair and the important cultural role it plays.

- **Alliteration**—Examples include *my Afro puffs proud and pretty; halo heavenly hair; framing faces full of friendship;* and *Heart happy hair happy.*
- **Descriptive language**—The lively rhythmic text perfectly complements the striking photographs of African American hair.
- **Effective ending**—The last line of the text echoes the title.
- **Metaphor**—Hair takes on its own aura; the author refers to diversity as *our rainbow tribe of heritage.*
- **Print features**—The font color alternates between black and white; the first letter of the first word is in a bright pink larger font; the last line of text, which echoes the title, is in an uppercase bright pink font.
- **Print layout**—Unique and meaningful placement of print evokes a lyrical read and directs the flow of the text.
- **Punctuation**—Following a poetic format, sentences do not have ending punctuation. The author uses parentheses to add an aside: *Strong hair growing into dreadlocks (caring hands make them love locks).*
- **Repetition**—Words repeat for emphasis and lyricism, as in *In a jump dance street dance friends dance feet dance—HAIR DANCE!* or *My nature hair real hair flower power strong hair.*
- **Rhyme**—The book contains a rhyme scheme.
- **Simile**—Hair is compared to water, friends, and art, in the following phrases: *Braids swing with me like water; Special like my friends; it looks like a work of art.*
- **Text features**—The book includes a Photographer's Introduction, in which Johnson

explains the inspiration for the book. A Writer's Note, found at the end of the book, highlights the role that hair plays in the African American culture; also included at the end of the book is a bibliography, For the Little Sisters and For the Ladies, which tells about hair and its history.

Hairs/Pelitos, written by Sandra Cisneros and illustrated by Terry Ybáñez. 1984. New York: Dragonfly, Random House. Fiction. (32 pp.)

>*Summary:* In this bilingual picture book, which originally appeared as a vignette in Cisneros's novel, *The House on Mango Street*, a young girl describes each of her family members' hair and the detailed differences that make each one's so special.
>
> • **Breaking the rules**—Many sentences begin with *And* or *But*. The author effectively uses fragments and run-on sentences to give the story a childlike voice. In fact, 10 of the 22 pages in the book contain just one continuous run-on sentence.
>
> • **Descriptive language**—Sensory images are used to capture the many diverse qualities of hair.
>
> • **Print features**—The first letter of the first word in the book is written in large boldface cursive font; some pages are written in black font, and others are in white.
>
> • **Print layout**—Lines of English text run along the top of the page with the corresponding Spanish line running along the bottom of the page.
>
> • **Simile**—Descriptions of hair are made more vivid by comparing hair to a broom or rosettes or candy circles.
>
> • **Text features**—The title and all of the text appear in both English and Spanish. Additionally, the author provides extending activities inside the front cover in English, and the inside of the back cover includes these same features in Spanish.

Hello, Harvest Moon, written by Ralph Fletcher and illustrated by Kate Kiesler. 2003. New York: Clarion, Houghton Mifflin. Fiction. (32 pp.)

>*Summary:* Prose becomes poetry as Fletcher paints a breathtaking picture of the full moon of autumn.
>
> • **Alliteration**—Evocative language is made even more lovely through the author's use of alliterative phrases such as: *wake and wonder; lonely lunar light; spilling out spores.*
>
> • **Descriptive language**—Beautiful language throughout creates imagery: *With silent slippers it climbs the night stairs, lifting free of the treetops to start working its magic, staining earth and sky with a ghastly glow.*
>
> • **Effective ending**—With the dawn of a new day, it is now time to say good night to the Harvest Moon, giving a little twist to the title.
>
> • **Hyperbole**—One good example is *a million ears of corn.*
>
> • **Metaphor**—In one instance, sand is compared to a blanket, and the author uses a few metaphors to describe the moon or moonlight: *the great lamp in the sky; a sparkling tablecloth.*
>
> • **Personification**—The entire book personifies the harvest moon. In addition, there are individual examples of this craft, such as *large luna moths performing their ballet.*
>
> • **Print features**—Italic print gives voice to the moon.
>
> • **Print layout**—Several pages have unique and meaningful placement of print which gives a poetic feel and paces the reader.
>
> • **Punctuation**—Ellipses slow down a moment, as in *Finally, it starts to ease lower…;* hyphens combine words, such as *double-dipped* or *hide-and-go-seek;* and dashes interject a clarification *Now it's bedtime—but not for everyone.*
>
> • **Simile**—Beautiful similes include the following: *spilling out spores like tiny moonlings floating up to their mother; sprinkling silver coins like a careless millionaire.*

Hello Ocean, written by Pam Muñoz Ryan and illustrated by Mark Astrella. 2001. Watertown, MA: Charlesbridge. Fiction. (32 pp.)

>*Summary:* The rhyming text rhythmically echoes the undulating motion of the ocean's waves as a young child describes, through her five senses, the wonders of a day at the beach. This book is also available in a bilingual version that alternates English and Spanish text.
>
> • **Alliteration**—Alliterative phrases add fun to the story: *squishy, sandy, soggy ground, slippery seaweed; tide that tickles.*
>
> • **Descriptive language**—The ocean comes alive with descriptive language that creates imagery through each of the five senses.
>
> • **Effective ending**—The closing sentence echoes the opening line by bidding farewell to the ocean.
>
> • **Lead**—The opening line is a greeting to an old friend.

- **Metaphor**—The ocean becomes *a chameleon* and *a bowl of skies*; its aroma becomes *fragrant ore*.

- **Personification**—The first and last sentences speak to the ocean in the second person and give it life as an *old best friend*; the ocean is personified throughout, as in *waves that kiss and pounce in rowdy play*; *surf gives chase, then wraps me in a wet embrace*. The five senses are depicted as friends who join the narrator for a day at the beach: *I'm here, with the five of me, again!*

- **Print features**—Each of the five senses is presented in boldface.

- **Print layout**—The rhyming poetic flow is encouraged by the placement of text among the brilliantly colored illustrations. The undulating movement of the seaweed is reflected in a line of wavy text.

- **Punctuation**—Dashes are used throughout. The final sentence ends with an ellipsis instead of a period, connoting the narrator's planned return to her beloved ocean.

- **Rhyme**—The book is written in rhyming text that captures the rhythm of ocean waves

- **Verbs and verb forms**—Ocean-inspired verbs include *shushing and rushing*, and *wafting*.

- **Wordplay**—Verbs and nouns have been altered into effective adjectives, such as *reeky* and *froggy*.

Hide and Seek Fog, written by Alvin Tresselt and illustrated by Roger Duvoisin. 1965. New York: HarperCollins. Fiction. (40 pp.)

Summary: A thick, gray fog rolls into a small seaside village and changes life for the occupants as it lingers for three days. (This is a Caldecott Honor Book.)

- **Alliteration**—Phrases such as *lazy lopping waves* and *sun slanted through* provide good examples of this craft.

- **Breaking the rules**—Sentences begin with *And*, as in *And the fog stayed three days*; or *But*, such as *But out of doors the fog twisted about the cottages like slow-motion smoke*.

- **Descriptive language**—Tresselt uses vivid imagery to describe the mysterious fog that envelops the town: *The streets of the town were so full of fog that the people bumped into one another with their arms full of bundles.*

- **Personification**—Waves and foghorns have voices: *chattery talk of the low tide waves; the mournful lost voices of the foghorns calling.*

- **Punctuation**—Hyphens create new words, and ellipses slow down a moment, as in *so they could do their marketing…creeping, creeping…along the strange and hidden roads.*

- **Repetition**—Words repeat for emphasis, such as *gently, gently, rolled back the fog*, or *creeping, creeping*, and a single word repeats at the beginning of several sentences to show immediacy of action: *Now the water of the bay was gray like the sky, and the end of the beach was gone. Now the afternoon sun turned to a pale daytime moon….*

- **Simile**—Comparisons create more vivid scenery, such as in the following: *the bay was gray like the sky*; *The sailboats bobbled like corks*; *the fog twisted about the cottages like slow-motion smoke.*

- **Verbs and verb forms**—Verbs such as *creep, bobbled, spoddled, scowled*, and *muffled* add to the fog imagery.

- **Wordplay**—Playful words include *sun-sparkle, blue-lipped, gray-wrapped*, and *cotton-wool*.

Hot City, written by Barbara Joosse and illustrated by R. Gregory Christie. 2007. New York: Philomel, Penguin. Fiction. (32 pp.)

Summary: A young girl and her little brother find respite from the scorching summer city heat by slipping into the silent air-conditioned library where the books and the children's imaginations combine to provide a magical escape.

- **Breaking the rules**—Incorrect grammar, sentences that begin with *and* or *but*, and the use of sentence fragments bring reality and rhythm to the urban voices of the children: *Me and Joe on the front porch steps, cement steps, hot as a fry pan, sizzlin'*; *"Watcha wanna do?"*; *But Joe can't do nothin'.*

- **Descriptive language**—Through the use of hyperbole, metaphor, simile, and visual imagery, the reader can almost feel the all-consuming urban heat. Then the whole feeling changes when the children enter the library: *In the library, I sit where I want, so I plop down in a big old chair, smooth and cool, like a throne. I turn the pages of my book slow, like a princess.*

- **Hyperbole**—Exaggerated descriptions written across red and orange illustrations dramatically convey the sweltering heat.
- **Metaphor**—Perspiration becomes rivers, as in *sweatin' out rivers*, and the author describes Joe's inability to sit still with a perfect metaphor: *He's got jumps in his skin.*
- **Print features**—The first letter of the first word in the book is in large white font outlined in red.
- **Punctuation**—Apostrophes used throughout to indicate a missing letter in a word and to convey the children's dialect, such as *bakin', fillin',* and *'cross.* Dashes cause the reader to pause in anticipation, as in *And then—, I look at the gowns and then—, We do—for Mama.* Hyphens are used to create new words, such as *the gold-sparkle edge.*
- **Repetition**—The phrase *"Blah blah…Blah blah blah…Blah blah"* indicates what is to Mimi and Joe the incessantly boring conversation of the older women. The word *black* is repeated for emphasis, as in *smoky black, stinky black,* and repetition of the simile *like a princess* underscores Mimi's fascination with princesses. The phrase *out there* repeats to emphasize the heat outside on the city streets as the children look out the library window: *There's people out there, sweatin' out rivers. There's buses out there, huffin' out hot. Still hot out there. Cool in here.*
- **Simile**—Some good examples include the following: *Wearin' a fancy dress. Like a princess; hot as a fry pan, sizzlin'; his eyes big as moons; Sweat runs like a river; a big old chair, smooth and cool, like a throne.*
- **Voice**—Through the dialogue between Mimi and her little brother Joe, the voices of these two city children on a hot summer's day emerge, and the tenderness this big sister feels for her younger brother comes through.

I Am the Dog, I Am the Cat, written by Donald Hall and illustrated by Barry Moser. 1994. New York: Dial, Penguin. Fiction. (32 pp.)

Summary: A dog and a cat take turns delighting the reader in the many contrasts that exist between these two most popular household pets. Anyone who has owned a dog and a cat will relate to this warm, funny (but mostly accurate) picture book.

- **Lists**—The book employs lists to show the characteristics of each animal and to highlight their differences. For example, *cats are at the same time independent, selfish, fearless, beautiful, cuddly, scratchy, and intelligent;* and *a dog is at the same time dignified, guilty, sprightly, obedient, friendly, vigilant, and soulful.*
- **Point of view**—Each animal speaks in first-person narration, providing the very distinct differences between a dog's view of the world and a cat's.
- **Print features**—The words *CAT* and *DOG*, which identify the speaker, are written in uppercase letters; italics are used for emphasis or when using the pronoun *they* or *them* to refer to the humans.
- **Print layout**—The text is laid out in a script-like format with the speakers of the lines identified.
- **Punctuation**—Colons set off the speaker, dashes are used to cause the reader to pause, and hyphens are used to create words such as *bed-in-the-house* or *pretend-nip.*
- **See-saw pattern**—The book alternates back and forth between the dog's view of the world and the cat's.
- **Voice**—Through first-person narration and some very amusing descriptions of their species, the distinctly opposing voices of the dog and the cat ring true for any reader who has owned either or both as pets.

If You Were Alliteration, written by Trisha Speed Shaskan and illustrated by Sara Gray. 2008. Minneapolis, MN: Picture Window. Nonfiction. (24 pp.)

Summary: A combination of information about, and unmistakable examples of, alliteration provide the reader with everything one needs to know about this craft.

- **Alliteration**—From *young yaks yodeling* to *chubby chickens chitchatting while they cha-cha* each page of this book highlights at least one alliterative sentence or phrase.
- **Print features**—The book employs varied font, font color, and print size.
- **Print layout**—Technical explanations and descriptions of alliteration are found on the top of the left pages of the book, and examples of the craft are scattered across all the pages to complement the text and the illustrations.
- **Punctuation**—Ellipses instruct the reader to pause, as in *If you were alliteration….*
- **Simile**—Examples of this craft include *pretty as a picture, busy as a bee,* and *fit as a fiddle.*

- **Text features**—At the top of the dedication page the author invites the reader to look for alliteration in the *big, colorful words in the example sentences*. A page toward the end of the book, titled Fun With Alliteration, explains to the reader how to create an acrostic name poem. The last page of the book includes a glossary, an index, a list of more books in the Word Fun series, a list of other alliterative books to read, and information about related Internet sites.

If You Were Onomatopoeia, written by Trisha Speed Shaskan and illustrated by Sara Gray. 2008. Minneapolis, MN: Picture Window. Nonfiction. (24 pp.)

Summary: A combination of information about, and unmistakable examples of, onomatopoeia provide the reader with everything one needs to know about this craft.

- **Onomatopoeia**—From the *CHOO CHOO* of a train to the *WHOOSH* of a waterfall, this book overflows with examples of this craft.
- **Print features**—Varied print features, such as font, font size, font color, and uppercase letters, are employed. Each instance of onomatopoeia is set in uppercase colorful font that distinguishes it from the rest of the sentence.
- **Print layout**—Technical explanations and descriptions of onomatopoeia are found on the top of the left pages of the book, and examples of the craft are scattered across all the pages to complement the text and the illustrations.
- **Punctuation**—Hyphens connect some onomatopoeic words, such as *KER-PLUNK* or *TSST-TUT-TAH*; ellipses instruct the reader to pause, as in *If you were onomatopoeia...*.
- **Simile**—Each example of onomatopoeia is presented through simile, such as *BOOM like thunder* or *SPLISH and SPLOSH like the rain*.
- **Text features**—At the top of the dedication page the author invites the reader to look for onomatopoeia by watching for *the big, colorful words in the example sentences*. Toward the end of the book, a page titled Fun With Onomatopoeia encourages the reader to grab a friend and a notebook to listen for and record at least 10 sounds that are heard outside; the last page of the book includes a glossary, an index, a list of more books in the Word Fun series, a list of more onomatopoeic books to read, and information about related Internet sites.

The Important Book, written by Margaret Wise Brown and illustrated by Leonard Weisgard. 1949. New York: HarperCollins. Fiction. (24 pp.)

Summary: A series of vignettes describes the importance of everyday things as they might be seen through the eyes of a child.

- **Breaking the rules**—Many sentences begin with *And* or *But*, and run-on sentences composed of simple language convey a childlike voice: *It is yellow in the middle, it has long white petals, and bees sit on it, it has a ticklish smell, it grows in green fields, and there are always lots of daisies.*
- **Effective ending**—The "important" thread that runs through the book concludes with a vignette about the importance of "you": *But the important thing about you is that you are you.*
- **Print features**—Vignettes are written in various fonts of different sizes and colors; there are also uppercase and cursive letters.
- **Print layout**—Unique and varied layout of the print on each page melds the text into the illustrations.
- **Repetition**—Each page begins with the phrase *The important thing about a...* and ends with the phrase *But the important thing about a...*, echoing the title word and serving as a thread to bind the vignettes.

In My New Yellow Shirt, written by Eileen Spinelli and illustrated by Hideko Takahashi. 2001. New York: Henry Holt. Fiction. (32 pp.)

Summary: While wearing his new yellow shirt, a little boy uses his imagination to transform himself into a variety of yellow things.

- **Alliteration**—The aural effect of the alliteration adds to the playful tone of this imaginative story with examples such as *Running and roaring* and *a daffodil dancing dizzily*.
- **Breaking the rules**—Sentences begin with *And* or *But*, and the author uses sentence fragments to effectively convey the childlike whimsy: *Then a butterfly fluttering away. Or a fancy tropical fish swimming round and round in Sam's backyard pool.*
- **Descriptive language**—Spinelli captures the little boy's imagination with vivid descriptions and metaphors: *When I'm tired of running and roaring, I become a lazy caterpillar taking a nap under a peach tree.*

- **Metaphor**—Using his imagination, the narrator turns into a variety of items that represent the color yellow, such as *I am a tennis ball*. Other great metaphors can be found, too, such as *a big puddle of sun*, or *a smile of moon*.

- **Onomatopoeia**—*ROAR! HONK! HONK! TOOT! TOOT!* are a few examples of this craft.

- **Personification**—The author effectively uses personification to continue the vivid imagery, with phrases such as *a daffodil dancing* or *a yellow submarine snorkeling*.

- **Print features**—Uppercase letters make sound words loud, such as *ROAR! HONK! HONK! TOOT! TOOT!*; black font switches to white on the dark illustrations that depict nighttime.

- **Punctuation**—Ellipses throughout instruct the reader to turn the page in anticipation. Dashes interject onomatopoeia into a sentence, as in *Now I'm a brass—TOOT! TOOT!* or *Now I'm a taxi—HONK! HONK!—zooming down the street*. Hyphens create clever wordplay, such as *bounce-bounce-bouncing*.

- **Repetition**—The title is repeated throughout and serves as the thread that carries the story. Also, single words repeat for emphasis, as in *hidden in the dark, dark attic*. Phrases repeat to create imagery and rhythm: *I wink here, I wink there. I wink past Sam's windows*.

- **Verbs and verb forms**—Creative use of verbs and participles creates imagery: *a silly banana thumping about the house, a taxi…zooming down the street, squawked; stalking,* and *fluttering*.

- **Wordplay**—Playful words and phrases such as *bounce-bounce-bouncing* or *a canary singing tweetily* enhance the imaginative nature.

In November, written by Cynthia Rylant and illustrated by Jill Kastner. 2000. Orlando, FL: Harcourt. Fiction. (32 pp.)

Summary: The changes in nature and the holiday traditions that November brings are evoked through Rylant's loving tribute.

- **Breaking the rules**—Rylant effectively uses sentence fragments such as *Hard times. No silly spring chirping now*. Many sentences begin with *And*.

- **Descriptive language**—This craft is used throughout to capture the sights, smells, tastes, sounds, and feel of November.

- **Metaphor**—The snow becomes the blankets of a winter bed: *The bed is white and silent, and much life can hide beneath its blankets*. Also, the change in season from autumn to winter is described as *winter's gate*.

- **Personification**—The earth and elements of nature are personified, adding to the rich descriptions: *the earth…is making its bed; the trees are standing all sticks and bones…spreading their arms…; And the world has tucked her children in, with a kiss on their heads, till spring*.

- **Repetition**—The title phrase introduces several sentences. Phrases and sentence patterns also repeat, as in this line: *Cats pile up in the corners of barns. Mice pile up under logs. Bees pile up in deep, earthy holes*.

- **Simile**—A good example of this craft is the following: *trees…spreading their arms like dancers*.

Journey Around Chicago From A to Z, written and illustrated by Martha Day Zschock. 2005. Beverly, MA: Commonwealth. Nonfiction. (28 pp.)

Summary: Experience all that Chicago has to offer through this alphabetical journey around the Windy City. This book is part of a geographic exploration series written by this author.

- **Alliteration**—Each page that introduces alphabetic information about Chicago contains a framed inset illustration with an alliterative fact, such as *Abstract art adorns the area* or *Many marvel at magnificent merchandise*.

- **Interesting format**—The book uses an alphabet book format to impart factual information about Chicago.

- **Print features**—The letter that starts each alliterative inset is written in large boldface font; the font used to describe the illustrated detail in the lower right corner is tiny; the first few words of the main text on each page appear in all uppercase letters; italics are used for titles of books and periodicals and for a Latin motto; italics are used for emphasis as well.

- **Print layout**—Each page contains an alliterative inset, a paragraph of information about the subject, a key to all the information featured on the page, and a tiny wavy line across the bottom of the page that describes the illustrated detail in the lower right corner; captions and environmental print can be found throughout many of the illustrations.

- **Punctuation**—Use of dashes throughout indicate an aside or clarification, or cause the reader to pause: *The DuSable Museum of African American History—named for Chicago's first settler, a Haitian fur trader—celebrates African Americans' experiences and achievements.* Hyphens are used to combine words to form new words, such as *steel-framed, four-wheeled,* or *Deep-dish.* Parentheses are used to add an aside, such as *The fire began on DeKoven Street when (some say) a cow kicked over a lantern…;* or to add clarifying information *Michael Jordan (Bulls) and Sammy Sosa (Cubs).* Quotation marks indicate nicknames for well-known Chicago place names: *Chicago's elevated train, the "L" or "El," circles "The Loop," Chicago's central business district.*
- **Text features**—The book begins with a section called Welcome to Chicago! wherein the author provides some introductory information about the city and invites the reader to join her on a journey around the city. The endpapers at the front and back of the book include captioned illustrations of some of Chicago's famous faces, features, and inventions.

Just Like Daddy, written and illustrated by Frank Asch. 1981. New York: Aladdin, Simon & Schuster. Fiction. (32 pp.)

Summary: A young bear recounts his day doing all the things that his father does, right through to the amusing twist at the book's end. This book is ideal for primary grades.

- **Breaking the rules**—Several sentences begin with *And,* and the book effectively uses sentence fragments.
- **Effective ending**—The surprise ending changes the pattern of the story.
- **Punctuation**—Ellipses instruct the reader to pause in anticipation.
- **Repetition**—The title is repeated throughout and serves as the thread that carries the story. Also, single words are repeated to slow down the narration.

A Kitten's Year, written by Nancy Raines Day and illustrated by Anne Mortimer. 2000. New York: HarperCollins. Fiction. (32 pp.)

Summary: Using a single unique verb for each month, Day chronicles the first year in the life of a playful kitten.

- **Lists**—This short text is one continuous list.
- **Print layout**—The entire text is one long sentence.
- **Punctuation**—Commas create the long list, and ellipses instruct the reader to pause in anticipation.
- **Verbs and verb forms**—Kitten-specific verbs bring the months to life: *stalks March, paws April,* and *spooks October.*

Last Night at the Zoo, written and illustrated by Michael Garland. 2001. Honesdale, PA: Boyds Mills. Fiction. (32 pp.)

Summary: The zoo animals are bored so they don disguises from the Lost and Found and sneak out for a rousing, rhyming night on the town.

- **Circular ending**—The book ends as it begins, with the animals planning an escape from the boredom of the zoo.
- **Lead**—The opening sentence repeats the title and engages the reader, while the ellipsis hints that more is to come: *Last night at the zoo there was nothing to do….*
- **Punctuation**—Dashes throughout cause the reader to pause. An ellipsis is used at the beginning and end to build anticipation.
- **Repetition**—The word *and* repeats instead of a comma to draw out a list of words for effect: *With coats and hats and shirts and ties* or *hooted and howled and screeched.*
- **Rhyme**—Clever use of rhyme creates a whimsical cadence.
- **Simile**—A playful sentence adds to the whimsy as the animals add a bustling night club to their escapade: *And the house was full up, like a busy beehive.*
- **Verbs and verb forms**—The verbs reflect their animal subjects, such as *hooted and howled and screeched, whisked, strolled, gobbled,* and *devoured.*

Leaf Jumpers, written by Carole Gerber and illustrated by Leslie Evans. 2004. Watertown, MA: Charlesbridge. Fiction. (32 pp.)

Summary: The leaves of autumn and the trees from which they fall are lyrically but factually described in this simple picture book.

- **Descriptive language**—Gerber's simple but perfectly chosen words capture the uniqueness of each autumn leaf: *The broad leaf of the sycamore is yellow with a coat of tan.*
- **Metaphor**—This craft vividly describes leaves with the following phrases: *Bright jewels from the crowns of trees; Stubby fingers, brown as dirt, reach from the slender white oak leaf;* and *Leaf hats settle on our heads.*
- **Print layout**—The majority of the pages contain only one sentence.
- **Rhyme**—The story is written with a rhyme scheme, which adds to the lyricism.
- **Simile**—Interesting leaf similes include the following: *vivid as a match, orange like pumpkins in a pumpkin patch, shaped like hearts with little teeth, oval as an egg,* and *shaped like a little fan.*
- **Text features**—The last page of the text provides information about what happens to the leaves during the fall and the eight leaves that are highlighted in the text are illustrated and labeled.
- **Wordplay**—Playful words capture the leaves' autumn hues: *sunny-side* and *yellow-green.*

Listen, Listen, written by Phyllis Gershator and illustrated by Alison Jay. 2007. Cambridge, MA: Barefoot. Fiction. (32 pp.)

Summary: The sights and sounds of the four seasons are captured in this lively rhyming book.

- **Alliteration**—This craft is used throughout to enliven the action and brighten descriptions: *Skaters spin, skiers glide. Zip, zoom, slip, slide.*
- **Circular ending**—The book opens with the sounds of summer insects singing and weaves through the year to come full circle to the singing of summer insects again.
- **Descriptive language**—The simple rhyming verse uses sensory details to capture the sights and especially the sounds of the seasons.
- **Onomatopoeia**—This is used throughout to capture the sounds of the four seasons, as in *Chirp, chirp, churr, churr, buzz, buzz, shirr, whirr; crick, crack;* and *Peep, peep….*
- **Personification**—In this book *Snowflakes whisper, Finches whistle,* and *flowers shout.*
- **Print layout**—Lines of print arc and bend to complement the unique illustrations.
- **Punctuation**—Ellipses cause the reader to pause in anticipation: *Listen, listen… after spring,*

summer comes and…. A dash creates the same effect: *In the air, on the ground, night and day—what's that sound?*)

- **Repetition**—The title is repeated as each season is introduced; many words, especially onomatopoeic terms, are presented in pairs to produce a patterned rhythm; the final onomatopoeic line echoes the first.
- **Rhyme**—Lines of rhyming text create a lively tempo.
- **Sequencing**—The sounds and sights of nature cycle through the change of seasons from summer to fall to winter to spring and back again to summer.
- **Text features**—At the end of the book there is a nature-search game wherein the reader is challenged to find 10 different objects depicted in each of four seasonal illustrations.

The Listening Walk, written by Paul Showers and illustrated by Aliki. 1961. New York: HarperCollins. Fiction. (32 pp.)

Summary: A little girl, her father, and their old dog Major share a "Listening Walk" as they take in all the sounds around them—tranquil and tumultuous, hushed and harsh.

- **Effective ending**—On the final page of the book the little girl invites you, the reader, to close the book and count how many different sounds you can hear.
- **Onomatopoeia**—The book is filled with onomatopoeia as it describes the different sounds the little girl hears as she walks: *bomp bomp bomp bomp, chuff chuff chuff chuff,* and *dop dup dop dup.*
- **Print features**—All of the onomatopoeic words are italicized.
- **Print layout**—Unique and meaningful placement of the print complements the text and illustrations and strengthens the onomatopoeia.
- **Punctuation**—Hyphens stretch out onomatopoeic words, as in *rat-tat-tat-tat-tat,* and colons introduce onomatopoeic words as in *A baby crying: waaaa awaaaa awaaaa awaaaa.*
- **Simile**—A great example of simile is the following: *The woodpecker sounds like a little hammer.*

The Little House, written and illustrated by Virginia Lee Burton. 1942. Boston: Houghton Mifflin. Fiction. (44 pp.)

Summary: A little house is given human emotions as she observes the urbanization of her world over a span of many years. Through her story, we are reminded of the age-old lesson that sometimes things are perfect just as they are. (This is a Caldecott Medal Winner.)

- **Descriptive language**—Though not a typical book cited for descriptive language, the simplicity of the language used to bring the sights and sounds of both the city and country make this an excellent choice for introducing this craft to our youngest writers.

- **Effective ending**—The final page is a rush of elliptical sentences that demonstrate the flurry of emotions felt by the Little House, with the final two lines slowing down for the happy ending.

- **Personification**—The little house is instilled with human emotions and characteristics throughout the book, as in *The Little House was very happy as she sat on the hill and watched the countryside around her.* Uppercase letters for *Little* and *House* further personalize the house with a proper name.

- **Point of view**—The changing seasons and the passing years with all their changes are witnessed through the point of view of a little house bearing the burden of urbanization.

- **Print features**—Italics emphasize a word, as in *only* that *Little House was way out in the country.*

- **Print layout**—Line breaks elicit phrasing that adds a lyrical quality.

- **Punctuation**—Ellipses throughout indicate the passing of time, as in *More houses and bigger houses…apartment houses and tenement houses…schools…stores…and garages spread over the land.* Ellipses also set up a parenthetical phrase, such as *big cellars…one on each side.* The final page is structured around a series of elliptical sentences: *Never again would she be curious about the city…Never again would she want to live there…The stars twinkled above her…A new moon was coming up…It was Spring…and all was quiet and peaceful in the country.*

- **Sequencing**—Strings of repeating phrases and frequent transitional words show the passing of time and the changes wrought: *Once again* appears four times, *Pretty soon* appears eight times, and *Now* is used to begin a sentence five times.

The Little Yellow Leaf, written and illustrated by Carin Berger. 2008. New York: Greenwillow, HarperCollins. Fiction. (40 pp.)

Summary: In this simple tribute to friendship, a little yellow leaf clings tenaciously to its tree when autumn comes, but ultimately finds the courage to let go after finding a lone red leaf with whom to soar away.

- **Alliteration**—Examples of this craft include the following: *The sun sank slow; the waiting wind;* and *a heavy harvest moon.*

- **Breaking the rules**—The author employs single-word sentence fragments such as *Alone.* or *Together.* Some sentences begin with *And,* as in *And one, two, three, they let go and soared.*

- **Descriptive language**—This craft is used throughout to capture the feel of autumn, as in *a heavy harvest moon bloomed amber in the starry sky.*

- **Effective ending**—A simple one-word sentence delivers a powerful message: *Together.*

- **Personification**—Elements of nature are given human characteristics, such as *a riot of fiery leaves chased and swirled around the tree, the afternoon sun beckoned and teased,* and *In the hush of the forest a lone yellow leaf clung to the branch of a great oak tree.*

- **Print features**—The first letter of the first word is in large boldface font; two pages of large bold font represent the raised voices of the two leaves as they call out to each other across the tree; italics are used throughout to show the Little Yellow Leaf's thoughts.

- **Print layout**—Minimal text on each page is purposefully laid out to complement the illustrations and significance of the words.

- **Punctuation**—Ellipses cause the reader to pause in anticipation, as in *Neither spoke. Finally…;* or to slow down a moment, such as *And then…and then,….*

- **Repetition**—The phrase *Not ready,* or some variation, repeats throughout as the Little Yellow Leaf voices his reluctance to drop from the branch. Other phrases repeat to slow down a moment; to add emphasis, as in *Not yet, not yet, not yet;* or to imply time and distance, as in *away and away and away.* Words repeat for emphasis, as well: *the bare, bare branches.*

Loki & Alex: Adventures of a Dog and His Best Friend, written and photographed by Charles R. Smith Jr. 2001. New York: Dutton, Penguin. Fiction. (32 pp.)

Summary: Alex thinks he knows exactly what his dog Loki is thinking, but we find out that this is not always the case as the book alternates between Alex's and Loki's views of the world. One thing they do agree on is their love for each other.

- **Breaking the rules**—The author uses vernacular to bring voice to Loki's words, with such phrasing as *Lemme climb up there…I wanna hang upside down, too!*

- **Point of view**—The story alternates back and forth so the reader can see the same actions from Alex's point of view and then Loki's point of view.

- **Print features**—Alex's viewpoint is printed in simple red font on an orange border; Loki's viewpoint is printed in a wild purple font on a green border; uppercase letters are used to indicate increased volume.

- **Punctuation**—There are several examples of multiple exclamation points for emphasis. Dashes link two parts of a sentence, as in *I fetched, I ran, I jumped—gimme MY treat!* Ellipses cause the reader to pause, as in *Gimme that rope…Gimme. Mine, mine, MINE!*

- **See-saw pattern**—The book alternates back and forth between Alex's point of view and Loki's.

- **Text features**—A photograph of Alex's head or Loki's head accompanies their thoughts on the alternating pages to further distinguish who is speaking. Alex's photographs are all in black and white because that's the way Loki sees him, while Loki's photographs are always in color to show the way Alex sees the world.

- **Voice**—This book provides an interesting contrast for children studying voice. Alex's personality barely comes through in his matter-of-fact descriptions, but Loki's personality "steals" the book.

The Lonely Scarecrow, written by Tim Preston and illustrated by Maggie Kneen. 1999. New York: Dutton, Penguin. Fiction. (24 pp.)

Summary: A kind but lonely scarecrow wishes that his scary face would not frighten off the birds and animals, until one day when a blanketing snowfall creates a surprising transformation.

- **Alliteration**—A lovely example of this craft is exemplified by *whispering of the wheat.*

- **Breaking the rules**—Sentences begin with *And* or *But*, and the author uses fragments.

- **Descriptive language**—Preston's poignant imagery captures the changing seasons and along with it, the scarecrow's transformation: A*s the warmth of spring stirred the brown earth, the scarecrow felt a bird peck at his hat and a mouse nestle in the folds of his coat.*

- **Metaphor**—The wheat field becomes *his golden sea;* the farmer's combine turns into a *monster* with *churning jaws.*

- **Personification**—Examples include the following: *whispering of the wheat* and *a sly breeze that stole the leaves from the trees and the light from the days.*

- **Print features**—The font is calligraphic rather than block.

- **Punctuation**—Ellipses cause the reader to pause in anticipation, as in *And then the snow began to thaw….* Dashes also direct the reader to pause, as in *The animals hid from its churning jaws—and the ravaged acres of mud and stubble that it left behind.*

- **Simile**—This is a good example for young writers to model: *he was as cheerful and bright as the sunny winter day.*

long night moon, written by Cynthia Rylant and illustrated by Mark Siegel. 2004. New York: Simon & Schuster. Fiction. (40 pp.)

Summary: Each month a full moon graces the sky. Through Rylant's lyrical text we learn the traditional Native American name and unique personality of each month's moon.

- **Breaking the rules**—The title of the book is written in lowercase letters.

- **Descriptive language**—Rylant creates imagery through the use of simple and soothing language in order to honor the Native American tradition of naming the full moons.

- **Metaphor**—The clouds of a January night are compared to a wild wolf; the chill of a February night is compared to cool breath. In June, the grass and buds are compared to a meal and thunderclouds are compared to drums.

- **Personification**—The different moons are given human characteristics. For example, the Sun is described as the Snow Moon's sister, the Sap

Moon is hopeful, the Flower Moon smiles, the Thunder Moon trembles and shudders, the Acorn Moon says good-bye, the Frosty Moon shivers and goes to sleep, the Long Night Moon waits like a faithful friend.

- **Print features**—All of the text is in cursive font of soft muted colors that complement the peaceful tone. The Native American name for each moon is written in a different color font from the rest of the text on the page and is shadowed in a contrasting color that creates a hazy effect like looking at the moon.
- **Print layout**—Each moon is described and illustrated on a new page; purposeful line breaks and word spacing pace the reader and create a calming poetic effect.
- **Repetition**—The same pattern repeats as each full moon is introduced with the month in which it appears. Certain words repeat to slow down a moment.
- **Sequencing**—The 12 full moons are described in order from January through December.
- **Simile**—In one of the best examples of this craft, a Harvest Moon is compared to a big ripe melon.

Max Found Two Sticks, written and illustrated by Brian Pinkney. 1994. New York: Aladdin Paperbacks, Simon & Schuster. Fiction. (40 pp.)

Summary: Max isn't in the mood to talk. Instead, he uses two sticks and a variety of objects to drum out rhythmic responses to the questions posed to him.

- **Breaking the rules**—The slow and easy words of the people whom Max meets on the city streets come alive through the use of dialogue that incorporates incorrect grammar.
- **Onomatopoeia**—This craft is used throughout as Max creates a pair of drumsticks out of two ordinary sticks.
- **Print features**—The first letter of the first word in the book appears in large red font; all onomatopoeic words are in italics; some onomatopoeic words are in all uppercase letters to represent increased volume.
- **Punctuation**—Ellipses are used to separate onomatopoeic words, and hyphens are used to create onomatopoeia.

Mojave, written by Diane Siebert and illustrated by Wendell Minor. 1988. New York: HarperCollins. Poetry. (32 pp.)

Summary: Written from the point of view of the Mojave Desert, this poetic text brings to life the natural beauty of the desert and the flora and fauna that flourish there.

- **Circular ending**—This book demonstrates a more sophisticated and subtle use of this craft: the first and final stanzas are identical, implying that the years will continue to pass and continue to leave their mark on the desert: *I am the desert. I am free. Come walk the sweeping face of me.*
- **Descriptive language**—Factual information and vocabulary about the physical characteristics of the desert are interwoven with sensory descriptions in first-person verse making the Mojave come alive for the reader.
- **Effective ending**—The opening line of the book, *I am the desert*, repeats as the opening line of the final three stanzas of this poem.
- **Lead**—The opening lines are powerful in their simplicity.
- **Personification**—The Mojave Desert is imbued throughout this book with human qualities as it speaks to the reader in first-person narration. One good example is the following: *Great mountain ranges stretch for miles / To crease my face with frowns and smiles.*
- **Point of view**—The reader experiences the desert environment and all that it encompasses through sensory details and the first-person narration of the Mojave Desert.
- **Rhyme**—The entire text is written in rhyming verse; in addition there are internal rhyming words within each stanza, such as *go gliding, hiding* or *walls of water grow, and flow* or *stumbling, bumbling tumbleweeds.*
- **Sequencing**—The physical changes that occur in the desert are traced through the cycle of changing seasons across the years.

The Moon Was the Best, written by Charlotte Zolotow and illustrated by Tana Hoban. 1993. New York: Greenwillow, William Morrow. Fiction. (32 pp.)

Summary: The magic and beauty of Paris are captured as a mother brings her memories of the city home to her daughter, including the message that the little girl was never far from her mother's heart.

- **Alliteration**—The following examples of this craft evoke images of Paris: *long loaves, glistening gods, parks like paintings and paintings like parks.*

- **Descriptive language**—This craft is used throughout to capture both the mundane and magical images of Paris.
- **Lead**—A simple first sentence brings a fairy tale quality to the opening.
- **Repetition**—Each page begins with *She remembered…*, as the mother stores her memories of Paris to bring home to her daughter. The single word *in* repeats to create the image of a profusion of flowers: *in all the stores, in every house, even in the window….*
- **Simile**—Good examples for young writers include: *unwrapped bread like sticks under their arms; a tiny carousel, like a birthday cake.* There is also a clever simile that reverses itself: *parks like paintings and paintings like parks.*
- **Text features**—Scenes of Paris are captured through a series of full-page photographs that appear on the left hand page. The camera then zooms in on a detail from the photograph, which then appears below the text on the right-hand page, making this an excellent book for teaching children to zoom in on small details.

Mud, written by May Lyn Ray and illustrated by Lauren Stringer. 1996. San Diego: Harcourt. Fiction. (32 pp.)

Summary: Ray's simple words couple with the vivid illustrations to paint a glorious tribute to mud and all it has to offer, including the promise of spring.

- **Alliteration**—Alliterative phrases are used throughout to capture everything about mud—its consistency, its magnificence, and the joy it brings to playful children: *Gooey, gloppy, mucky, magnificent mud.*
- **Breaking the rules**—Sentences begin with *But*. The author uses fragments mixed in with some longer sentences to create a playful, rhythmic effect.
- **Descriptive language**—Ray's simple yet eloquent words make ordinary mud seem magical.
- **Lead**—The opening line immediately engages the reader.
- **Onomatopoeia**—One two-page spread captures all the squishy and slurpy sounds of mud.
- **Personification**—Leaves run; the sun sees; hills remember; mud is happy—These are just a few examples of the way natural elements receive human qualities.
- **Print features**—Font is large with some pages in black font and others in white.

- **Print layout**—Most pages have just one sentence. Text placement varies from page to page, with some lines of print shaped to complement the text and illustration.
- **Repetition**—Word and sentence patterns repeat to create a rhythmic effect.
- **Simile**—The season's first thaw brings with it a welcome earthy aroma that is compared to the sugary smell of sap.
- **Wordplay**—The author makes up a few nonsense words to add to the fun and descriptiveness.

My Dog Is as Smelly as Dirty Socks: And Other Funny Family Portraits, written and illustrated by Hanoch Piven. 2007. New York: Schwartz & Wade, Random House. Fiction. (40 pp.)

Summary: A little girl uses everyday objects to adorn her family drawing, carefully selecting each for its ability to convey a particular family member's traits.

- **Breaking the rules**—Sentences begin with *And* or *But* giving a childlike quality.
- **Print features**—Font size, uppercase, italics, and boldface are all used effectively to direct the reader's phrasing and emphasis, as well as to bring out the narrator's voice.
- **Punctuation**—Ellipses cause the reader to pause in anticipation; parentheses allow the narrator to share an aside with the reader.
- **Simile**—The entire book is a series of similes that describe the narrator's family, herself, and her dog Smutz.
- **Text features**—There is an Author's Note on the copyright page wherein the author describes three days spent conducting a workshop in a pediatric oncology department. The workshop, Drawing with Objects, allowed the children to create family portraits using everyday objects and served as the inspiration for this book; pictures made by the children appear inside the front and back covers on the endpapers; at the end of the book the author encourages readers to make their own family portraits and provides objects that might be used within similes to exemplify traits.
- **Voice**—The narrator's voice comes through loud and clear throughout the book, but never more so than when she begins to describe herself.

My Little Island, written and illustrated by Frané Lessac. 1984. New York: HarperCollins. Fiction. (48 pp.)

Summary: A young boy invites his best friend to visit the little island where he was born. Lessac perfectly captures Caribbean life in this sweet story about coming home.

- **Alliteration**—Alliterative phrases such as *flipping and flopping fish* or *a breeze begins to blow* convey the spirit of the island.

- **Breaking the rules**—The infusion of unconventional spellings captures the dialect of the Caribbean islands. Examples include, *"Wha de mangoes?" "Wha de nuts?"* people ask.

- **Descriptive language**—Sensory details create imagery and evoke a strong sense of place.

- **Lists**—Several long lists fill the text with the sights, sounds, and tastes of Caribbean life.

- **Onomatopoeia**—Sound words such as *Tootle-tu-whooo!* and *Ding dong…ding dong* add depth to descriptions.

- **Personification**—A Caribbean sunrise comes to life: *The sun is just peeking over the mountaintops.*

- **Print features**—The titles of the illustrations are in very small font; italics are used for proper nouns and for onomatopoeia; the first letter of the first word of the book is in large boldface font.

- **Print layout**—The title of each of the paintings that serve as the illustrations for the story may be found in the lower right-hand corner of the accompanying text page; many of the illustrations contain environmental print and, in some cases, the artist's signature.

- **Punctuation**—Colons and commas are used for lists, as in *Lucca and I can't decide what to get: soursops, guavas, christophines, mangoes, coconuts, or juicy orange pawpaws*; quotation marks designate idiomatic expressions, such as *Our friends call the barking frogs "mountain chickens"* and onomatopoeia: *People hear the "Tootle-tu-whooo!" and run to the beach.* Dashes direct the reader to pause in order to separate one object from a group, as in *We choose mango jam, guava cheese, lime squash—and some very hot pepper sauce for Lucca's father.* Ellipses separate repetitive phrases, such as *Ding dong…ding dong* or *Jump up! Jump up!*

- **Simile**—The island is seen from the air as the plane descends: *it looks like a giant green turtle.* And the brightly painted houses are seen from the car window: *they look like little rainbows sitting on the hills.*

My Mama Had a Dancing Heart, written by Libba Moore Gray and illustrated by Raúl Colón. 1995. New York: Orchard. Fiction. (32 pp.)

Summary: An adult ballerina reminisces about her childhood and how her mother instilled in her a love of dance.

- **Breaking the rules**—Many long run-on sentences mirror the energetic pace of the dances; more than half of the sentences begin with *And*.

- **Descriptive language**—Through playful imagery, the first-person narration evokes the joyful, free-spirited times shared by the narrator and her mother.

- **Effective ending**—The final sentence repeats the first and underscores the influence that the narrator's mother has had on her life.

- **Flashback**—Much of the story is told in flashback as the narrator recalls special childhood times with her mother who nurtured her love of dance.

- **Lead**—The first line echoes the title capturing the essence of the story and sets the flashback format wherein an adult woman reminisces about her mother.

- **Print features**—As an adult ballerina, the narrator imagines hearing her mother's voice echo across the years; her mother's words appear in italics.

- **Print layout**—Rather than through indented paragraphs, the text is set up to resemble stanzas of poetry, with purposeful line breaks that prompt a lyrical reading.

- **Punctuation**—Ellipses are used to slow down the reading; hyphens are used throughout to create wordplay.

- **Repetition**—The first line of the book repeats as the last line, and the mother's words from years ago appear at the start of the story and then again at the end.

- **Sequencing**—The author uses the changing seasons to move the narrator's memories of her childhood from spring to summer to autumn to winter and then to leap across the years to the narrator as an adult ballerina stepping onto the stage.

- **Simile**—The narrator remembers a winter day when she and her mother danced through the snow like snowmen decked out in mittens and galoshes.

- **Wordplay**—This book is filled with this craft! The author creates wonderful images using playful hyphenated words such as *frog-hopping leaf-growing flower-opening hello spring ballet.*

My Map Book, written and illustrated by Sara Fanelli. 1995. New York: HarperCollins. Fiction. (32 pp.)

Summary: A young child draws a series of maps that present a perfect childlike view of the world with the places and things that are special.

- **Interesting format**—The book is a compilation of childlike maps of things that are special to the narrator, such as *My Bedroom*, *My Family*, and *My Tummy*.
- **Print features**—All of the map labels appear in childlike script—complete with arrows and cross-outs.
- **Print layout**—The print, which primarily consists of labels on each map, is scattered about each two-page spread very much as a child might do.
- **Text features**—The book jacket unfolds to a poster-sized map. The front flap challenges the reader to find specific things in the map.
- **Voice**—With very limited text, the author manages to convey the narrator's voice, not only through the choices of maps and their components, but also through parenthetical asides, such as *More Vegetables (To Make Mommy Happy!)*, *Saturdays + Sundays (No School!)*, and *Red Cheek (shy…)*. Particularly touching is the *Map of My Heart* which is so full that its contents spill out into the space around the map's borders.

Night in the Country, written by Cynthia Rylant and illustrated by Mary Szilagyi. 1986. New York: Aladdin Paperbacks, Simon & Schuster. Fiction. (32 pp.)

Summary: What happens on a country night when people are fast asleep? Rylant brings the nocturnal sights and sounds to life.

- **Breaking the rules**—Sentences begin with *And* or *But*, and Rylant effectively uses fragments.
- **Descriptive language**—The highly descriptive language and use of the second-person narrative allow the author to invite the reader to accompany her on a visit to the country at night.
- **Effective ending**—A unique reversal takes place at the end when day breaks and the now-sleeping nocturnal animals listen to the sounds of people.

- **Lead**—The descriptive opening sentence immediately immerses the reader in the setting.
- **Metaphor**—This craft is used to create imagery, such as in *marble eyes.*
- **Onomatopoeia**—Great examples of sound words add to the vivid descriptions.
- **Print features**—All text is in yellow font imprinted directly on the illustrations; use of italics throughout highlights onomatopoeia.
- **Print layout**—Many pages have a single line of text, and one page has a single word.
- **Punctuation**—Colons are used in interesting ways, usually to introduce new sounds. Ellipses cause the reader to pause in anticipation. Dashes help the reader zoom in on important details.
- **Repetition**—Individual words repeat in several sentences for rhythmic effect. The word *and* repeats instead of commas to group words and indicate ongoing action.

Night Rabbits, written by Lee Posey and illustrated by Michael G. Montgomery. 1999. Atlanta, GA: Peachtree. Fiction. (32 pp.)

Summary: Elizabeth's father has worked on the lawn at the cabin all summer long and now the rabbits are eating it. Elizabeth loves the rabbits, so she devises a plan that will maintain her father's carefully tended lawn and still allow the rabbits to dance in the night.

- **Descriptive language**—This craft is used throughout to evoke a lyrical tone and to create imagery: *His eyes sparkle like the lake when the setting sun turns the water gold.*
- **Lead**—Through the use of an urgent line of dialog written in large boldface font, the author immediately grabs the reader's attention.
- **Metaphor**—Morning is compared to *a picture waiting for the colors to be painted in.*
- **Onomatopoeia**—The nighttime noises of the crickets can be heard—*hum zzzz mmm, zzzz mmm*—while the frogs add their chorus—*ruumph, ruumph.*
- **Print features**—The only deviation in font, with the exception of onomatopoeic words which are italicized, is in the opening sentence, which is in large boldface—the singular use of this technique makes it particularly effective.
- **Simile**—Good examples of this craft include the following: *The noise keeps me awake, sticking in my mind the way warm sheets stick to my*

body; *They are quick as moonbeams; bare brown spots will grow like frowns; Their leaps are soft as shyness.*

On the Same Day in March: A Tour of the World's Weather, written by Marilyn Singer and illustrated by Frané Lessac. 2000. New York: HarperCollins. Nonfiction. (40 pp.)

Summary: Singer takes us on a journey to 17 different locations around the world where we experience the weather as well as snippets of life, all on the same day.

- **Alliteration**—Two effective examples include *Only the weather wears a watch* and *crocodiles crouched.*

- **Breaking the rules**—The book is made up mostly of long run-on sentences interspersed with some short sentences and meaningful line breaks to create a lyrical effect.

- **Descriptive language**—The engaging images evoke a simple but strong sense of setting: *Fog threads through the temples. The sun slips out, still winter pale.*

- **Metaphor**—Hailstones become magical through a young girl's eyes: *the moon has broken and scattered its necklace of pearls.* Clouds become puffs of wool from the shorn sheep: *"Catch the wool,"* Mama teases her youngest son.

- **Personification**—Elements of weather are given unusual but fitting human traits: *the sun's shy smile; Only the weather wears a watch;* and *The rain is always on time.*

- **Print features**—The name of each place appears in a unique font that characterizes each locale; italics are used for foreign words or to add emphasis, as in *But it's not too hot to spell R-I-C-E….*

- **Print layout**—The book is divided into a series of vignettes with purposeful print layout to create rhythm.

- **Punctuation**—Ellipses instruct the reader to pause before each page turn. A colon leads to a series of questions, such as *In the park the old men and small children guess: What will the wind carry today?* Dashes instruct the reader to pause before a continuation of a sentence, as in *They said it was just a tiny twister—not big enough to spin a horse or hoist a cow.* Hyphens create wordplay such as *dragon-shaped, blue-winged,* and *willy-willies.*

- **Repetition**—The title is the last line of each page and serves as the cohesive thread. Individual words and phrases repeat for emphasis, as in *Fog threads through temples. Fog settles on the swamp;* and *It's too hot to plant rice. It's too hot to pick rice.*

- **Rhyme**—Several of the vignettes contain rhyme schemes.

- **Sequencing**—The book is sequenced in such a way that time remains constant throughout each vignette, while the setting changes.

- **Simile**—Good examples of this craft include the following: *that wild chinook blows in like a dragon, autumn shears the clouds like a flock of sheep,* and *kites shaped like butterflies.*

- **Text features**—A world map at the beginning and end of the book highlights the locations included in the story. A Note From the Author at the conclusion of the book sums up the information presented in a more technical manner.

- **Verbs and verb forms**—Exciting verbs such as *scramble, vanish, crouched,* and *dazzles* enhance the imagery.

- **Wordplay**—The author creates new words to add to the imagery. For example, *the six-month sun, a dragon-shaped patch, Clouds of blue-winged swallows.*

The Other Way to Listen, written by Byrd Baylor and illustrated by Peter Parnall. 1997. New York: Aladdin Paperbacks, Simon & Schuster. Fiction. (32 pp.)

Summary: This is the story of an old man who is intimately in touch with his natural surroundings and of the child who learns to follow in his footsteps by being very quiet and just listening.

- **Breaking the rules**—Sentences begin with *And* or *But.*

- **Descriptive language**—The text evokes a strong sense of setting, vividly describing images such as a star-filled sky and a blooming cactus.

- **Lists**—Several long lists highlight the elements of the desert.

- **Personification**—Elements of nature, such as rocks, corn, and trees are given human qualities or actions.

- **Print features**—Italics and boldface uppercase letters are used for emphasis.

- **Print layout**—Unique and meaningful placement of text on the page gives this book a poetic feel.

- **Punctuation**—Ellipses instruct the reader to pause; colons indicate directives; dashes instruct the reader to pause; parentheses are used to create an aside.

- **Repetition**—A particular line is repeated throughout the book and it also serves as the final sentence. A phrase repeats for emphasis; the words *and* or *or* repeat instead of using commas to create a list.

- **See-saw pattern**—The dialogue between the boy and the old man creates a see-saw effect.

Out of the Ocean, written and illustrated by Debra Frasier. 1998. San Diego, CA: Voyager, Harcourt. Fiction. (40 pp.)

Summary: A mother teaches her young daughter the importance of appreciating nature and all its beauty as they stroll along the beach and wonder at the treasures the ocean has wrought. Although this is a fiction book, it is filled with factual information. (This book was voted Best Book of the Year by the Southeast Booksellers Association.)

- **Breaking the rules**—The author writes with sentence fragments and begins sentences with *And* or *But*. Also, although there is much dialogue between the mother and her daughter, there are no quotation marks used.

- **Lists**—A long list that spans three pages names the treasures one can find when walking along the beach. Another list offers the nontangible treasures that the beach offers.

- **Print features**—The first three words in the book are in uppercase red font; one sentence on a dark blue background is printed in white font.

- **Punctuation**—Dashes are used to add parenthetical remarks and to cause the reader to pause for more to come. Ellipses continue a list at a page break.

- **Text features**—At the end of the book, the author writes a brief personal note to the reader and includes An Ocean Journal, with photographs and factual information about treasures one might discover at the beach. The author's biography on the final page of the book includes some photographs of the author's childhood home near the Atlantic Ocean and a photograph of her with a loggerhead turtle.

Over and Over, written by Charlotte Zolotow and illustrated by Garth Williams. 1957. New York: HarperCollins. Fiction. (32 pp.)

Summary: A mother teaches her very young daughter about time as she helps her look forward to each special time of the year. As the year draws to a close and the little girl blows out her birthday candles, she wishes for it all to happen again.

- **Breaking the rules**—Sentences begin with *And* or *But*. The author also uses fragments and run-on sentences that capture the voice of a very young child reveling in all the joy a holiday brings: *That afternoon her grandmother and grandfather and uncles and aunts all came to her house for dinner and afterward they sat in front of the fire and cracked open walnuts and ate the soft sweet kernels.*

- **Circular ending**—The end of the story echoes the title and makes it clear that this all will be happening over and over again: *And of course, over and over, year after year, it did.*

- **Descriptive language**—Zolotow creates imagery by capturing the sights and sounds of the changing holidays and seasons: *Then one morning the air was soft and warm and the birds were singing outside and the little girl went downstairs, and there was a big basket full of shiny green paper grass and a big chocolate egg with white icing on it.*

- **Lists**—Three lists on the very first page (the days of the week, the months of the year, and the seasons of the year) introduce the theme of time passing. Several other lists are used throughout the book to build the excitement that comes with the arrival of each special time of the year, for instance, *she asked the ghosts and witches and tigers and tramps and devils who came* or *She remembered a snowman and a pumpkin, and a Christmas tree, and a birthday cake, a Thanksgiving dinner and valentines.*

- **Repetition**—Individual words repeat to suggest a large quantity, as in *There were red packages and white packages and green packages and everyone opened everything* or to demonstrate the passing of time, as in *She woke up many mornings and went for many walks and had many baths.*. The word *and* repeats instead of commas to create a list, such as the following: *That afternoon her grandmother and grandfather and uncles and aunts all came to her house for dinner.* A variation of the same question repeats at the start of almost every page and acts as a thread that carries the little girl through the year: *What comes next? What comes now?*

- **Sequencing**—Through the use of transitional words and phrases, the time span of one year passes.

Owl Moon, written by Jane Yolen and illustrated by John Schoenherr. 1987. New York: Philomel. Fiction. (32 pp.)

Summary: On a cold clear winter night, by the light of the round full moon, a young girl goes owling with her father for the very first time. Yolen has crafted a tribute to the special traditions shared by a parent and child. (This is a Caldecott Medal Winner.)

- **Alliteration**—This craft appears in phrases such as *long and low, like a sad, sad song; wet and warm*.

- **Breaking the rules**—Sentences begin with *And* or *But*, and the author relies on sentence fragments, even in the final sentence.

- **Descriptive language**—Beautiful language creates imagery and provides sensory details: *The moon was high above us. It seemed to fit exactly over the center of the clearing and the snow below it was whiter than the milk in a cereal bowl*.

- **Effective ending**—The final powerful sentence is a beautifully crafted fragment whose last two words echo the book title: *The kind of hope that flies on silent wings under a shining Owl Moon*.

- **Hyperbole**—Yolen makes time stand still as the narrator and the owl finally come face to face: *For one minute, three minutes, maybe even a hundred minutes, we stared at one another*.

- **Metaphor**—A shadow metaphor is used effectively to describe both the owl as it alights on a branch (*The shadow hooted again*) and the young girl as she walks home after her night of owling (*But I was a shadow*). Another effective example of metaphor is when the moon casts its glow on Pa's face: *The moon made his face into a silver mask*.

- **Onomatopoeia**—*Whoo-whoo-who-who-who-whooooooo* is repeated throughout.

- **Personification**—Sophisticated examples include the following: *an echo came threading its way through the trees; and little gray footprints followed us*.

- **Print layout**—Long, narrow columns of text look like poems and encourage a rhythmic, lyrical reading.

- **Repetition**—A variation of the phrase *If you go owling…* or *When you go owling…* repeats throughout to create a thread that carries the story. Individual words repeat for emphasis, as in *like a sad, sad song* and *I had been waiting to go owling with Pa for a long, long time* or for lyrical effect, such as *We watched silently with heat in our mouths, the heat of all those words we had not spoken*. The word *or* repeats for rhythmic effect and to zoom in and slow down the action: *just as if he and the owl were talking about supper or about the woods or the moon or the cold*. Certain phrase patterns repeat to create balance between actions in the story: *I put my mittens over the scarf over my mouth* and *I took my mitten off the scarf off my mouth*.

- **Simile**—Setting is evoked through effective use of this craft: *it was as quiet as a dream*, and *trees stood still as giant statues*. The owl's flight is perfectly captured: *and lifted off the branch like a shadow without sound*.

- **Verbs and verb forms**—Yolen chooses interesting verbs that bring this special night to life, as in the following examples: *Our feet crunched; and my short, round shadow bumped after me; an echo came threading*; and *the owl pumped its great wings*.

- **Voice**—First-person narration and repetition of phrases such as *that's what Pa always says* give powerful voice and a sense of wonder to the little girl.

Parade, written and illustrated by Donald Crews. 1983. New York: Greenwillow, HarperCollins. Fiction. (32 pp.)

Summary: Through sparse text and colorful illustrations, Crews lists all the components of a parade.

- **Alliteration**—Some simple examples of this craft add to the parade's rhythm: *baton twirlers, twirling and turning; Flags flying*.

- **Breaking the rules**—The author uses fragments throughout.

- **Circular ending**—The book begins and ends with the Sanitation Department truck cleaning up: first getting the streets ready for the parade to start and later, cleaning up after the parade is over.

- **Lists**—Lists of varying length throughout the book highlight the elements of a parade: *Trombones, clarinets, saxophones, cornets, trumpets, flutes,*

French horns, sousaphones, field drums, cymbals, and last the big bass drums.

- **Print features**—Story text is printed in large grey font. Examples of environmental print appear in different fonts of various size and colors.
- **Print layout**—Story text is purposefully placed and spaced at the top of the page—sometimes as a line that runs across the top, sometimes in columns. Examples of environmental print can be found in many illustrations.
- **Punctuation**—Commas create a list; ellipses instruct the reader to pause in anticipation before turning the page.

Potluck, written by Anne Shelby and illustrated by Irene Trivas. 1991. New York: Orchard. Fiction. Note: this book is out of print but can be found in many classrooms, as well as school and public libraries. (32 pp.)

> **Summary:** The children are having an alliterative potluck celebration. There's a child's name and food for every letter of the alphabet!
>
> - **Alliteration**—The children's names, their actions, and the food they bring follow an alliterative pattern from A to Z: *Acton appeared with asparagus soup. Ben brought bagels. Christine came with carrot cake and corn on the cob.*
> - **Print layout**—Most alliterative sentences have their own page; line breaks complement the illustrations and pace the reader; some lines are written in undulating font that complements the illustrations.
> - **Punctuation**—Dashes cause the reader to pause in anticipation: *and set their table—for thirty one.* Ellipses have the same effect: *Then at the last minute…*
> - **Repetition**—Single words repeat for emphasis: *So they all sat down and ate and ate and ate and ate and ate.*
> - **Sequencing**—The children's names and their contributions to the potluck dinner are sequenced in alphabetical order.

Psssst! It's Me…the Bogeyman, written by Barbara Park and illustrated by Stephen Kroninger. 1998. New York: Aladdin Paperbacks, Simon & Schuster. Fiction. (40 pp.)

> **Summary:** In this hilarious story, a young boy discovers the Bogeyman living under his bed. The Bogeyman, who claims he has been misunderstood all these years, makes a tactical error when he gives away the secret of how to get rid of him.

- **Alliteration**—This craft is used extensively to add to the Bogeyman's humorous banter.
- **Breaking the rules**—The author uses fragments and begins sentences with *And* or *But*. Grammatically incorrect language and lazy pronunciation add to the Bogeyman's voice.
- **Circular ending**—The text is identical on the first and final pages, leading the reader to believe the Bogeyman will continue on with his antics.
- **Lead**—The suspenseful opening lines immediately draw the reader in.
- **Metaphor**—The Bogeyman uses a marshmallow metaphor to describe his ability to tiptoe up to children unseen and unheard.
- **Print features**—Use of italics, boldface, enlarged print, uppercase letters, and varied font color add to the story's frenetic tone. Plus, purposeful selection of typeface adds to the creepy-crawly feeling and complements the text.
- **Print layout**—Unique and meaningful placement of the print complements the text and illustrations, sometimes quickening the pace, sometimes slowing down the pace to add suspense, and sometimes creating a playful rhythm.
- **Punctuation**—Ellipses cause the reader to pause and build suspense. Hyphens between words create clever wordplay, and parentheses are used to interject sarcasm and voice.
- **Text features**—The front page of a newspaper headlining one of the Bogeyman's escapades and an "Official Bogeyman Contract" are incorporated into the story.
- **Voice**—The spirit of the book is captured through the Bogeyman's voice with shouts and whispers, tinged with humor, sarcasm, clever wordplay, and a bit of fright.
- **Wordplay**—Some examples of lively, Bogeyman-inspired words include the following: *silly-willy, jiggle-jam-jelly,* and *creepy-crawly.*

Puddles, written by Jonathan London and illustrated by G. Brian Karas. 1997. New York: Puffin. Fiction. (32 pp.)

> **Summary:** What does every child long to do on the morning after a rain? Why, puddle-jump, of course! London captures all the joy and exuberance of this favorite childhood pastime.

- **Circular ending**—After getting all warm and dry, the children go full circle and return outside to puddle-jump.

- **Descriptive language**—Through the use of sensory details, London slows down the moment by building anticipation of the puddle-jump. He also creates vivid imagery with simple yet precise language: *Mud sucks at our boots….*

- **Hyperbole**—Use of this craft underscores the beauty of the raindrops glistening on rooftops and tree branches: *Look—the sparkle of a million suns in a million drops!*

- **Lead**—The opening lines create setting and mood that capture the reader's attention.

- **Metaphor**—The phrase *pieces of sky on the ground* is used throughout to describe puddles, and an implied metaphor compares the sky to a blackboard: *A sky wiped clean of the last cloud.*

- **Onomatopoeia**—The thunder claps with a *Ka-BOOM!* Mud sucks at the children's boots—*slup slup slup*—as they puddle-jump—*Splash splash splash!*

- **Personification**—This craft is shown in the following examples: *the trees are applauding!* and *worms…learning the ABCs of weather.*

- **Print features**—Onomatopoeic words are written in italics.

- **Print layout**—Spacing between words and purposeful line breaks prompt a lyrical read.

- **Punctuation**—Ellipses zoom-in and slow down a moment, as in *On a morning after rain it's time to soak in a hot bath…wiggle dry in a warm towel… get dressed and drink hot chocolate…then run outside again.* Dashes instruct the reader to pause, as in *Look—the sparkle of a million suns…* or *Needles glisten—listen—the drip drip drip from the eaves and the leaves.*

- **Repetition**—Individual words repeat to create a rhythmic effect, such as *Big ones, little ones, long ones, skinny ones* or to add emphasis, as in *Splash Splash Splash!* A cluster of sentences appears twice, supporting the book's theme: *Puddles! Big ones, little ones, long ones, skinny ones—pieces of sky on the ground. It's time to puddle-jump!*

- **Rhyme**—There are several instances of internal rhyme as in the following examples: *slash…flash*; *Hop…Flop-plop!*; *glisten…listen*; *eaves…leaves.*

- **Simile**—The sunrise after the rain is *like a curtain rising on a shiny new day* and earthworms rising up from the ground *leave tiny trails in the muck like sloppy writing.*

- **Verbs and verb forms**—Interesting verbs such as *rattling, hollers, glisten, trickling, snaking,* and *slog* add to the imagery.

- **Wordplay**—The word *puddle-jump* creates the perfect mind-picture.

The Pumpkin Book, written and illustrated by Gail Gibbons. 1999. New York: Holiday House. Nonfiction. (32 pp.)

Summary: This simple book contains everything you need to know about pumpkins including their history, how to grow them, and most important, how to carve and decorate them for Halloween.

- **Breaking the rules**—The author uses sentence fragments throughout.

- **Punctuation**—Ellipses instruct the reader to pause in anticipation, as in *Over time it becomes bigger…and bigger…and bigger* and serve in place of a colon, such as in the following example: *It weighed about as much as a small car…1061 pounds.*

- **Repetition**—Individual words repeat to suggest a large quantity and add a rhythmic effect: *Small pumpkins. Big pumpkins. Round pumpkins. Tall pumpkins.* or *Funny pumpkins. Scary pumpkins. Beautifully carved pumpkins.*

- **Text features**—The book contains diagrams with labels; a how-to page; definitions; and, on the last page, a quick reference guide to the facts presented throughout the book.

A Quiet Place, written by Douglas Wood and illustrated by Dan Andreasen. 2002. New York: Aladdin Paperbacks, Simon & Schuster. Fiction. (32 pp.)

Summary: A young boy describes the quiet places, both real and imaginary, that one can find when some silent, peaceful solitude is needed.

- **Breaking the rules**—Sentences begin with *And* or *But*, and the author uses run-on sentences or fragments to demonstrate the cacophony from which one might need to escape.

- **Descriptive language**—All the quiet places of the boy's imagination are vividly captured through sensory details and lush language.

- **Effective ending**—After pages of imagined places and adventures, the book ends softly and sweetly with an explanation that the best place to go is the quiet place inside of you, which is always there no matter where you go.

- **Hyperbole**—Sitting quietly by the pond, the young boy imagines himself to be the quintessential fisherman pulling in a fish of gargantuan proportion.
- **Lead**—One short simple sentence sets the theme of all that is to come.
- **Lists**—Lists are used for emphasis and to stretch out time so that it moves slowly.
- **Metaphor**—The woods are compared to a green mansion; a timber wolf becomes a gray ghost; and paintings are compared to magic windows for your imagination.
- **Onomatopoeia**—This craft effectively describes noises, such as *drip, drip* and *shhhh*.
- **Personification**—Elements of nature, such as wind and snow, are given human traits such as singing and whispering.
- **Print features**—The first letter of the first word (on all but the first and last pages) is in large fancy font; italics are used to emphasize an individual word or to indicate onomatopoeia.
- **Print layout**—Line breaks instead of commas create lists; all but the first and last pages are laid out in the same format resembling stanzas of poetry instead of paragraphs; one elliptical phrase is set at the bottom of each page to allow the reader to anticipate what is to follow.
- **Punctuation**—Ellipses cause the reader to pause, and ellipses at the end of each page cause the reader to anticipate the new imaginary place to be revealed when the page turns. Dashes frame a clarifying phrase. Hyphens create wordplay.
- **Repetition**—Individual words repeat to emphasize a point; the words *and* or *or* repeat instead of commas to create lists. A pattern repeats that carries the story from one quiet place to another: each page begins with the words *You could* as it introduces the imaginary adventure and then ends with an elliptical phrase (usually beginning with *But*) that introduces an alternative suggestion in case the one described does not work.
- **Simile**—Several evocative examples of simile create a sense of setting, as when distant desert thunderclouds are compared to flowers in the sky and hilltop clouds are compared to boats and animals. A sense of stillness is conveyed as a shore bird is compared to a tree branch and

a pond is compared to a mirror. Stalactites in a cave are compared to icicles and sculptures.
- **Verbs and verb forms**—Verbs such as *shrieking, roaring,* and *blaring* convey the noises one hears all around.
- **Wordplay**—A lovely example of this craft is the word *sky-flowers*.

Rain, written and illustrated by Manya Stojic. 2000. New York: Crown, Random House. Fiction. (32 pp.)

Summary: It is the dry season on the parched African savannah, but the animals sense the coming rain. Their exultation at its arrival is contagious, short-lived though it may be.

- **Circular ending**—The story ends, just as it began, with the air so hot and dry that the red soil cracks, leaving the reader to believe that the rains will come again.
- **Cumulative text**—As the animals sense the coming rain, one animal's reaction builds upon another's, creating a cumulative text and a sense of anticipation.
- **Descriptive language**—Stojic creates imagery through sensory details and onomatopoeic words as the animals await the coming rain.
- **Effective ending**—The last page of this circular story contains two lines: One in the center of the page and the other at the bottom of the page in a smaller font leading the reader to feel the calm before the storm.
- **Print features**—A large bold font is used throughout.
- **Repetition**—Individual words repeat for emphasis and rhythm. Many sentence patterns repeat throughout this cumulative story, as each sentence builds upon the prior.
- **Verbs and verb forms**—The author uses descriptive verbs such as *flashed, boomed, gushed,* and *gurgled* to describe the rain and water.

Roller Coaster, written and illustrated by Marla Frazee. 2003. San Diego: Harcourt. Fiction. (32 pp.)

Summary: All the thrill and delicious terror of riding a roller coater are captured by Frazee's simple descriptive text and vivid illustrations that zip and loop across the pages.

- **Breaking the rules**—Sentences begin with *And* or *But*.
- **Circular ending**—The story ends with the anticipation of another ride on the roller coaster.
- **Descriptive language**—Although the vocabulary is simple, the author truly captures how one feels while riding a roller coaster by zooming in on the small moments, from the anticipation of the ride to that combination of post-ride queasiness and exhilaration.
- **Lead**—The opening line draws you in with the anticipation of the ride.
- **Onomatopoeia**—Examples of this craft include the following examples: *WHEEEEEEEEEEEEEEEEEEEE!*; *Clickety, clackity*; and *WHOOSH!*
- **Print features**—The first letter of the first word of the book is in a large, colorful, distinct font that echoes the title's font; the text changes to an uppercase red font when the ride begins.
- **Print layout**—The red text mimics the movements of the roller coaster as it curves and loops across the page.
- **Punctuation**—Parentheses indicate an aside; ellipses instruct the reader to turn the page in anticipation; hyphens stretch out words, such as *s-l-o-w-l-y*.
- **Verbs and verb forms**—Roller-coaster specific verbs include *zip, dip, dive,* and *zoom.*

Rosie and Michael, written by Judith Viorst and illustrated by Lorna Tomei. 1974. New York: Atheneum, Simon & Schuster. Fiction. (40 pp.)

Summary: A true friend is there for you through the good and the bad. Rosie and Michael share that special kind of bond.

- **Effective ending**—The two voices that see-saw throughout the book come together on the last page for a heartwarming ending.
- **Hyperbole**—Viorst employs this craft to demonstrate the depth of affection that Rosie and Michael share for each other.
- **Repetition**—The children's declaration of friendship is repeated throughout the story and carries the theme.
- **See-saw pattern**—The book alternates back and forth between Rosie's point of view and Michael's.
- **Voice**—First-person narration, humor, and the honesty of youth give voice to the two main characters.

Saturdays and Teacakes, written by Lester L. Laminack and illustrated by Chris Soentpiet. 2004. Atlanta, GA: Peachtree. Fiction. (32 pp.)

Summary: The narrator lovingly reminisces about his boyhood Saturdays in the South when he would bike to his Mammaw's house to spend the day helping out and building special memories like baking and eating teacakes together.

- **Alliteration**—Examples of the use of this craft include the following: *a fistful of flour, sputtered and spit,* and *mixed and mashed and mixed and mashed.*
- **Breaking the rules**—Many sentences begin with *And.* The use of fragments accentuates the narrator's voice and adds emphasis: *No one else. Just me.*
- **Descriptive language**—Laminack creates imagery and captures the tiny details of the young boy's childhood tradition: *Every Saturday she spread a cloth over the red countertop and scattered a fistful of flour across it. Sending a cloud into the air.*
- **Effective ending**—The young boy bids a poignant farewell to his Mammaw as he pedals away from her house: *Don't worry, Mammaw. I won't ever forget.* The dedication that Laminack makes to his grandmother in the front of the book is testament to the fact that he did *not* forget.
- **Metaphor**—Morning's dew turns into gems, as in *the dew-pearls were gone*; gravel sprayed into a garden becomes *a shower of tiny pebbles.*
- **Onomatopoeia**—Use of sound makes those long-ago Saturdays come to life: *whoosh!* is used to convey the narrator speeding downhill on his bicycle; *Criiick-craaack-criiick-craaack* creates the rhythmic sound of the glider squeaking back and forth.
- **Personification**—Two effective examples of this craft include: *From time to time the mower choked on mouthfuls of wet grass…*and *This is where my tires gave up their humming on pavement….*
- **Print features**—Italics are used to indicate dialogue and onomatopoeic words.
- **Punctuation**—Ellipses slow down a moment, as in *One…two…three…*; insert an aside, such as *In our little town everyone knew everybody…and told everything to anyone who would listen*; and add clarification, as in *and pull that shell apart over the bowl…like this.* Parentheses are used to indicate an aside or explanation: *You go on ahead*

to the car house. *(That's what Mammaw called the garage.)* Hyphens stretch out onomatopoeic words and dashes interject onomatopoeia in a sentence, as in the following example: *sitting on her old metal glider—criiick-craaack-criiick-craaack—sipping a cup of Red Diamond Coffee and waiting.* Dashes also instruct the reader to pause while the narrator clarifies a point: *and put them in the oven to bake—375 degrees for fifteen minutes.*

- **Repetition**—The phrase *Every Saturday* is repeated throughout and serves as a thread that carries the story; the three-word phrase *Pedal, pedal, pedal* is repeated six times to emphasize the distance the young boy biked to get to his Mammaw's house. Certain phrases repeat for emphasis, such as *mixed and mashed and mixed and mashed.* The same phrases begin and end the young boy's visit with his Mammaw.

- **Simile**—Some good examples of this craft are the following: *sunlight poured through the windows like a waterfall; I gobbled mine down like a hungry dog. But she nibbled at hers like a bird; She let the mixture drift through her hand like I sifted sand at the beach.* When describing the dough that would become the teacakes, the author writes *It was smooth and pale yellow and smelled like fresh cotton candy at the county fair.*

- **Verbs and verb forms**—Interesting verbs include *coasted, sputtered, trudged,* and *flopped.*

- **Voice**—Mammaw's Southern voice comes through loud and clear creating nostalgia and bringing the young boy's memories to life. For example, *I 'spect we need a bit more sugar in this; I reckon we can call that half an egg;* and *You better wait, buddy. They gonna be mighty hot just yet.*

- **Wordplay**—The author creates unique words that describe his memories of Saturdays with Mammaw, such as *dew-wet grass* or *flour-dusted.*

Scarecrow, written by Cynthia Rylant and illustrated by Lauren Stringer. 1998. San Diego, CA: Voyager, Harcourt. Fiction. (32 pp.)

Summary: A wise and gentle scarecrow with an abundance of self-awareness is happy with his lot in life because he has the privilege of being close to nature.

- **Breaking the rules**—Sentences begin with *And* or *But*, and the author relies on fragments.

- **Descriptive language**—Simple, rhythmic, beautiful language is used throughout to create imagery.

- **Hyperbole**—There's a great example of hyperbole to describe pumpkin and bean crops.

- **Personification**—This craft is used to describe the crows, as well as the sun and moon.

- **Punctuation**—Examples of colons and ellipses are used to cause the reader to pause in anticipation.

- **Repetition**—Sentence patterns repeat for emphasis. The word *and* is used to create a list.

- **Simile**—A good example of this is the following: *a web like lace.*

- **Verbs and verb forms**—Verbs specific to nature, such as *yellowed, greened,* and *blossomed,* add to the imagery.

- **Wordplay**—Words are combined to create playful adjectives, such as *pie-pan hands* and *button-borrowed eyes.*

Scoot!, written and illustrated by Cathryn Falwell. 2008. New York: Greenwillow, HarperCollins. Fiction. (32 pp.)

Summary: The harried pace of life in and around the pond seems to have little effect on six turtles who sit silent and still on a sunny summer day.

- **Alliteration**—Effective examples create an unmistakable and pleasing aural effect: *on a sunny summer day* and *six silent turtles sit still as stones.*

- **Print features**—The verbs appear in a large bold font.

- **Print layout**—The seemingly scattered placement of the verbs within the illustrations echoes the frenetic pace at the pond.

- **Punctuation**—Ellipses instruct the reader to pause.

- **Repetition**—The phrase *But six silent turtles sit still as stones* is repeated three times throughout the text.

- **Rhyme**—The text is rhythmic and contains a rhyme scheme.

- **Simile**—The simile that compares the turtles to stones, *sit still as stones,* is repeated throughout.

- **Text features**—A two-page spread titled Notes from Frog Song Pond at the end of the book provides information about the different creatures that the author sees from her own tree house on the pond. The final page of the book, titled Printing Textures, shows how to use paint and various materials to create artistic textures.

- **Verbs and verb forms**—The book is filled with playful effective verbs such as *perch, scamper, wriggle, scuttle,* and *hover.*

Shortcut, written and illustrated by Donald Crews. 1992. New York: Greenwillow, HarperCollins. Memoir. (32 pp.)

Summary: Crews effectively captures the suspense, fear, and relief experienced by a group of children who come to recognize the foolishness and danger of their choice to take a shortcut along the train tracks.

- **Breaking the rules**—Sentences begin with *And* or *But.*
- **Descriptive language**—Pacing empowers the story as the author zooms in on a childhood event to stretch out a moment in time and then uses many short sentences to quicken the story's pace as the sense of urgency builds.
- **Lead**—The opening lines immediately engage the reader and foreshadow what is to come.
- **Onomatopoeia**—*Klakity-Klak-Klak-Klak-Klakity* and *Whoo-Whoo* are a few of the sound words used to describe the scene.
- **Print features**—Boldface and uppercase letters add emphasis during the story's climax.
- **Print layout**—Various onomatopoeic versions of *Whoo-Whoo* appear in the upper left corner apart from the main text and become increasingly larger as the danger grows.
- **Repetition**—The sentence, *We should have taken the road* is repeated throughout and adds to the reader's sense of foreboding.

Sky Tree: Seeing Science Through Art, written and illustrated by Thomas Locker (with Candace Christiansen). 1995. New York: HarperCollins. Nonfiction. (40 pp.)

Summary: Locker's words are as effective as his paintbrush in this lyrical but informative book that chronicles a lone tree and its surroundings through the four seasons of the year.

- **Circular ending**—The tree goes through a full year cycle that begins and ends with summer and

the phrase, *its leaves fluttered in the soft summer breeze.*

- **Descriptive language**—Locker creates imagery that supports the beautiful oil illustrations: *One morning, light glistened on a thin silver frost.*
- **Sequencing**—Transitional phrasing shows the passage of time through the seasons.
- **Text features**—Questions at the bottom of each page prompt the reader to make connections and lead to a discussion in the back of the book, connecting art with science.
- **Verbs and verb forms**—*Fluttered, glistened, squabbled,* and *huddled* are a few of the lovely descriptive verbs in this book.

Small Green Snake, written by Libba Moore Gray and illustrated by Holly Meade. 1994. New York: Orchard. Fiction. (32 pp.)

Summary: A curious and impetuous little snake ignores his mother's warnings and slithers across the garden wall where his adventure nearly ends in disaster.

- **Alliteration**—This craft is used throughout, creating a toe-tapping rhythm.
- **Metaphor**—To Small Green Snake, trapped in a jelly jar, the sudden appearance of a stalking a cat becomes a huge vision of colorful fur.
- **Onomatopoeia**—This craft is used throughout to create rhythm and add drama to Small Green Snake's adventure.
- **Print features**—Many of the words (especially onomatopoeia) are printed in large colorful playful fonts.
- **Print layout**—Most onomatopoeic words and much of the dialogue are set apart from the text and some pages have purposeful line breaks to support the rhythmic reading.
- **Punctuation**—Dashes and ellipses are used to cause the reader to pause for dramatic effect. Hyphens are used to create onomatopoeia.
- **Repetition**—Words and phrases repeat throughout the story to support the slick, hip-hop rhythm of the text.
- **Rhyme**—Inconsistent rhyme patterns can be found throughout, adding to this book's unique rhythmic quality.
- **Simile**—One particularly effective simile is used to describe Small Green Snake's mother.

Snow, written by Cynthia Rylant and illustrated by Lauren Stringer. 2008. Orlando, FL: Harcourt. Fiction. (40 pp.)

Summary: Rylant has crafted a celebration of the many different kinds of snow, evoking the beauty and distinctiveness of each, while pointing out that children love them all.

- **Breaking the rules**—Sentences begin with *And*, and there are examples of sentence fragments.

- **Descriptive language**—This craft is used throughout to capture the many different kinds of snowfall, such as soft snow, peaceful snow, cheerful snow, light snow, and heavy snow.

- **Effective ending**—One short simple sentence captures the essence of the book: the wonder of snow.

- **Personification**—The snow itself is given life, as are snowflakes, flowers, gardens, and the sun.

- **Punctuation**—A single colon is used to introduce the book's heartfelt message.

- **Simile**—This craft is used to describe the way the snow comes *like a shy friend*.

Snow Is Falling, written by Franklyn M. Branley and illustrated by Holly Keller. 1986. New York: HarperCollins. Nonfiction. (32 pp.)

Summary: This science book for young children describes the snow and all the benefits of a snowfall while pointing out that it also can be dangerous.

- **Lists**—Lists interspersed throughout the text highlight the properties and benefits of snow: *Melted snow gives us water for wells, our streams, and our rivers.*

- **Repetition**—Qualities of snow are described in short simple sentences that include repeated words that reinforce the concept: *Lawns are white. Trees are white, and so are the roofs of houses. Everything is covered. Everything is white. Everything is quiet and cold.*

- **Simile**—A good example of this craft is the following: *The snow is like a blanket.*

- **Text features**—Additional resources at the end of the book include Snow Experiments, Snow Websites, and Books About Snow.

Snow Music, written and illustrated by Lynne Rae Perkins. 2003. New York: Greenwillow, HarperCollins. Fiction. (40 pp.)

Summary: When a young boy opens the front door to see the snow that fell throughout the night, his dog gets loose. As the boy searches for his pet, he experiences the sights and especially the sounds that surround him—snow music!

- **Alliteration**—Good examples include *quick, and as quiet* and *Snow came singing a silent song.*

- **Descriptive language**—This book has an uneven rhythm that is very effective in evoking the sights, the feel, and especially the sounds of a winter snow.

- **Effective ending**—The book ends with a call for a choral reading of the sound of snow: *Everyone whisper: fep fep fep fep fep fep fep fep fep.*

- **Lead**—The book begins with a call for a choral reading of the sound of snow: *Everyone whisper: peth peth peth peth peth peth peth.*

- **Onomatopoeia**—This is used throughout to describe snow music: *Click, fep fep fep fep, poot poot poot poot, plop, huff huff huff huff jingle jingle jingle jingle,* and *peth peth peth peth.*

- **Personification**—Both clouds and night are brought to life: *Clouds crept in* and *Night was here, but she left at dawn.*

- **Print features**—The first letter of the first word that begins the story is in large soft blue font; the word *dawn* appears in pastel pink, as does the word *Shhhhhhhhhh*; several pages have fonts of varied colors; use of uppercase letters.

- **Print layout**—Some onomatopoeic words appear as snow falling in the illustrations; some lines appear in type that arcs upward, some in type that arcs downward; several lines mimic the movement of the animals in the illustrations or the footsteps of two children meeting in the snow; some lines are laid out as if lines of music.

- **Punctuation**—Dashes and ellipses are used effectively to enhance a squirrel's frenetic search for a buried nut: *I think—I think I left it—I think I left it here—somewhere…I think. I think I—I know I left it here… No, wait—.*

- **Rhyme**—Although most of the book does not rhyme, there are some lines of rhyming text that enhance the lyrical quality of this book.

- **Simile**—Some examples of this craft include the following: *quick, and as quiet as a bunny; Swift, and as silent as the shadow of a crow;* and *Soft as our nests when day has gone.*

Snow Sounds: An Onomatopoeic Story, written and illustrated by David A. Johnson. 2006. Boston: Houghton Mifflin. Fiction. (32 pp.)

Summary: With only the sounds of the snowy morning to help the illustrations carry the story, the reader meets a young boy anxious to get to school for his holiday party.

- **Alliteration**—Examples include the following: *Swish Slush Smoosh* or *Crash Crush Clank*.

- **Onomatopoeia**—The entire story is carried by a series of sounds that move the boy from his cozy morning bed, *Snore*, to his bus ride to school for the holiday party, *Vroom*.

- **Print features**—Purposeful choice of font, case, color, and size complement each onomatopoeic word.

- **Print layout**—Playful layout of the onomatopoeic text within the illustrations helps to carry the nearly wordless story.

- **Punctuation**—The only punctuation in the book is a pair of quotation marks and an exclamation point—*"Wait!"*—as the boy's mom chases after him.

The Snow Speaks, written by Nancy White Carlstrom and illustrated by Jane Dyer. 1995. Boston: Little, Brown. Fiction. (32 pp.)

Summary: No one knows snow better than a child, and what snow could be more glorious than the snow that falls on Christmas?

- **Alliteration**—Some good examples include the following: *warmed and waiting, The snow speaks in sparkling stars,* and *dark, drear night*.

- **Breaking the rules**—Sentences begin with *And* or *But;* the author also uses sentence fragments. Uppercase letters are sometimes used mid-sentence to support the print layout, as in *Tired*.

- **Descriptive language**—This craft is used throughout to capture all the magic of a first snowfall.

- **Personification**—This resonates in the title as well as in the imagery throughout: *words freeze, stubborn snow,* and *Day climbs into night*.

- **Print layout**—Paragraph alignment resembles stanzas of poetry, which prompt a lyrical reading.

- **Repetition**—Individual words repeat for emphasis and lyricism, as in *Hello Hello Hello* or *Cold Cold Cold*, as well as to express the amount of snow, *snow on snow on snow*.

- **Simile**—Good examples of this include the following: *light as feathers; endless as a winter sky; swerves along the curve of road like a ship at sea;* and *as bold as salt sea air*.

The Snowy Day, written and illustrated by Ezra Jack Keats. 1962. New York: Viking. Fiction. (n.p.)

Summary: The excitement and promise of the season's first snowfall are seen through the eyes of a little boy in a bright red snowsuit. (This is a Caldecott Medal Winner.)

- **Circular ending**—The boy goes to bed after his Snowy Day but awakens the next morning to have it all begin again.

- **Descriptive language**—Keats captures the innocence of a snowy day through simple and concise language: *Snow had fallen during the night. It covered everything as far as he could see*.

- **Onomatopoeia**—*Crunch, crunch, crunch* and *plop!* are some of the sound words used to describe the day.

- **Punctuation**—Colons are used to incorporate the illustrations and the text, as with the line *He walked with his toes pointing out, like this:* which is followed by an illustration of footprints in the snow. Hyphens are used to stretch out a word, as in *dragged his feet s-l-o-w-l-y*, and dashes instruct the reader to pause before the continuation of a sentence: *Down fell the snow—plop!*

- **Repetition**—Words repeat for emphasis and to slow down a moment: *And he thought and thought and thought about them*.

Some Smug Slug, written by Pamela Duncan Edwards and illustrated by Henry Cole. 1996. New York: HarperCollins. Fiction. (32 pp.)

Summary: A smug slug refuses to heed the warnings of the other creatures and continues to slither up the steep slope, where he meets a surprising but unfortunate end in this alliterative tale.

- **Alliteration**—Words that begin with the letter *s* repeat throughout the story, for instance, *One summer Sunday while strolling on soil....*

- **Descriptive language**—The craft of alliteration creates a poetic effect when coupled with the unique and interesting vocabulary: *For one single second in a sunbeam it slumbered* or *as its sapphire tail swished*.

- **Effective ending**—The surprise ending catches the reader off guard.

- **Simile**—Good examples of this include the following: *stringing behind it scribble sparkling like silk* and *its sleek skin was soft like shantung*.
- **Text features**—On the final page after the story ends, the author includes two challenges for the reader: to find several animals hidden in the illustrations and to find the hidden *S* shape in each picture.
- **Verbs and verb forms**—Fun slug verbs include *snickered, sauntered, slithered, slumbered, skewing,* and *shambled*.

Someday, written by Eileen Spinelli and illustrated by Rosie Winstead. 2007. New York: Dial, Penguin. Fiction. (32 pp.)

Summary: A spunky young girl imagines a future filled with great accomplishments and contrasts it to her present ordinary existence in this humorous story about endless possibilities.

- **Breaking the rules**—The author uses fragments and begins sentences begin with *And* or *But*, as in *But I will smile*.
- **Descriptive language**—Although the book doesn't contain the lyrical, beautiful language typically cited for this category, the narrator's descriptions in this book include many details, creating mental imagery of the scene.
- **Hyperbole**—This book is brimming with exaggeration as the narrator imagines her larger-than-life future. For example, *I will count Macaroni Penguins—all five million of them. It will take a very, very long time. My hair will turn gray. I will return home to a ticker-tape parade. Five million people will cheer.*
- **Print features**—The word or phrase that indicates whether the narrator is imagining the future or describing the present is written in a different font that is larger and darker than the rest of the text; occasional asides also are written in this same font.
- **Print layout**—Purposeful line breaks support the childlike narration; lines of wavy and down-slanted print mirror the illustration of the narrator's cartwheels and final collapse into the mud; the narrator's asides are sometimes set apart from the text in wavy lines that complement the illustrations.
- **Punctuation**—Each time the narrator imagines a future adventure, the page ends with *Someday…* with ellipses used to prompt the reader's voice to fall off as if dreaming along with the little girl.

Parentheses indicate asides. Hyphens create words such as *frog-print pajamas* or *pointy-eared cats*. Dashes are used to add parenthetical remarks, as in *I will count Macaroni Penguins—all five million of them,* and in place of commas: *As for today—I am practicing cartwheels in the backyard.*

- **Repetition**—The title repeats at the top and bottom of each page where the narrator dreams of the future; the words *Right now* or *Today* repeat at the top of most pages where she is describing the present; the phrase *I will* repeats throughout the narrator's musings.
- **See-saw pattern**—The young narrator alternates back and forth between her dreams of the future and the things she can do as a child: *Someday I will be invited to the White House to have lunch with the president…In the meantime I'm having lunch with my brother Roger.*
- **Simile**—Good examples of this include the following: *as gracefully as any ballerina* and *his breath smells like a camel's*.
- **Voice**—The first-person narration perfectly captures the voice of an imaginative young girl who has big dreams for the future and a humorously realistic view of the present.

Spots (Counting Creatures From Sky to Sea), written by Carolyn Lesser and illustrated by Laura Regan. 1999. New York: Scholastic. Fiction. (32 pp.)

Summary: This counting book of spotted animals includes a glossary of biomes describing the creatures' habitats, making it an ideal text for inclusion in a study of ways to incorporate nonfiction elements into a work of fiction.

- **Alliteration**—Simple examples introduce this craft to young writers: *sunning, slipping* and *warming, waiting*.
- **Print layout**—Unique positioning of print throughout the text follows the movement of each creature.
- **Rhyme**—The book begins and ends with rhyming patterns.
- **Verbs and verb forms**—Three unique participles are used to describe the actions of each spotted creature, as in *slinking, prowling, hunting spots* and *sloshing, wiggling, lurking spots*.

The Squiggle, written by Carole Lexa Schaefer and illustrated by Pierr Morgan. 1996. New York: Crown, Random House. Fiction. (32 pp.)

Summary: In this tribute to childhood imagination, a little girl on a walk with her class discovers a piece of string, which is cleverly transformed into a variety of objects.

- **Alliteration**—Some examples of this craft include the following: *Slither slish* and *the full fat moon.*
- **Onomatopoeia**—This is used throughout to describe the sounds of the string in the little girl's imagination.
- **Print features**—The first letter of the first word is in large boldface print; use of uppercase letters indicates a loud noise, as in *KA-BOOM!*
- **Print layout**—Words of a sentence are separated to slow down the reader's pace as the narrator shows her classmates each thing that the string has become.
- **Punctuation**—Ellipses at the end of a page prompt the reader to pause in anticipation; hyphens create onomatopoeic words.
- **Wordplay**—Playful words such as *bunched-up*, *push-a-pat*, and *tah-dah* add to the sense of childlike wonder.

The Storm Book, written by Charlotte Zolotow and illustrated by Margaret Bloy Graham. 1952. New York: HarperTrophy, HarperCollins. Fiction. (32 pp.)

Summary: The book begins with the anticipation of the coming summer storm, which then engulfs the residents of the countryside, the city, the seashore, and the mountains in all its thundering fury before the calm settles once again with the appearance of a rainbow in the nearly cloudless sky. (This is a Caldecott Honor Book.)

- **Alliteration**—This craft is demonstrated in the following examples: *silver sighing stretch* and *the wild white wolf.*
- **Breaking the rules**—Many complex run-on sentences combine with occasional purposeful short sentences to capture the reader's attention and convey the pacing of the storm: *A little cool wind suddenly races through the trees, sways the rambler roses, bends the daisies and buttercups and Queen Anne's lace and the long grass until they make a great silver sighing stretch down the hill. Then it happens!*

- **Descriptive language**—The first 265 words zoom in to slow down the action in anticipation of the storm's arrival. Beautiful language creates imagery throughout, such as *Everything is the same color—one enormous listless gray world where not a breath stirs and the birds don't sing.*
- **Onomatopoeia**—Sound words bring the storm to life: *pitpatpitpatting* rain and *swish-swishing* of the tires on the wet road.
- **Personification**—Good examples of this craft include *the flowers straining into the storm wind*; *A little cool wind suddenly races through the trees*; *as they toss in the cool huge arms of the storm.*
- **Repetition**—The little boy's repeated question of *What's that?* provides a vehicle for the mother's descriptive responses.
- **Simile**—Examples include *Shooting through the sky like a streak of starlight*; and *The lightning was like a wild white wolf running free in the woods and the lamp like the gentle white terrier.*
- **Verbs and verb forms**—*Buffet, strain, splatter*, and *skids* are among the interesting storm-related verbs in this story.
- **Wordplay**—Playful words add to the descriptive language and imagery, as in the following examples: *loop-fenced circles*; *storm-darkened city*; *cloud-rending light*; *wind-driven sweet-smelling petals*; *clean-smelling, bird-singing mountains.*

Storm in the Night, written by Mary Stolz and illustrated by Pat Cummings. 1988. New York: HarperCollins. Fiction. (32 pp.)

Summary: Thomas, his grandfather, and their cat Ringo are sitting in the darkness waiting for a terrible thunderstorm to pass and for the electricity to be restored. While they wait, Grandfather tells Thomas about a time when he was afraid of thunderstorms and Thomas learns that sometimes it's OK to admit when you are afraid.

- **Alliteration**—Phrases like *whooped windily*, *brandishing branches*, and *Horns honked and hollered* provide good examples of this craft.
- **Breaking the rules**—The first seven sentences (five declaratory and two interrogative) are all fragments.
- **Descriptive language**—The lyrical tone is established through the vivid images that bring the tale to life. The images often can be subtle yet highly effective, as in the following example

where Stolz expresses *orange* in two different ways without ever using the word: *Except for Ringo's shining mandarin eyes and the carrot-colored flames in the wood stove....*

- **Flashback**—The author moves the action back and forth between the present and the past.
- **Lead**—The opening sentence is a fragment that echoes the title.
- **Onomatopoeia**—This craft is exemplified by sound words such as *Ping, ping, ping...ping-a-ling* or *Ticktickticktickticktickety.*
- **Personification**—This craft is exemplified by the following: *Lightning licking the navy-blue sky; A siren whined; Horns honked and hollered.*
- **Print features**—Italics are used for onomatopoeia and to add emphasis to words within dialogue.
- **Print layout**—There's no paragraphing in this book; each sentence starts a new line.
- **Punctuation**—Use of ellipses and dashes throughout instruct the reader to pause.
- **Simile**—Examples of this craft include *Thomas had a chin as smooth as a peach. Grandfather had a voice like a tuba. Thomas's voice was like a penny whistle.*
- **Verbs and verb forms**—Verbs such as *creaked, swished, drenched,* and *commanded* convey the action in an interesting way.
- **Voice**—Dialogue interspersed throughout the narrative brings voice to the characters of Thomas and Grandfather.
- **Wordplay**—The author evokes imagery by creating adjectives such as *rain-wet streets* or *carrot-colored flames.*

Summersaults, written and illustrated by Douglas Florian. 2002. New York: Greenwillow, HarperCollins. Poetry. (48 pp.)

Summary: This book of 48 short poems is a collective ode to summer and those fun-filled magical childhood days that seem like they will never end.

- **Alliteration**—Examples of this craft include *Bullfrogs belch beneath moonlight; hideous horrible; The temperature's torrid, sparse and spare.*
- **Metaphor**—Good metaphors include the following: *I am an otter: a streamlined torpedo; June's a bright blue butterfly;* and *September is the net.* Also, a series of metaphors are used to describe the sea in the poem "The Sea."

- **Onomatopoeia**—*Sizzle* and *zinging* are just two examples of onomatopoeic words that add life to the language.
- **Print layout**—The collection includes a poem for two voices, titled "Double Dutch Girls," which is set up in two columns to allow for a shared reading between two people. Some poems demonstrate unique and meaningful placement of print that mirrors the poem's action, such as "Summersaults," "Fireflies," and "The Swing."
- **Repetition**—Individual words repeat to imply a large quantity, as in *There's flocks and flocks and flocks and flocks;* and to add a lyrical, rhythmic effect such as *Some summers blaze. Some summers haze. Some summers simmer. Some summers....*
- **Rhyme**—Some poems contain rhyme schemes, as well as internal rhyme.
- **Simile**—The dandelion, unlike a lion, is *quiet as a closet door.*
- **Text features**—A table of contents helps the reader navigate.
- **Wordplay**—There are many examples of clever wordplay, such as *snow-packed day, rosy-fingered dawn, dande-lying,* and *sky-light de-lights.*

Sun Dance, Water Dance, written by Jonathan London and illustrated by Greg Couch. 2001. New York: Dutton, Penguin. Fiction. (40 pp.)

Summary: The children alternate between the scorching summer heat and the refreshing coolness of a river swim or an ice cold summer drink in this celebration of a summer's day and all its delicious sensations.

- **Descriptive language**—London creates imagery and captures the magic of summer through the use of sensory details, as in *we giggle with the tickle of our skin tightened into goose bumps....*
- **Hyperbole**—A good example of this craft is the following: *our bones turn to icicles.*
- **Metaphor**—A pool is compared to glass; the trees' roots become feet, as in *the willows with their feet in the water;* the river becomes *green worlds of icy light.*
- **Personification**—*Watch the moon float, Orion march across the sky,* and *the sharp bite of rocks* are all good examples of this craft.
- **Print features**—Italics are used for exclamations; text is printed in both black and white font; on a

page of black print on blue background, the single white word, *star* seems to be shining in the sky.

- **Print layout**—Unique and meaningful placement of print creates the effect of a lyrical poem.
- **Punctuation**—The author uses no punctuation except for four lines of dialogue that include quotation marks and ending punctuation.
- **Simile**—Examples of this craft include the following: *twist and roll like a river otter, watch the moon float like a great boat,* and *We play in the sun like a dance.*
- **Verbs and verb forms**—Verbs such as *radiating, plunge, ripple, topple, angling, dally,* and *dash* convey the mood and action.
- **Wordplay**—Fun words include *hand-paddle, too-bright, foot-slap,* and *snowmelt water.*

A Swim Through the Sea, written and illustrated by Kristin Joy Pratt. 1994. Nevada City, CA: Dawn. Nonfiction. (44 pp.)

Summary: In this colorful and informative plea for environmental consciousness, Seamore the seahorse invites the reader on a fascinating alphabetic tour of the undersea world.

- **Alliteration**—Each alphabetic animal is introduced with an alliterative sentence or phrase, as in *He'd greet a gargantuan Grouper gladly getting groomed,* or *He'd peer at a pokey puffed-up Porcupine Fish.*
- **Interesting format**—The book uses an alphabet book format to impart factual information about sea creatures.
- **Print features**—The alliterative line that introduces each animal is in large font with the animal's name emphasized in boldface.
- **Print layout**—The print is found in different spots on each page so that it appears to meld with the illustrations.
- **Text features**—The book contains an author's introduction that talks about the importance of the oceans and the need for environmental awareness; in the back of the book there's an About the Author segment that gives biographical information about the teenage author, including the fact that she had two books published before graduation from high school; around each page there is a border that incorporates the names of additional sea creatures whose names begin with the featured letter.

This Place in the Snow, written and illustrated by Rebecca Bond. 2004. New York: Dutton, Penguin. Fiction. (32 pp.)

Summary: In this lyrical picture book Bond has managed to capture both the playful and the almost spiritual wonder of a blanketing snowfall.

- **Alliteration**—Examples of this craft include *silent snow; It capsuled the cars; It hatted the houses; rumbling, rattling…rolling and rounding.*
- **Breaking the rules**—Most sentences begin with *And,* linking all that occurs on this long winter day and making it seem like one long continuous stream of activities; the final line of the book is a highly effective sentence fragment: *This place, full of grace, in the snow.*
- **Descriptive language**—The pages of this book are filled with the vivid and lovely imagery of a blanketing snowfall coming softly to life through the eyes of the children who are captivated by its wonder.
- **Effective ending**—A single lyrical fragment containing rhyme returns the reader to the quiet, almost reverent tone set in the opening line.
- **Lead**—A simple and lyrical first line creates the mood and anticipates what will follow.
- **Metaphor**—The snow becomes *creamy waves of white;* shoveled snow becomes *big spoonfuls of white;* the children in their snow creation become *kings in a kingdom uncovered.*
- **Print features**—The first word of the book is written in large bold red font; uppercase letters are used to increase the volume of the reader's voice, as in *And noisy turned LOUD;* increasingly larger font is used for the same effect.
- **Print layout**—The print is spread out—often one line per page with breaks between phrases of a sentence—causing the reader to slow down and zoom in on details; some lines of print are shaped to conform to the illustrations, thereby mirroring the children's movements in the snow.
- **Punctuation**—Dashes make the reader pause, as in *at what this might be—this place they would make in the snow;* indicate unfinished thoughts, such as *And could we—;* and appear in place of a colon, for example *at what they could see—This place, full of grace, in the snow.* Hyphens combine words to create new words such as *sun-snow* or *sky-high.* Ellipses slow down the moment and allow the reader to anticipate what will follow.

- **Repetition**—The word *and* repeats at the beginning of sentences and is used instead of commas to link words. Lines of dialog repeat to demonstrate the children's increasing excitement. Sentences repeat and are expanded to build upon an image: *They tunneled. They hollowed. They tunneled deep pockets. They hollowed large holes.*

- **Simile**—Good examples include the following: *It lay like lace, Like springs being sprung, sun-snow like lemon.*

- **Wordplay**—Nouns are creatively transformed into surprisingly effective verbs, such as *It capsuled the cars* and *It hatted the houses.* Words are combined to form hyphenated imagery, such as *sun-snow like lemon, shade-snow light blue,* and *gauzy-white night.*

Tigress, written by Nick Dowson and illustrated by Jane Chapman. 2004. Cambridge, MA: Candlewick. Fiction. (32 pp.)

Summary: An attentive mother tiger raises her two cubs, providing them with all they will need to know to survive on their own. This little gem of a book works on two levels: It provides factual information about endangered tigers and relates a universal story about motherhood. (This book has received many honors, including an International Reading Association/Children's Book Council Children's Choice selection; a Bank Street College Best Children's Book of the Year designation; and an Oppenheim Toy Portfolio Platinum Award Winner.)

- **Alliteration**—There are many good examples of this craft, including *strong muscles stretch, cracks and crevices, plate-sized paws press the ground, snuggled deep in shaded sleep,* and *soft, slow steps.*

- **Breaking the rules**—Sentence fragments and sentences that begin with *And* or *But* run throughout.

- **Descriptive language**—Dowson's perfectly chosen words create imagery while capturing the appearance and the actions of these exotic creatures: *Like fire, the roaring tigress leaps and falls in a crush of teeth and muscle.*

- **Lead**—The book begins with a series of questions that create a sense of mystery.

- **Metaphor**—The tiger is described as *A pattern of gliding stripes.*

- **Personification**—A good example of this craft is exemplified by the following: *She watched the forest swallow her tail.*

- **Print features**—The book employs bold print and varied font size to emphasize words and phrases. Italics indicate the factual information about tigers found on each page.

- **Print layout**—The factual information about tigers is set apart from the realistic fictional story on each page.

- **Simile**—This craft is used beautifully to describe the tigress and her cubs. For example, *Bright as torches, her large yellow eyes gleam all around; Smooth as a river she moves; Their bright white ear spots wink like magic eyes.*

- **Text features**—An index, About the Author, About the Illustrator, and information about the threat of tiger extinction are all found at the back of the book; in addition, the author encourages the reader to look for "both kinds of words," reminding the young reader to read the factual information as well as the story.

- **Verbs and verb forms**—Tiger-specific verbs include *stalk, stretch, and snarl; snuffles; crouch; quiver; gleam; ripple; wriggling;* and *nuzzles.*

- **Wordplay**—The author creates new words to describe the tigers and their environment, such as *stripy coat, plate-sized paws,* and *oven-hot.*

Treasures of the Heart, written by Alice Ann Miller and illustrated by K.L. Darnell. 2003. Chelsea, MA: Sleeping Bear, Gale. Fiction. (16 pp.)

Summary: A child's most treasured possessions are amassed under the bed. Will mom understand that they are precious and not a mess to clean up?

- **Effective ending**—The book ends with a heartfelt question: *You wouldn't want to break my heart and throw it out...Mom? Would you?*

- **Lists**—A list of the child's treasures amassed under the bed makes up the heart of this book.

- **Print features**—The first letter of the first word is a childlike, handwritten large red *C.* The author also uses uppercase letters for exclamation, as in *YUK!*

- **Print layout**—The book employs purposeful playful placement of print to guide the reader's phrasing.

- **Rhyme**—This craft is employed throughout to add a childlike sing-song quality.

- **Voice**—With little more text than a list of treasures, the child's voice comes through despite the fact that the reader never discovers whether the child is a boy or a girl.

Turtle Splash! Countdown at the Pond, written and illustrated by Cathryn Falwell. 2001. New York: Greenwillow, HarperCollins. Fiction. (32 pp.)

Summary: A peaceful day of lolling by the pond is interrupted as, one by one, 10 turtles are startled from their log by the noises and activities around them. This reverse counting book provides factual information about life at a pond.

- **Alliteration**—Examples of alliteration include *Ten timid turtles, lounging in a line* and *Six sunning turtles.*
- **Onomatopoeia**—A single example of this craft is used at the end of the book when the last turtle jumps into the pond: *Splash!*
- **Print features**—The numbers are in a large blue font; the single word *Splash!* is written in large blue arcing font that mirrors the turtles' dive into the pond.
- **Print layout**—The print see-saws between the extreme left and right margins and helps to create the countdown rhythm.
- **Punctuation**—Ellipses are found on almost every page to instruct the reader to pause in anticipation before turning to the next page.
- **Rhyme**—The text is rhythmic and contains a rhyme scheme.
- **Text features**—A page at the end of the book titled Life at the Pond provides information about the pond animals found in the book; the final page of the book shows the reader How to Make Leaf Prints like those found among the illustrations throughout the book.
- **Verbs and verb forms**—Good verbs capture the scene and actions, such as *lounging, rustles, scampers, flutters,* and *lolling.*

Twilight Comes Twice, written by Ralph Fletcher and illustrated by Kate Kiesler. 1997. New York: Clarion, Houghton Mifflin. Fiction. (32 pp.)

Summary: The twilight of dawn and the twilight of dusk are beautifully depicted through Fletcher's characteristic poetic prose.

- **Alliteration**—*Millions of mosquitoes* and *deepening dusk* are examples of this craft.

- **Descriptive language**—Eloquent images of twilight are vividly captured through sensory details and lush language: *The air is still moist from the cool of the night and your own skin feels all tingly clean.*
- **Metaphor**—Interesting metaphors include *dusk pours the syrup of darkness into the forest; the blackboard of night; Dawn slowly brightens the empty baseball field, polishing the diamond until it shines.*
- **Personification**—Dusk and dawn are both personified throughout the book: *With invisible arms dawn erases the stars; dawn drinks up night's leftover darkness.* In addition, there are many other individual examples of this craft, such as *Crows gather in the trees for last-minute gossip before nightfall.*
- **Print layout**—Rather than through indented paragraphs, the text is set up to resemble stanzas of poetry with purposeful line breaks that prompt a lyrical reading.
- **Repetition**—The first three lines begin with the same word, *Dusk.*
- **Simile**—A beautiful example of this craft is the line *Dawn is like a seed that will grow into daylight.*

Twister, written by Darleen Bailey Beard and illustrated by Nancy Carpenter. 1999. New York: Farrar, Straus and Giroux. Fiction. (32 pp.)

Summary: The peaceful opening scene of two children swinging on the porch belies the sheer, heart-pounding terror that follows as a tornado rips through the rural countryside.

- **Descriptive language**—Sensory details evoke a strong sense of setting and allow the reader to experience the emotion of surviving a tornado: *We sit on folding chairs in the dark, spidery room, which smells of old rain and earthy potatoes.*
- **Metaphor**—For the young brother and sister, the porch swing becomes different things in their playful imagination: *Our porch swing…is our throne.*
- **Onomatopoeia**—Sound words such as *Screeeek scraaawk* communicate the tornado noise.
- **Personification**—Elements of the twister are given human characteristics, which add to the ominous tone: *Then, with a ferocious roar, the twister strikes. It claws and chomps and pulls at our cellar door.*

- **Print features**—Italics emphasize individual words.
- **Punctuation**—A dash replaces a colon, as in *We give him our royal handshake—up, down, touch elbows, high-five*; hyphens create wordplay, such as *fence-hopping* and *belly-full*.
- **Repetition**—Onomatopoeia is written in pairs. The final lines echo lines from the opening paragraph.
- **Rhyme**—Pairs of rhyming words provide internal rhyme, as in *banging clanging porch swing*.
- **Simile**—This craft is used to convey the children's observations of a twister, as well as to add to the descriptions. Examples include *the sky looks green, like Mama's guacamole. Hail cracks onto the roof and bounces in the grass like popcorn popping.*
- **Verbs and verb forms**—A number of interesting verbs convey the action, such as *hobbles*, *crackles*, and *skitters*.
- **Wordplay**—The author creates specific words to describe scenes, such as *his fence-hopping scar* or *Natt lifts the hem of his T-shirt and stuffs it belly-full.*

Up North at the Cabin, written by Marsha Wilson Chall and illustrated by Steve Johnson. 1992. New York: Lothrop, Lee & Shepard, William Morrow. Fiction. (32 pp.)

Summary: A young girl heads north for her family's annual summer trip to the cabin by the lake. This beautifully written book captures the anticipation, wonder, and joy of a special summer place that provides a year full of memories until summer comes once again.

- **Alliteration**—The lyrical tone of this beautifully written book is enhanced by alliterative phrases such as: *serves my sunnies* and *skimming over sand that swirls behind me.*
- **Descriptive language**—The use of multiple crafts creates poetic prose that captures the setting and experiences of a summer by the lake: *We eat at the long table on the screen porch, sitting next to one another on the same side so we can all watch the loons dance down the sun.*
- **Effective ending**—The last line of the book echoes the title, *and once again I am up north at the cabin.*
- **Lists**—One particular list describes much of the setting: *I look all around me—at the screen porch, at the creaky branch I hear at night, at the chipmunk hole under the stoop, at the tufted island in the bay, at the spot in the sky where the North Star shines.*
- **Metaphor**—The antlers of a moose are described as *rocking branches of bone*; two characters carrying a canoe over their heads become *an armored beetle homeward bound.* Other good metaphors include *I am a great gray dolphin. The lake is my ocean; I am an acrobat in a perfect handstand; I float on a carpet of waves; I am a fearless voyageur.*
- **Onomatopoeia**—*Kawishiwee...Kawishiwee* describes the whisper of the river.
- **Personification**—The elements of nature and animals are given human traits, which add to the wonder. Examples include *the sunshine sits in my lap all morning, we can all watch the loons dance down the sun,* and *The river spills over rocks and whispers to me.*
- **Punctuation**—A colon introduces a clarification, as in *I know the way by heart: past the big walleye statue on Lake Mille Lacs....* Dashes instruct the reader to pause, such as in *Grandpa tries pink spinners, leeches, and dragonflies—but I know what fish like*; and interject onomatopoeia, as in *and whispers to me—Kawishiwee... Kawishiwee—.* Dashes are also used in place of a colon, for instance, *I fall three times—a flip, a somersault, the splits.* Hyphens are used to create new words, such as *peanut-butter-and-worm sandwiches* and *air-bubble balloons.* Ellipses connect onomatopoeic words.
- **Repetition**—The title is repeated eight times throughout the book and is the thread that carries the story.
- **Simile**—Descriptive similes add to the imagery of the sights and sounds that abound "Up North at the Cabin" such as *houses are made from logs that look like shiny pretzels; Like a house on stilts, a bull moose stands in the shallows; blood thumps through my head like old Ojibway drums.*
- **Text features**—The information about the author, found on the book jacket, reveals her inspiration for the book.
- **Verbs and verb forms**—*Trudge, heaves and rumbles, bellows, sputters,* and *thumps* are a few examples of verbs that effectively convey the story's action.
- **Wordplay**—The young girl refers to the bait on her fishing hook as *peanut-butter-and-worm sandwiches.*

Uptown, written and illustrated by Bryan Collier. 2000. New York: Henry Holt. Fiction. (32 pp.)

Summary: Collier has painted a colorful tribute to Harlem through the eyes of a young boy who calls it home. (This book won the Coretta Scott King Award and the Ezra Jack Keats Book Award.)

- **Descriptive language**—The narrator uses sensory images to provide the reader with the sights, sounds, and even tastes of Harlem.

- **Effective ending**—After the detailed and colorful descriptions of all that Harlem is, the simple ending heightens the poignancy of the statement *Uptown is home.*

- **Metaphor**—The sites and sounds of Harlem become metaphors for this New York community, as in *Uptown is chicken and waffles; Uptown is a stage; Uptown is jazz.* The Metro-North train becomes *a caterpillar…as it eases over the Harlem River.*

- **Personification**—Canvas awnings on the windows become clothing as *the buildings are all dressed up.*

- **Print features**—Colorful fonts mirror the excitement of Harlem as the narrator lovingly describes it.

- **Print layout**—Some lines are written in wavy or slanted text that complement the illustrations.

- **Punctuation**—Dashes are added to clarify a point, as in *I saw a picture from before my dad was even born—a picture of my grandparents' wedding day!* Ellipses prompt the reader to pause, as in *Uptown is Harlem….*

- **Repetition**—The phrase *Uptown is* repeats throughout the text as the young boy relates the sights and sounds of his world. Another important word repeats to express the theme: *Harlem world, my world.*

- **Simile**—Rows of brownstones are compared to candy: *They look like they're made of chocolate.* The voices of the Boys Choir of Harlem resonate as *Each note floats through the air and lands like a butterfly.*

- **Voice**—After each metaphor, the narrator offers a small aside, several of which allow his voice to come through. For example, *Uptown is chicken and waffles served around the clock. At first it seems like a weird combination, but it works.*

Very Last First Time, written by Jan Andrews and illustrated by Ian Wallace. 1985. Toronto: Groundwood. Fiction. (32 pp.)

Summary: Andrews uses the special experience of a small Inuit girl to describe the peculiar and extraordinary world between the Arctic ice and the bottom of the sea. (Fiction)

- **Descriptive language**—Sensory details create beautiful imagery throughout and slow down the moment as the story focuses on the combination of trepidation and thrill that comes with experiencing something for the very first time.

- **Effective ending**—The title is echoed in the powerful last sentence.

- **Onomatopoeia**—Descriptions of waves lend themselves perfectly to this craft: *lap lap, whoosh.*

- **Personification**—The tide and the ice are given human traits such as roaring and shrieking, respectively.

- **Punctuation**—Dashes throughout instruct the reader to pause in anticipation while hyphens are used to create wordplay.

- **Verbs and verb forms**—The author uses unique verbs such as *rumbled, echoed, wedged, darted,* and *skittered.*

- **Wordplay**—The author creates unique adjectives, such as *blue-black mussel shells, gold-bright flame,* and *a pinky-purple crab.*

Vroomaloom Zoom, written by John Coy and illustrated by Joe Cepeda. 2000. New York: Crown, Random House. Fiction. (32 pp.)

Summary: Carmela is not ready for bed so her dad takes her on an onomatopoeic car ride through city and swamp and sea and stream in an effort to lull her to sleep.

- **Breaking the rules**—For some of the lengthier sentences, the author uses page breaks instead of commas.

- **Effective ending**—Part of the title is echoed on the book's final page.

- **Onomatopoeia**—This craft is found on every page of the book: *cackle lackle, wurgle lurgle,* or *SWOOSH AWOOSH.*

- **Print features**—The onomatopoeic words, found on each page, are in unique playful fonts that vary in color and size while complementing the text.

- **Print layout**—Unique and meaningful placement of the print complements the text and illustrations; several sentences span four pages.
- **Repetition**—A cluster of sentences repeats several times throughout the text—*Ready? Not yet, Daddy. Keep driving*—carrying the story's premise. A portion of the title is repeated on the first and last pages of the book.
- **Wordplay**—A summer's evening is described as *cake-bake hot*.

The Wacky Wedding: A Book of Alphabet Antics, written by Pamela Duncan Edwards and illustrated by Henry Cole. 1999. New York: Hyperion. Fiction. (32 pp.)

Summary: All the insects and animals attend the alliterative wedding of the queen ant one April afternoon. A series of disasters ensues before the party ends and the happy couple retires for the night to their honeymoon "sweet" in a box of chocolates.

- **Alliteration**—Each page playfully introduces another letter of the alphabet that carries the story alliteratively: *"Magnificent marriage," murmured a mole, his head emerging from a mossy mound.*
- **Hyperbole**—*Zillions of fireflies* gives the impression of a night filled with these sparkling little insects.
- **Onomatopoeia**—*Plipity-plop* announces the bride's ungraceful fall into a puddle. *Yik-yakity* conveys the excited chatter of the insects.
- **Print features**—The first letter on each page (in alphabetical order) is written in fancy boldface; onomatopoeic words appear in italics.
- **Text features**—The copyright page challenges the reader to find the hidden letter and an object beginning with the featured letter in the artwork on each page of this alphabet book; the insides of the front and back covers have two-page spreads depicting playful cartoon ants in conversation as a way of imparting factual information about ants.

Walk On! A Guide for Babies of All Ages, written and illustrated by Marla Frazee. 2006. Orlando, FL: Harcourt. Fiction. (40 pp.)

Summary: This hilarious how-to book, told from a baby's point of view, includes everything babies need to know when learning to take their first steps.

- **Lead**—The book opens with two questions that immediately establish the baby narrator's voice.

- **Point of view**—The complicated process of learning to walk is explained humorously through a baby's first-person narration.
- **Print features**—Font color alternates between blue and red; font style varies and includes both cursive and manuscript font; font size is varied to allow the reader to bring voice to the baby narrator.
- **Print layout**—Unique and varied layout of the print on each page melds the text into the illustrations; speech bubbles are used to incorporate the voices of encouraging onlookers.
- **Voice**—A unique use of this craft captures a baby's point of view through adult-like humor.

Walter Was Worried, written and illustrated by Laura Vaccaro Seeger. 2005. New Milford, CT: Roaring Brook, Holtzbrinck. Fiction. (40 pp.)

Summary: Letters of the alphabet cleverly form the features of the children's faces, as well as the names of their emotions, as the boys and girls anticipate and experience a storm in this simple alliterative book.

- **Alliteration**—Each of the names of the eight characters depicted in this story is paired with an alliterative reaction to the weather. For example, *Walter was worried* and *Priscilla was puzzled*.
- **Print features**—Each individual letter of the alliterative verb describing the children is in its own distinct large font and color, which then can be found in the illustrations of the children's faces.
- **Print layout**—Each page has a single line of text with the final word of each sentence set apart on the next page, making this a good participatory read-aloud.
- **Punctuation**—Ellipses after transitional words cause the reader to pause in anticipation.
- **Sequencing**—The simple language and use of transitional words and ellipses sequence the change in weather from a storm that is impending, to raging, and, ultimately, to clearing.

Watch William Walk, written and illustrated by Ann Jonas. 1997. New York: Greenwillow, HarperCollins. Fiction. (24 pp.)

Summary: Two children, William and Wilma, take an alliterative walk with Wally the dog and Wanda the duck.

- **Alliteration**—Every word in this book begins with the letter *W*, giving this book a tongue-twister quality.
- **Print layout**—Unique and meaningful positioning of print throughout the text paces the reader and complements the movement of the children and animals as they walk along.
- **Punctuation**—Exclamation points punctuate all one-word sentences—*Water! Waves! Whirlpools!*—as well as the last sentence of the book, *Wanda won't wait!*
- **Verbs and verb forms**—Some of the alliterative verbs include *whittles, whimper, waddles, whiffs,* and *wallows.*

Water Hole Waiting, written by Jane Kurtz and Christopher Kurtz and illustrated by Lee Christiansen. 2002. New York: Greenwillow, HarperCollins. Fiction. (32 pp.)

Summary: A mother monkey teaches her young son the importance of patience in this story about the life that abounds in and around a water hole on the African savanna.

- **Alliteration**—Good examples of this craft include *lumpy log, skips and slips, thirsty throat, squeaking, squirming,* and *herding hippopotami.*
- **Breaking the rules**—The author relies on fragments throughout.
- **Descriptive language**—Imagery evokes a strong sense of setting: *Evening slinks across the savanna, pulling shadows behind it.*
- **Lists**—A single rhyming, rhythmic list captures the sights and sounds around the water hole: *The grasslands fill with birdcalls, wails, a loud buzz-buzzing of insects, a great swish-swishing of tails.*
- **Metaphor**—There's a great metaphor used to describe a crocodile: *The log sinks back and waits.*
- **Onomatopoeia**—Sound words such as *buzz-buzzing; swish-swishing; Snort and grunt; Slash, snap!;* and *Thrum, thrum* enhance the descriptions.
- **Personification**—Natural occurrences such as morning, evening, and silence, as well as animals and nature, are given human characteristics, which add to the sense of wonder. Examples include *Morning slinks onto the savanna and licks up the night shadows one by one. Evening sighs. The silence pokes Monkey's ear. Sun cartwheels slowly up the sky. Monkey's feet nibble the ground. The grasses start to whisper.*

- **Print features**—Onomatopoeia appears in italics, as does a single emphatic word: *Wait!* Print on three pages is in white font that complements the illustrations.
- **Print layout**—Unique and meaningful placement of print evokes a lyrical read and paces the reader. A column of single words is used to create a list.
- **Punctuation**—Ellipses stretch out a word, as in *slo...o...owly.* Hyphens are used for onomatopoeic words, as in *cha-chug-chug* and *chitter-chatter.*
- **Repetition**—Words repeat for emphasis: *Time to jump. Time to swing. Time for morning foraging.* The interjection *Wait!* is repeated several times throughout as Mama Monkey warns Monkey of danger.
- **Rhyme**—Although the book does not contain a rhyme scheme, there are some lines of rhyming text that enhance its lyrical quality.
- **Simile**—Effective use of this craft includes a description of the sun reaching its zenith at noon: *Sun climbs the sky like an acrobat,* and a description of the deafening sound of the elephants' arrival: *A grumble like thunder.*
- **Text features**—An author's note, found at the end of the book, provides information about vervet monkeys (the main characters in the story) and water holes.
- **Verbs and verb forms**—Action is conveyed with verbs such as *splay, slinks, scamper, ripples, foraging,* and *bristles.*

Water Music: Poems for Children, written by Jane Yolen and illustrated with photographs by Jason Stemple. 1995. Honesdale, PA: Boyds Mills. Poetry. (40 pp.)

Summary: Yolen has crafted a collective ode to water in all its forms through this book of poems inspired by the breathtaking photographs taken by her son.

- **Alliteration**—A tangle of water reeds is described alliteratively: *A muddle, a meddle; Knotted and knitted.*
- **Descriptive language**—Yolen breathes life into water and all its forms, creating imagery through personification, sophisticated similes and metaphors.
- **Metaphor**—Used throughout to describe water in its many forms. Several entire poems are extended metaphors.

- **Personification**—Several beautifully crafted examples include *Listen to the water groaning through the pipes; Pond lotus, open up your face; the whisper of water; Where water sings across the rocks.*

- **Print layout**—The book relies on unique and meaningful placement of print, such as in the poem "Waterfall," where the letters cascade off the line, and in "Icicle," where the title and the poem are presented in a thin vertical line representative of an icicle.

- **Simile**—Bath water groaning and complaining its way through the pipes is compared to an old woman, as in *like an old woman home with her shopping.*

- **Text features**—The book starts off with a scientific definition of water, includes a table of contents, and concludes with a Note From the Author.

Welcome to the Green House, written by Jane Yolen and illustrated by Laura Regan. 1993. New York: Paperstar, Putnam. Nonfiction. (32 pp.)

Summary: Through this lyrical and rhythmic picture book, Yolen invites the reader to experience the rain forest with all its unique flora and fauna. This book is part of a series by the author.

- **Breaking the rules**—The combination of fragments, as in *A bright house. A day house. A night house.* and run-on sentences create a lyrical effect; sentences begin with *And* or *But.*

- **Descriptive language**—Factual information is imparted through beautiful poetic language that brings the rainforest to life: *There are no windows in the greenhouse, yet ropey vines frame the views.*

- **Lists**—Several long lists highlight the elements of the rain forest, as in *a lunge of waking lizards, a plunge of silver fish, a slide of coral snake through leaves, a glide of butterflies through air.*

- **Metaphor**—The entire book uses the greenhouse metaphor to describe the rain forest.

- **Onomatopoeia**—The sounds of the many creatures living in the rain forest echo throughout the pages of this book: *a-hoo, a-hoo, a-hoo, crinch-crunch, Chitter-chitter-rrrr,* and *grrrrrrrroooooowl.*

- **Punctuation**—Colons introduce an example, such as *But it is not all green in the hot green house: a flash of blue hummingbird, a splash of golden toad....*

- **Repetition**—The first three lines of the book begin with the phrase *Welcome to the...* and the four sentences that follow begin with *There are no....* Single words repeat to create rhythm, as in *A bright house. A day house. A night house. A wet house. A warm house.*

- **Rhyme**—Internal rhyme runs throughout and creates a poetic feel, for instance *of chorusing frogs from limbs and logs, from trunks and leaves, from the water's edge, from the rocky ledge....*

- **Text features**—The final page of the book, titled Did You Know?, encourages the reader to learn more about the destruction of the rain forests and provides an address for The Rainforest Action Network.

- **Verbs and verb forms**—Verbs are used as nouns, as in *a slide of coral snake through the leaves* and *a glide of butterflies through the air.*

- **Wordplay**—Unique words include *slow-quick ways, ever-new green house,* and *green-coated sloth.*

What's Up, What's Down?, written by Lola M. Schaefer and illustrated by Barbara Bash. 2002. New York: Greenwillow, HarperCollins. Nonfiction. (32 pp.)

Summary: Schaefer has crafted a unique format for this picture book journey around the world that allows the reader a variety of perspectives.

- **Alliteration**—Good examples of this craft include the following: *A playful pod; swelling, surging, splashing; twisting and twirling;* and *flashing and flickering.*

- **Breaking the rules**—All of the sentences are fragments, such as *The trailing legs of a startled toad leaping out of sight.*

- **Cumulative text**—The answer to each question leads to a new question.

- **Descriptive language**—The author imparts factual information through beautiful poetic language: *Whisper-thin butterfly wings fluttering above petal cups....*

- **Interesting format**—Set up in a question-and-answer format, the book must be turned in different directions in order to read the text: half of the book is read from bottom to top, and the other half from top to bottom.

- **Metaphor**—Not typically found in a work of nonfiction, these beautifully crafted metaphors create visual imagery: *A sea of wildflowers rising and falling in tides of color; Tall trees spreading* *leaves into umbrellas of shade; The traffic of birds rushing here and there on invisible highways.*

- **Personification**—Grass is given human emotion: *Proud, new grass.* Seaweed becomes a dancer turning in the currents: *A ballet of seaweed.*
- **Print features**—Large font is used for questions, uppercase letters are used for emphasis, and arrows are used to direct the reader through the book's unique format.
- **Simile**—A single example of this craft creates an immediate visual image: *Prickly sea urchins dotting rocks like black pincushions.*
- **Verbs and verb forms**—Strong and creative verbs add to the imagery, as in these examples: *A sleek octopus jetting; An undersea park…hosting; Rows of ocean waves, swelling, surging, splashing, crashing; blue sky wrapping the world.*

Wordplay—Unique words create imagery. For example, *whisper-thin butterfly wings, thread-fine roots, wing-like fins, ink-black waters.*

When I Was Little: A Four-Year-Old's Memoir of Her Youth, written by Jamie Lee Curtis and illustrated by Laura Cornell. 1993. New York: HarperCollins. Fiction. (32 pp.)

Summary: A "grown-up" 4-year-old is proud of how far she has come in four short years.

- **Lead**—The opening line immediately engages the reader by stating the obvious in a playful way: *When I was little, I was a baby.*
- **Lists**—Several lists capture the world and voice of a 4-year-old, as in *Now I eat pizza and noodles and fruit and Chee-tos.*
- **Print features**—Playful font throughout complements the tone of the book; one effective example of large boldface font adds dramatic emphasis and voice.
- **Repetition**—The title repeats throughout the book and serves as a cohesive thread. The words *and* or *or* repeat instead of commas to create lists, such as *Now I go to nursery school and I have teachers and cubbies and naptime and secrets* or *Now I can wear it in a ponytail or braids or pigtails or a pom-pom.*
- **See-Saw pattern**—The story see-saws back and forth between the girl as a baby and the girl as a 4-year-old *When I was little, I cried a lot. Now I use words.*
- **Voice**—First-person narration effectively captures the voice of a 4-year-old.

When Marcus Moore Moved In, written and illustrated by Rebecca Bond. 2003. New York: Megan Tingley, Little, Brown. Fiction. (32 pp.)

Summary: Marcus's first day in his new home on MacDougal Street changes from one of boredom and loneliness to one filled with bright possibilities when he meets a lively new friend.

- **Alliteration**—In addition to the alliterative title, alliteration is sprinkled throughout, as in these examples: *There were only beds and boxes. There were only rolls of rugs; She lifted high her heels; steps and stoops and sidewalks.*
- **Breaking the rules**—The word *and* is used instead of commas in lists, as in *there were dogs and trucks and trees,* and several sentences begin with *And.* The author relies on run-ons; the final sentence contains 68 words.
- **Effective ending**—The opening line becomes the perfect ending to bring closure to Marcus Moore's moving day.
- **Lead**—*At 44 MacDougal Street when Marcus Moore moved in…* immediately captures the playful spirit and rhythmic feel of the book.
- **Onomatopoeia**—Sound words occur throughout, as in the following examples that capture the joyful sounds of Marcus and his new friend at play: *tap! Ta-Tap! Ta-tap!; Ringle! Jingle! Jangle!* and *Ker-UNCH! Ker-UNCH! Ker-UNCH!*
- **Print features**—The first letter of the first word of the book is in boldface; several onomatopoeic terms include uppercase letters, such as *Ka-LOMP!* or *BOOM-BA-DEE!*; italics indicate emphasis, as in *Like* that *she banged her drum….*
- **Print layout**—Meaningful placement and shaping of lines of print complement the illustrations; spacing of words in mid-sentence cause the reader to slow down.
- **Repetition**—The phrases *there was* or *there were* repeat 14 times. The opening line, which echoes the title, appears seven times.
- **Sequencing**—The story's action is carried through the periods of the day from morning to afternoon to evening.
- **Simile**—An upbeat example of this craft is the line *like a sunny sidewalk dancer,* which describes the entrance of Marcus's newfound friend and changes his attitude about the move from gloom to glee.

When the Fireflies Come, written by Jonathan London and illustrated by Terry Widener. 2003. New York: Dutton, Penguin. Fiction. (32 pp.)

Summary: London has crafted the perfect summer evening—one that the characters, as well as the readers, do not want to end.

- **Alliteration**—Summery examples of alliteration include *Bird chirp and bee buzz* and *A bullfrog booms.*

- **Breaking the rules**—Extensive use of fragments throughout, and many sentences begin with *And* or *But.*

- **Descriptive language**—This craft is used throughout to capture the playful and unhurried sights, sounds, smells, tastes, and feels of summer with some truly noteworthy images, such as, *The fingernail moon hangs low in the sky* and *The smell of torn summer grass on the warm night.*

- **Effective ending**—The events of the day are encapsulated in the narrator's dream.

- **Lead**—A simple sentence, followed by onomatopoeia, literally and figuratively opens the door to this celebration of childhood summer.

- **Lists**—The numerous sentence fragments create a list of summer images and then within the fragments, the author zooms in on detailed lists, such as *Drumsticks, push-ups, and ice-cream sandwiches.*

- **Metaphor**— This craft is used to describe jars, as in *Our jars are lanterns that blink,* and shadows, as in *The fingers of night creep across the grass.*

- **Onomatopoeia**—This craft is used throughout to capture the sounds of summer, as in *Slam-bang. Slam-bang; thong-thong; Ching-a-ling. Ching-a-ling; Pock!;* and *Brahnk! Brahnk!*

- **Personification**—Evening stars take on magical human qualities, as in *The evening star dances* and *The stars are sending a message….*

- **Print features**—Italic print is used for all onomatopoeia, to indicate excitement, and to emphasize a single word in a sentence: *Still* we *play ball.*

- **Punctuation**—Hyphens are used to create onomatopoeiac words such as *Cricket-cricket* and to slow down a moment, as in *Day-night. Day-night. Day-night.* Dashes create parenthetical effect, as in *And off we run with sticky hands— me out front, 'cause I'm the fastest.* Ellipses are used in several places to slow down the moment and build anticipation, as in *I drift into sleep….*

- **Repetition**—Onomatopoeic words are frequently hyphenated and repeated for effect, as in *Hoo-hoo-hoo-hoo-hoo!* The word *and* repeats to link a series of verbs, such as *We crouch and stalk and pounce.* Individual words repeat to simulate the blinking of the fireflies, as in *Day-night. Day-night. Day-night;* and one line runs throughout to create a thread: *Still we play ball.*

- **Simile**—The playful antics of the children are conveyed with simile: *I swing from the trees like an ape.* The darting movement of the fireflies is captured through a vivid comparison: *They flit like sparks from a bonfire at a marshmallow roast.* And, finally, a feeling with which we all can identify at the end of a busy day: *my pillow as soft as owl feathers.*

- **Voice**—Through the use of dialogue and through the narrator's thoughts, the voices of children on a summer evening ring loud and true: *"Ah, darn. Time to go home!"* and *Ah, the feel of a bat hitting a hardball to the outfield!*

When the Moon Is Full: A Lunar Year, written by Penny Pollock and illustrated by Mary Azarian. 2001. Boston: Little, Brown. Poetry with factual information. (32 pp.)

Summary: A collection of lyrical poems pays tribute to the Native American tradition of naming each month's full moon.

- **Alliteration**—The use of this craft enhances the poetic rhyme scheme: *cloud's crest, mirrors moon, forgetting all our foes.*

- **Descriptive language**—Pollack's quaint lyrical poems create imagery and bring beauty to the monthly moons: *Moonbeams touch the cornfield, laying shadows stripe by stripe down the endless rows of corn, tall and green and ripe.*

- **Metaphor**—Beautiful examples of this include the following: *Lilies of the valley ring each silent bell* and *We feast all night in moon's spotlight….* Metaphor is also used to describe snow as *a curtain of winter's lace* and to describe a deer's antlers: *Moonbeams slanting down show them velvet soft.*

- **Personification**—Nature comes to life through the use of this craft: *Old Man Moon hides his face; Furry-footed creatures scurry here and there dancing to the music they can hear quite well; Snow falls all day into the night snuggling the world in downy white.*

- **Rhyme**—All of the poems contain a rhyme scheme.

- **Sequencing**—The 12 poems are titled and arranged by month, beginning with January and spanning the entire year while following the path of the moon.

- **Simile**—This craft is used effectively in describing a squirrel as September's chill brushes the air: *tail wrapped round her like a cloak*.

- **Text features**—A question-and-answer section, found at the end of the book, provides information about the moon's surface, lunar eclipses, and the true meaning of a blue moon. Beneath each monthly poem, there is a an anecdotal sentence or two about characteristics of that particular month.

When the Sky Is Like Lace, written by Elinor Lander Horwitz and illustrated by Barbara Cooney. 1975. New York: Viking, Penguin. Fiction. (32 pp.)

Summary: Poetic prose describes the surprising *splendidiferous* things that can happen on a *bimulous* night when the sky is like lace.

- **Alliteration**—This craft adds to the wonder of this magical book. For example, *The wind was rather whistly* as the children lay in their beds listening on a *bimulous* night. Outside the trees were *Swishing and swaying, swaying and swishing*.

- **Breaking the rules**—Sentences begin with *And* or *But*; use of frequent fragments such as *Because you don't want to miss a thing*, interspersed with occasional run-ons, creates a lyrical flow.

- **Descriptive language**—Rich vocabulary and unique phrasing create imagery throughout: *You will also find that, on bimulous nights when the sky is like lace, the grass is like gooseberry jam. It's not really squooshy like jam, because then the otters' feet would slurp around and the snails might drown….But if you walk barefoot, it feels like the velvet inside a very old violin case.*

- **Lists**—Each of two consecutive pages contains a unique child-like list that is set apart from the rest of the text and is in perfect keeping with the mood of the book.

- **Onomatopoeia**—*KA-BOOM!* is used to describe that exact moment when a night goes from ordinary to *bimulous*.

- **Personification**—The lyrical and mystical tone of this book is enhanced through the use of this craft: *the otters are tuning their voices; the trees dance; the snails usually sulk under the cinnamon bush.*

- **Print features**—Uppercase letters, italics, and boldface print are all used to emphasize words and phrases.

- **Print layout**—Unique and meaningful placement of print supports the flow of the text.

- **Punctuation**—Hyphens create clever wordplay. Dashes are used in place of an ellipsis to instruct the reader to pause before turning the page; to direct the reader to pause a second longer before reading on, *Because—you never know*; and to zoom in and slow down a moment, as in *and the sky—the sky—OH, LOOK AT THE SKY!* Question marks are used as the author effectively poses a series of questions for the reader, such as *Did you see the sky was like lace? Or did you fall asleep and miss it?*

- **Repetition**—*On bimulous nights when the sky is like lace* is repeated throughout and is the thread that carries the story. The word *and* repeats to create a list. Individual words repeat to slow down a moment: *back and forth, forth and back, swishing and swaying, swaying and swishing.*

- **Simile**—Some unusual yet highly effective examples of this craft include *the sky is like lace; the grass is like gooseberry jam; it feels like the velvet inside a very old violin case.*

- **Wordplay**—*Strange-splendid, plum-purple, fern-deep*, and, of course, *bimulous* are all creative examples of this craft.

Where Once There Was a Wood, written and illustrated by Denise Fleming. 1996. New York: Henry Holt. Fiction. (32 pp.)

Summary: This simple picture book offers an important message about what happens to wildlife when a habitat is destroyed by development.

- **Alliteration**—Good examples of this craft include *the brown snake slithered and slipped out of sight* and *the raccoons rambled and rummaged.*

- **Breaking the rules**—There is no punctuation except for one final period at the end of the book.

- **Descriptive language**—With very limited text, the author captures the beauty of wildlife: *Where once the ferns unfurled and purple violets grew.*

- **Effective ending**—The ending, which is anticipated from the very first page, remains powerful because it presents such a dramatic shift from the beauty of nature that is portrayed throughout the book.

- **Lead**—The first line echoes the title and begins the single run-on sentence that makes up the text.
- **Repetition**—The title phrase is repeated as the opening line; the phrase *where once...* begins nearly every page of text; the first three pages of text, *Where once there was a wood a meadow and a creek* repeat at the end.
- **Rhyme**—Lines of rhyming text lend a rhythmic quality.
- **Text features**—At the end of the book there are two informational features that support the book's theme. Welcome Wildlife to Your Backyard Habitat suggests ways to provide space, shelter, water, and food to support wildlife and More Information provides contact information for the National Wildlife Federation, as well as a bibliography of books that address the topic.

White Snow, Bright Snow, written by Alvin Tresselt and illustrated by Roger Duvoisin. 1947. New York: Lothrop, Lee & Shepard, William Morrow. Fiction. (32 pp.)

Summary: The anticipation, realization, and ultimate departure of a blizzardous winter snowfall impacts the lives of children, grown-ups, and wildlife—all in different ways. (This book is a Caldecott Medal Winner.)

- **Alliteration**—Tresselt's signature lyrical prose includes the aural effect of melting water as spring arrives: *gurgled in gutters*.
- **Breaking the rules**—Sentences begin with *And* or *But*.
- **Descriptive language**—Despite the cold subject, Tresselt's words exude a feeling of warmth and coziness and create poetic imagery: *icy cold snowflakes sparkled in the light of the street lamps* and *Silently, the frost made pictures of ice ferns on the window panes*.
- **Lead**—The book begins with a rhyming poem that describes the overnight arrival of a blizzard.
- **Lists**—Two effective lists add emphasis: *Fields and stone walls, roads and gutters, lawns and sidewalks* coveys the extent to which all is blanketed in snow; and *The children made a snowman, a snow house, a snow fort, and then had a snowball fight* conveys all the fun that children experience after a snowfall.
- **Metaphor**—Throughout the book, the author captures the wonder of snow through the use of this craft, with beautiful metaphors such as the following: *It filled the cold tree branches with great white blossoms* and *Houses crouched together, their windows peeking out white from under great white eyebrows*.
- **Personification**—This craft can be soft and lovely as in *soft powdery snowflakes, whispering quietly as they sifted down*, or playful and whimsical as in *Even the church steeple wore a pointed cap on its top*.
- **Print layout**—Paragraph alignment prompts a lyrical reading.
- **Punctuation**—Commas build anticipation, as in *One flake, two flakes, five, eight, ten, and suddenly the air was filled with soft powdery snowflakes*; hyphens are used to slow down an action, as in *drip-drip-dripped*.
- **Repetition**—Words and phrase patterns repeat for emphasis: *under the ground, under the snow...under the roof-tops, under the snow*.
- **Rhyme**—The first page of the book, before the story begins, contains a lovely rhyming poem about snow.
- **Simile**—A playful simile creates a whimsical image: *Automobiles looked like big fat raisins in snowdrifts*.
- **Text features**—At the end of the book is a page titled *About White Snow, Bright Snow*, in which Tresselt describes his inspiration for writing the book.
- **Verbs and verb forms**—Melting rain *gurgled*, rabbits *scurried*, and snowflakes *sifted*.
- **Wordplay**—The barn is brightened by *snow-light*.

Whoosh Went the Wind, written by Sally Derby and illustrated by Vincent Nguyen. 2006. Tarrytown, NY: Marshall Cavendish. Fiction. (32 pp.)

Summary: A boy tries (unsuccessfully) to convince his teacher that his lateness for school can be blamed on the wind and all the havoc it caused. Derby's funny and clever book takes childhood excuses to a whole new level.

- **Alliteration**—The title itself is alliterative as are a number of phrases throughout the book, such as *I whizzed down the street while the wind zigzagged ahead, whisking dandelions; a clatter and clang; drivers dithered; on the wings of that wandering wind*.
- **Breaking the rules**—To add to the voice of a young child whose words are spilling out, many sentences begin with *And* or *But*.

- **Descriptive language**—The boy's dramatic recount of his morning is described in vivid detail: *…the wind sighed a foggy breath. The fog grew deep, the park grew dark. Soon all I could see was gray. A ghostly figure loomed, and I shook with fright…*

- **Effective ending**—The surprise ending in this book is presented through a wordless illustration.

- **Hyperbole**—The boy's increasingly exaggerated excuses for being late are filled with hyperbole: *The post office flag was flapping so hard its stars fluttered down to the sidewalk. I picked up stars till my pockets were full….*

- **Lead**—The opening sentence bursts on the page with a line of dialogue in large bold font: *I'm late! I'm late, but it's not my fault.*

- **Metaphor**—Blowing dandelions become a *golden hill.*

- **Personification**—The wind takes on a personality all it's own in sentences such as these: *It snatched laundry from our clothesline…*; or *the wind caught its breath and blew away the fog.*

- **Print features**—The boy's words are written in black font; the teacher's in red or white. The opening sentence is in large boldface font to indicate increased volume.

- **Print layout**—The teacher's words and the boy's words are set apart on the page.

- **Punctuation**—Ellipses prompt the reader to pause in anticipation.

- **Simile**—Two examples of this craft create interesting contrasting images: the force of the wind as it gusts and wrenches open the doors of a millinery shop blowing *hats like flowered Frisbees* and the gentle calm that characterizes the end of a windstorm: *softly as a kitten's breath.*

- **Verbs and verb forms**—Verbs such as *whooshed, whizzed, whisking, dithered, nestling,* and *loomed* support the frenetic pace of the boy's story—and help to convey the power of the wind.

- **Voice**—The boy's desperation to convince his teacher is carried through his first-person narration. However, although she's given very few words, the teacher's skeptical voice may actually be the stronger of the two, with remarks such as *Flying traffic signs? You must be kidding me!*; or *A hill of dandelions? Now, really…*; or *Free pets at Dippy Deli? Now you're going too far.*

Winter: An Alphabet Acrostic, written by Steven Schnur and illustrated by Leslie Evans. 2002. New York: Clarion, Houghton Mifflin. Fiction presented as an acrostic poem. (32 pp.)

Summary: Schnur has crafted a collection of A to Z acrostic poems that celebrate all that winter has to offer. This book is part of a series that highlights each of the four seasons in acrostic poem format.

- **Descriptive language**—Rich images capture the sights, sounds, smells, and chill of winter.

- **Personification**—Images of winter come to life as do the trees in this illustrative example of this craft: *Evergreens that seem to dance.*

- **Print features**—The first letter of each word that begins a new line in each acrostic poem is in uppercase blue font, which highlights the vertical word that is the subject of each poem.

- **Print layout**—Each page (from A to Z) has a separate acrostic poem set in a black-bordered text box.

- **Sequencing**—The stand-alone acrostic poems are sequenced to flow from the beginning to final days of winter.

- **Simile**—Lovely winter images are made through soft and gentle comparisons: *crystals of ice as delicate as lace* and *white flakes…glittering like diamonds.*

Winter Is the Warmest Season, written and illustrated by Lauren Stringer. 2006. Orlando, FL: Harcourt. Fiction. (40 pp.)

Summary: A young boy revels in all the delicious ways to stay warm in winter.

- **Alliteration**—A cozy, aural effect is created as Stringer describes the child's mittens.

- **Breaking the rules**—Sentences begin with *And* or *But.*

- **Descriptive language**—The boy's love of winter is captured through vivid sensory details.

- **Effective ending**—The twist on the common perception of winter as the coldest season is carried through with a twist at the end when the boy says he will have to cool off by dreaming of summer.

- **Lead**—The simple opening sentence echoes the title and contradicts a common belief.

- **Metaphor**—Nature stays warm under blankets of snow and radiators become dragons.

- **Personification**—Snowmen, hats, pants, pajamas, and gloves all take on human characteristics.
- **Print features**—The first letter of the first word is in large fancy red font.
- **Punctuation**—Ellipses prompt the reader to pause in anticipation.
- **Wordplay**—The author creates words such as *oven-hot* and *candleplaces* to describe winter warmth.

the wonderful happens, written by Cynthia Rylant and illustrated by Coco Dowley. 2000. New York: Simon & Schuster. Fiction. (40 pp.)

Summary: Rylant has crafted an homage to the wonder of life's simple things.

- **Breaking the rules**—No use of uppercase letters throughout the book—not even the title; sentences begin with *and* or *but*.
- **Descriptive language**—Rylant creates a child-like innocence by showing us how imagery can be created through even the simplest language.
- **Lists**—The entire book is a series of lists in different formats.
- **Print features**—Font is in a variety of colors; use of boldface for emphasis.
- **Print layout**—Placement of the print guides the reader's phrasing and emphasis; many pages contain only one word and one page contains a column of single words to create a list.
- **Punctuation**—Colons are used to introduce a word or a list; ellipses instruct the reader to anticipate before the page turn.
- **Repetition**—The title repeats throughout and is the thread that carries the story; individual words and sentence patterns repeat to create a rhythmic or lyrical effect or to add emphasis.
- **Simile**—The book ends by describing that most wonderful of all things: a child who grows quickly and exquisitely as does a rose, and who is soft and wonderful like peaches and snow.
- **Text features**—The words *each day,* which begin the story, precede the title page.

The World That We Want, written and illustrated by Kim Michelle Toft. 2005. Watertown, MA: Charlesbridge. Nonfiction. (32 pp.)

Summary: Cumulative text combines with luminescent illustrations to weave this cautionary picture book that extols the interconnectedness of Earth's many habitats and warns about their fragility in our constantly developing world.

- **Cumulative text**—As each habitat is introduced, the connection to the previous habitats is apparent through the use of the patterned cumulative text structure.
- **Print features**—Each new habitat that is introduced is in italics so it stands out from the rest of the text. The entire text is in white font, which serves as the perfect complement to Toft's magnificent luminescent illustrations.
- **Print layout**—The rhythmic flow of the cumulative text is encouraged by the placement of the text on the page.
- **Repetition**—Many sentence patterns repeat throughout this cumulative story, as each sentence builds upon the last.
- **Text features**—Before the title page is an invitation to find 45 creatures throughout the book. A two-page fold out, found at the end, is an illustration that includes all of the habitats mentioned throughout the book. Following the two-page fold out are brief descriptions of each habitat with a thumbnail of each page identifying and providing information about each of the 45 creatures.

The Worrywarts, written by Pamela Duncan Edwards and illustrated by Henry Cole. 1999. New York: HarperCollins. Fiction. (32 pp.)

Summary: Wombat, Weasel, and Woodchuck worry about everything—but will they allow their constant fretting to interfere with their alliterative adventure?

- **Alliteration**—The intentional exaggerated use of words beginning with the letter *W* creates a playful, tongue-twister effect.
- **Circular ending**—The ending leads the reader to believe that the wombats will continue their incessant worrying.
- **Onomatopoeia**—Woodchuck whirls a dictionary at Owl—*WHANG!*—and Owl responds with glee—*Whoopee!*
- **Personification**—The reader can envision the sun's face when reading that Wombat was awakened when *the sun winked* through her window.
- **Print features**—Use of uppercase letters and bold print adds emphasis.

- **Repetition**—The interjection *WAIT!* and the phrases *WHAT IF...* and *WATCH OUT!* are repeated throughout the book.
- **Verbs and verb forms**—The author chooses specific and fun *W* verbs, such as *waltzing*, *wallops*, *whizzed*, and *warbled*.

Reproducible Student Recording Sheets

Descriptive Language

Show—Don't Tell

Title	Author	Excerpt (first few words…)	Season

Hyperbole

Title	Author	Hyperbolic excerpt

Lead

Title	Author	Lead	Type of lead

Onomatopoeia

Sound	Onomatopoeia

Print Features and Print Layout

Title	Author	Print Feature	Reason	Print Layout	Reason

Additional Reading Lists

Children's Books About Writing

Once again, we encourage you to allow authors to be your teaching partners. Read these books aloud to your students and talk about the messages that the authors impart. Within the pages of the following books are countless references and reminders you can use as you confer with your students throughout the year.

Amelia's Notebook, written and illustrated by Marissa Moss. 1995. New York: Scholastic. Fiction. (40 pp.)

> Nine-year-old Amelia is unhappy about her family's move to a new state. Her mom gives her a notebook to record her thoughts and make her feel better. Designed to look like a black-and-white notebook with hand-lettered text and childlike illustrations, this book can serve as a model for children on how to use a writer's notebook to gather seeds for writing ideas. This is part of a series of notebooks that young Amelia writes.

Aunt Isabel Tells a Good One, written and illustrated by Kate Duke. 1992. New York: Penguin. Fiction. (32 pp.)

> Penelope asks her Aunt Isabel to tell her a goodnight story. Through this story-within-a-story, Aunt Isabel teaches Penelope all about the various elements that combine to tell a really good story. This book provides young children with a lively introduction to the ingredients of the fiction genre. (This has been an IRA–CBC Children's Choices selection.)

Author: A True Story, written and illustrated by Helen Lester. 1997. Boston: Houghton Mifflin. Biography. (32 pp.)

> Through cartoon-like illustrations and simple language, children's author Helen Lester describes her writing life beginning with helping her mother write grocery lists at the age of 3 and ending as a published author. Along the way, she discusses how she writes and shares the joys and frustrations that writing has brought to her life. (This has been an IRA–CBC Children's Choices selection.)

The Boy Who Loved Words, written by Roni Schotter and illustrated by Giselle Potter. 2006. New York: Schwartz & Wade, Random House. Fiction. (40 pp.)

> This is a celebration of the power of words. Selig is a young boy who loves words. He collects his favorites on slips of paper and stores them everywhere. When he is misunderstood and ridiculed by classmates, he sets out on a journey of self-discovery, wherein he meets a genie who helps him find his purpose in life.

If You Were a Writer, written by Joan Lowery Nixon and illustrated by Bruce Degen. 1995. New York: Aladdin, Simon & Schuster. Fiction. (32 pp.)

> Young Melia tells her author-mother that she, too, would like to be a writer. Melia's mother teaches her that a writer starts with an interesting idea and then must find words to "show" rather than "tell" a story. Melia comes to understand that a writer can write for herself or to share her writing with others.

Look at My Book, written and illustrated by Loreen Leedy. 2004. New York: Holiday House. Nonfiction. (32 pp.)

> This book is a guide for children on how to create a book. Cartoon illustrations with plenty of speech bubbles and thought bubbles combine with simple text to explain all aspects of publication from planning to drafting to revising to illustrating to formatting to binding.

Max's Words, written by Kate Banks and illustrated by Boris Kulikov. 2006. New York: Frances Foster, Farrar, Straus and Giroux. Fiction. (32 pp.)

Max's brothers refuse to share with him their collections of coins and stamps. Max decides to build a collection of his own—a collection of words. He discovers, as do his nosy brothers, that his collection is unique. When put together, his words can create a story. Max's brothers realize the value of his collection and suddenly are willing to swap their coins and stamps for a handful of words.

"Meet the Authors" series, various authors. Katonah, NY: Richard C. Owen. Biographies. (32 pp.)

This series of autobiographies by 35 popular children's authors provide insight to the writing process. Writing specifically for 7- to 10-year-olds, the authors share personal photographs and information about how they structure their writing days. The authors and titles in this series include the following:

Aardema, Verna. *A Bookworm Who Hatched*

Adler, David A. *My Writing Day*

Ancona, George. *Self Portrait*

Arnosky, Jim. *Whole Days Outside*

Asch, Frank. *One Man Show*

Bruchac, Joseph. *Seeing the Circle*

Bunting, Eve. *Once Upon a Time*

Cherry, Lynne. *Making a Difference in the World*

Ehlert, Lois. *Under My Nose*

Fleming, Denise. *Maker of Things*

Florian, Douglas. *See for Your Self*

Goble, Paul. *Hau Kola Hello Friend*

Heller, Ruth. *Fine Lines*

Hopkins, Lee Bennett. *The Writing Bug*

Howe, James. *Playing With Words*

Hurwitz, Johanna. *A Dream Come True*

Kimmel, Eric A. *Tuning Up*

Kuskin, Karla. *Thoughts, Pictures, and Words*

Locker, Thomas. *The Man Who Paints Nature*

London, Jonathan. *Tell Me a Story*

Lyon, George Ella. *A Wordful Child*

Mahy, Margaret. *My Mysterious World*

Martin, Rafe. *A Storyteller's Story*

McKissack, Patricia. *Can You Imagine?*

Numeroff, Laura. *If You Give an Author a Pencil*

Pallotta, Jerry. *Read a Zillion Books*

Polacco, Patricia. *Firetalking*

Pringle, Laurence. *Nature! Wild and Wonderful*

Rylant, Cynthia. *Best Wishes*

Simon, Seymour. *From Paper Airplanes to Outer Space*

Thaler, Mike. *Imagination*

Van Leeuwen, Jean. *Growing Ideas*

Wong, Janet. *Before It Wriggles Away*

Yolen, Jane. *A Letter From Phoenix Farm*

Nothing Ever Happens on 90th Street, written by Roni Schotter and illustrated by Kyrsten Brooker. 1997. New York: Orchard. Fiction. (32 pp.)

Eva discovers the essential ingredients to a great story with the help of the colorful and lively cast of characters that live and work in her neighborhood. She comes to the realization that she was mistaken…things really do happen on 90th Street!

Punctuation Takes a Vacation, written by Robin Pulver and illustrated by Lynn Rowe Reed. 2003. New York: Holiday House. Fiction. (28 pp.)

Frustrated with and tired of teaching punctuation, Mr. Wright decides to take a break and give punctuation a vacation—much to the delight of his students. Unfortunately, the punctuation marks get wind of this and are extremely offended. They decide to teach the class a lesson. The students soon discover that nothing makes sense without punctuation and they realize what must be done in order to return the punctuation to its rightful place.

Show, Don't Tell! Secrets of Writing, written by Josephine Nobisso and illustrated by Eva Montanari. 2004. Westhampton Beach, NY: Gingerbread House. Nonfiction. (40 pp.)

This book focuses on using specific nouns and revealing adjectives to create sensory details. This allows a writer to "show" rather than "tell" a story, incorporating both figurative language and literal expression. (This book has received the following commendations: IRA–CBC Children's Choice Award, Parents' Choice Recommended, Independent Bookseller Book Sense Pick, and the National Parenting Publications Awards—NAPPA Gold.)

What Do Authors Do?, written and illustrated by Eileen Christelow. 1995. New York: Clarion, Houghton Mifflin. Fiction. (40 pp.)

Eileen Christelow shows us the arduous process of bringing a book to publication. Where do authors get ideas? What do editors do? How is a book made? What happens after books are published? All of these questions (and more) are answered in this enjoyable book, which uses a comic strip-like format to impart its valuable information.

Willie's Word World, written by Don L. Curry and illustrated by Rick Stromoski. 2005. New York: Children's Press. Fiction. (32 pp.)

Willie loves words! Nevertheless, he's in a panic when his teacher gives a class assignment for each child to write an alliterative sentence using his or her own name. Suddenly, Willie is at a loss for words. Will he come up with the W words he needs, or will he be embarrassed in front of his classmates?

Written Anything Good Lately?, written by Susan Allen and Jane Lindaman and illustrated by Vicky Enright. 2006. Minneapolis, MN: Millbrook, Lerner. Fiction. (32 pp.)

Through the words of a young boy, this alphabet book explores the many different types of writing one can do. The simple text and inviting illustrations make this the perfect book for young writers to explore the various forms of both functional and creative writing.

You Have to Write, written by Janet S. Wong and illustrated by Theresa Flavin. 1997. New York: Margaret K. McElderry, Simon & Schuster. Poetry. (40 pp.)

We've all experienced this panic-stricken feeling: The teacher has given an assignment. You look around the room. Everyone is writing furiously, but you're staring at a blank page. This sensitive book offers encouragement for young writers who believe they have nothing to say, and it imparts further encouragement to those writers who get the words on the paper but are not happy with what they've written.

Suggested Professional Readings

Fletcher, R. (2004). *Teaching the qualities of writing.* Portsmouth, NH: Heinemann.

Harwayne, S. (2001). *Writing through childhood.* Portsmouth, NH: Heinemann.

Laminack, L.L. (2007). *Cracking open the author's craft: Teaching the art of writing.* New York: Scholastic.

Portalupi, J., & Fletcher, R.J. (2001). *Nonfiction craft lessons: Teaching information writing K–8.* York, ME: Stenhouse.

Ray, K.W. (2002). *What you know by heart.* Portsmouth, NH: Heinemann.

Ray, K.W., & Cleaveland, L.B. (2004). *About the authors.* Portsmouth, NH: Heinemann.

Ray, K.W., & Laminack, L.L. (2001). *The Writing Workshop: Working through the hard parts (and they're all hard parts).* Urbana, IL: National Council of Teachers of English.

Ruzzo, K., & Sacco, M.A. (2004). *Significant studies for second grade.* Portsmouth, NH: Heinemann.

Arnberg, A. (1999). A study of memoir. *Primary Voices K–6, 8*(1), 13–21.

Calkins, L.M. (1994). *The art of teaching writing* (2nd ed.). Portsmouth, NH: Heinemann.

Calkins, L.M., & The Teachers College Reading and Writing Project. (2003). *Units of study for primary writing: A yearlong curriculum*. Portsmouth, NH: Heinemann.

Davis, J., & Hill, S. (2003). *The no-nonsense guide to teaching writing*. Portsmouth, NH: Heinemann.

Fletcher, R., & Portalupi, J. (1998). *Craft lessons: Teaching writing K–8*. York, ME: Stenhouse.

Fletcher, R., & Portalupi, J. (2001). *Writing workshop: The essential guide*. Portsmouth, NH: Heinemann.

Laminack, L.L. (2007). *Cracking open the author's craft: Teaching the art of writing*. New York: Scholastic.

Parsons, S. (2005). *First grade writers: Units of study to help children plan, organize, and structure their ideas*. Portsmouth, NH: Heinemann.

Ray, K.W. (1999). *Wondrous words: Writers and writing in the elementary classroom*. Urbana, IL: National Council of Teachers of English.

All the Colors of the Earth, written and illustrated by Sheila Hamanaka. (New York: Morrow Junior Books, HarperCollins, 1994). © 1994 by HarperCollins.

All the Places to Love, written by Patricia MacLachlan, illustrated by Mike Wimmer. (New York: HarperCollins, 1994). © 1994 by HarperCollins.

All You Need for a Snowman, by Alice Schertle. (New York: Harcourt, 2002). © 2002 by Harcourt.

Atlantic, by G. Brian Karas, copyright © 2002 by G. Brian Karas. Used by permission of G.P. Putnam's Sons, a division of Penguin Young Readers Group, a member of Penguin Group (USA) Inc., 345 Hudson Street, New York, NY 10014. All rights reserved.

Aunt Flossie's Hats (and Crab Cakes Later), by Elizabeth Fitzgerald Howard. (New York: Clarion, Houghton Mifflin, 1991). © 1991 by Clarion, Houghton Mifflin.

Autumnblings, by Douglas Florian. (New York: Greenwillow, HarperCollins, 2003). © 2003 by Greenwillow.

Bat Loves the Night, by Nicola Davies. (Cambridge, MA: Candlewick Press, 2001). © 2001 by Candlewick Press.

Bats at the Beach, by Brian Lies. (Boston: Houghton Mifflin, 2006). © 2006 by Houghton Mifflin.

Bats at the Library, by Brian Lies. (Boston: Houghton Mifflin, 2008). © 2008 by Houghton Mifflin.

Beach Day, by Karen Roosa. (New York: Clarion, Houghton Mifflin, 2001). © 2001 by Clarion, Houghton Mifflin.

Bigmama's, by Donald Crews. (New York: HarperCollins, 1991). © 1991 by William Morrow Children's Books.

Birthday Presents, by Cynthia Rylant. (New York: Orchard, 1987). © 1987 by Orchard.

Busy Toes, by C.W. Bowie. (Watertown, MA: Charlesbridge, 1988). © 1988 by Charlesbridge. Used with permission by Charlesbridge Publishing, Inc.

Butternut Hollow Pond, by Brian J. Heinz. (Brookfield, CT: The Millbrook Press, Lerner, 2000). © 2000 by The Millbrook Press.

Candy Corn, by James Stevenson. (New York: Greenwillow, William Morrow, 1999). © 1999 by William Morrow.

Clara Caterpillar, by Pamela Duncan Edwards. (New York: HarperCollins, 2001). © 2001 by HarperCollins.

Cloud Dance, by Thomas Locker. (New York: Harcourt, 2000). © 2000 by Harcourt.

Colors! ¡Colores!, by Jorge Luján. (Toronto: House of Anansi Press, Groundwood, 2008). © 2008 by Groundwood.

Come to the Ocean's Edge : A Nature Cycle Book, by Laurence Pringle. (Honesdale, PA: Boyds Mills Press, 2003). © 2003 by Boyds Mills Press.

Creatures of Earth, Sea, and Sky, by Georgia Heard. (Honesdale, PA: Boyds Mills Press, 1992). © 1992 by Boyds Mills Press.

Crocodile Listens, by April Pulley Sayre. (New York: Greenwillow, 2001). © 2001 by Greenwillow.

Dear Mrs. LaRue: Letters From Obedience School, by Mark Teague. (New York: Scholastic, 2002). © 2002 by Scholastic.

Dear Tooth Fairy, by Pamela Duncan Edwards. (New York: Katherine Tegen, HarperCollins, 2003). © 2003 by HarperCollins.

Diary of a Worm, by Doreen Cronin. (New York: HarperCollins, 2003). © 2003 by HarperCollins.

Dirty Laundry Pile: Poems in Different Voices, selected by Paul B. Janeczko, illustrated by Melissa Sweet. (New York: HarperCollins, 2001). © 2001 by HarperCollins.

Dogs Rule!, by Daniel Kirk. (New York: Hyperion, 2003). © 2003 by Hyperion.

Earthdance, by Joanne Ryder. (New York: Henry Holt, 1996). © 1996 by Henry Holt.

Farmer's Garden: Rhymes for Two Voices, by David L. Harrison (Honesdale, PA: Wordsong, Boyds Mills Press, 2000). © 2000 by Boyds Mills Press.

Fishing in the Air, by Sharon Creech. (New York: HarperCollins, 2000). © 2000 by HarperCollins.

Four Famished Foxes and Fosdyke, by Pamela Duncan Edwards. (New York: HarperCollins, 1995). © 1995 by HarperCollins.

Freight Train, by Donald Crews. (New York: HarperCollins, 1978). © 1978 by HarperCollins. Fiction.

Gentle Giant Octopus, by Karen Wallace. (Cambridge, MA: Candlewick Press, 1998). © 1998 by Candlewick Press.

The Gift of the Tree, by Alvin Tresselt. (New York: Lothrup, Lee & Shepard, William Morrow, 2003). © 2003 by William Morrow.

Gilberto and the Wind, by Marie Hall Ets, copyright © 1963 by Marie Hall Ets, renewed © 1991 by Marjorie M. Johnson. Used by permission of Viking Penguin, a division of Penguin Young Readers Group, a member of Penguin Group (USA) Inc., 345 Hudson Street, New York, NY 10014. All rights reserved.

Granddad Bill's Song, by Jane Yolen, copyright © 1994 by Jane Yolen, text. Used by permission of Philomel Books, a division of Penguin Young Readers Group, a member of Penguin Group (USA) Inc., 345 Hudson Street, New York, NY 10014. All rights reserved.

Grandpa Loved, by Josephine Nobisso, illustrated by Maureen Hyde. (Westhampton Beach, NY: Gingerbread House, 1989). © 1989 by Josephine Nobisso.

Grandpa Never Lies, by Ralph Fletcher. (New York: Clarion, Houghton Mifflin, 2000). © 2000 by Houghton Mifflin.

Grandparents' Song, by Sheila Hamanaka. (New York: HarperCollins, 2003). © 2003 by HarperCollins.

H Is for Home Run: A Baseball Alphabet, by Brad Herzog. (Chelsea, MI: Sleeping Bear Press, 2004). © 2004 by Sleeping Bear Press.

Hair Dance!, by Dinah Johnson. (New York: Henry Holt, 2007). © 2007 by Dinah Johnson.

Hello, Harvest Moon, by Ralph Fletcher. (New York: Clarion, Houghton Mifflin, 2003). © 2003 by Houghton Mifflin.

Hello Ocean, by Pam Muñoz Ryan. (Watertown, MA: Charlesbridge, 2001). © 2001 by Charlesbridge. Used with permission by Charlesbridge Publishing, Inc.

Hide and Seek Fog, by Alvin Tresselt. (New York: HarperCollins, 1965). © 1965 by HarperCollins.

Hot City, by Barbara Joosse, copyright © 2004 by Barbara Joosse, text. Used by permission of Philomel Books, a division of Penguin Young Readers Group, a member of Penguin Group (USA) Inc., 345 Hudson Street, New York, NY 10014. All rights reserved.

I Am The Dog, I Am The Cat, by Donald Hall, copyright © 1994 by Donald Hall, text. Used by permission of Dial Books for Young Readers, a division of Penguin Young Readers Group, a member of Penguin Group (USA) Inc., 345 Hudson Street, New York, NY 10014. All rights reserved.

If You Were Alliteration, by Trisha Speed Shaskan. (Minneapolis, MN: Picture Window, 2008). © 2008 by Picture Window.

If You Were Onomatopoeia, by Trisha Speed Shaskan. (Minneapolis, MN: Picture Window, 2008). © 2008 by Picture Window.

The Important Book, by Margaret Wise Brown. (New York: HarperCollins, 1949). © 1949 by HarperCollins.

In My New Yellow Shirt, by Eileen Spinelli. (New York: Henry Holt, 2001). © 2001 by Eileen Spinelli.

Journey Around Chicago From A to Z, by Martha Day Zschock. (Beverly, MA: Commonwealth Editions, 2005). © 2005 by Commonwealth Editions.

A Kitten's Year, by Nancy Raines Day. (New York: HarperCollins, 2000). © 2000 by HarperCollins.

Last Night at the Zoo, by Michael Garland. (Honesdale, PA: Boyds Mills Press, 2001). © 2001 by Boyds Mills Press.

Leaf Jumpers, by Carole Gerber. (Watertown, MA: Charlesbridge, 2004). © 2004 by Charlesbridge. Used with permission by Charlesbridge Publishing, Inc.

Listen, Listen, by Phyllis Gershator. (Cambridge, MA: Barefoot Books, 2007). © 2007 by Barefoot Books.

The Listening Walk, by Paul Showers. (New York: HarperCollins, 1961). © 1961 by HarperCollins.

The Little House, by Virginia Lee Burton. (Boston: Houghton Mifflin, 1942). © 1942 by Houghton Mifflin.

The Little Yellow Leaf, by Carin Berger. (New York: Greenwillow, HarperCollins, 2008). © 2008 by HarperCollins.

Loki and Alex, by Charles R. Smith, Jr., copyright © 2001 by Charles R. Smith, Jr. Used by permission of Dutton Children's Books, a division of Penguin Young Readers Group, a member of Penguin Group (USA) Inc., 345 Hudson Street, New York, NY 10014. All rights reserved.

The Lonely Scarecrow, by Tim Preston, copyright © 1999 by The Templar Company plc. Used by permission of Dutton Children's Books, a division of Penguin Young Readers Group, a member of Penguin Group (USA) Inc., 345 Hudson Street, New York, NY 10014. All rights reserved.

Mojave, written by Diane Siebert, illustrated by Wendell Minor. (New York: HarperCollins, 1988). © 1988 by HarperCollins.

The Moon Was the Best, by Charlotte Zolotow. (New York: Greenwillow, William Morrow, 1993). © 1993 by William Morrow.

My Little Island, by Frané Lessac. (New York: HarperCollins, 1984). © 1984 by HarperCollins.

My Map Book, by Sara Fanelli. (New York: HarperCollins, 1995). © 1995 by HarperCollins.

Night Rabbits, by Lee Posey. (Atlanta, GA: Peachtree, 1999). © 1999 by Peachtree.

On the Same Day in March: A Tour of the World's Weather, by Marilyn Singer. (New York: HarperCollins, 2000). © 2000 by HarperCollins.

Over and Over, by Charlotte Zolotow. (New York: HarperCollins Publishers, 1957). © 1957 by HarperCollins Publishers.

Owl Moon, by Jane Yolen, copyright © 1987 by Jane Yolen, text. Used by permission of Philomel Books, a division of Penguin Young Readers Group, a member of Penguin Group (USA) Inc., 345 Hudson Street, New York, NY 10014. All rights reserved.

Parade, by Donald Crews. (New York: Greenwillow Books, an imprint of HarperCollins Publishers, 1983). © 1983 by Greenwillow.

Puddles, by Jonathan London, copyright © 1997 by Jonathan London, text. Used by permission of Viking Penguin, a division of Penguin Young Readers Group, a member of Penguin Group (USA) Inc., 345 Hudson Street, New York, NY 10014. All rights reserved.

The Pumpkin Book, by Gail Gibbons. (New York: Holiday House, 1999). © 1999 by Holiday House.

Saturdays and Teacakes, by Lester L. Laminack. (Atlanta: Peachtree Publishers, LTD., 2004). © 2004 by Peachtree Publishers.

Scoot!, by Cathryn Falwell. (New York: Greenwillow Books, 2008). © 2008 by Greenwillow Books.

Shortcut, by Donald Crews. (New York: Greenwillow Books, HarperCollins Publishers, 1992). © 1992 by Greenwillow.

Sky Tree: Seeing Science Through Art, by Thomas Locker with Candace Christiansen. (New York: HarperCollins Publishers, 1995). © 1995 by HarperCollins Publishers.

Snow Is Falling, by Franklyn M. Branley. (New York: HarperCollins Children's Books, 1986). © 1986 by HarperCollins Children's Books.

Snow Music, by Lynne Rae Perkins. (New York: Greenwillow Books, An imprint of HarperCollins Publishers, 2003). © 2003 by Greenwillow Books.

Snow Sounds, by David A. Johnson. (Boston: Houghton Mifflin Company, 2006). © 2006 by Houghton Mifflin Company.

The Snow Speaks, by Nancy White Carlstrom. (Boston: Little, Brown and Company, 1992). © 1992 by Little, Brown and Company.

The Snowy Day, by Ezra Jack Keats, copyright © 1962 by Ezra Jack Keats, renewed © 1990 by Martin Pope, Executor. Used by permission of Viking Penguin, a division of Penguin Young Readers Group, a member of Penguin Group (USA) Inc., 345 Hudson Street, New York, NY 10014. All rights reserved.

Some Smug Slug, by Pamela Duncan Edwards. (New York: HarperCollins Publishers, 1996). © 1996 by HarperCollins Publishers.

Someday, by Eileen Spinelli, copyright © 2007 by Eileen Spinelli, text. Used by permission of Dial Books for Young Readers, a division of Penguin Young Readers Group, a member of Penguin Group (USA) Inc., 345 Hudson Street, New York, NY 10014. All rights reserved.

Spots (Counting Creatures From Sky to Sea), by Carolyn Lesser. (New York: Scholastic, 1999). © 1999 by Scholastic.

The Storm Book, by Charlotte Zolotow. (New York: HarperTrophy, HarperCollins Publishers, 1952). © 1952 by HarperCollins Publishers.

Storm in the Night, by Mary Stolz. (New York: HarperCollins Publishers, 1988). © 1988 by HarperCollins Publishers.

Summersaults, by Douglas Florian. (New York: Greenwillow Books, HarperCollins Publishers, 2002). © 2002 by HarperCollins Publishers.

Sun Dance, Water Dance, by Jonathan London, copyright © 2001 by Jonathan London, text. Used by permission of Dutton Children's Books, a division of Penguin Young Readers Group, a member of Penguin Group (USA) Inc., 345 Hudson Street, New York, NY 10014. All rights reserved.

A Swim Through the Sea, written and illustrated by Kristin Joy Pratt. (Nevada City: Dawn Publications, 1994). © 1994 by Dawn Publications.

This Place in the Snow, by Rebecca Bond, copyright © 2004 by Rebecca Bond. Used by permission of Dutton Children's Books, a division of Penguin Young Readers Group, a member of Penguin Group (USA) Inc., 345 Hudson Street, New York, NY 10014. All rights reserved.

Tigress, by Nick Dowson. (Cambridge: Candlewick Press, 2004). © 2004 by Candlewick Press.

Treasures of the Heart, by Alice Ann Miller. (Chelsea: Sleeping Bear Press, an Imprint of Gale Group, Inc., 2003). © 2003 by Sleeping Bear Press.

Turtle Splash! Countdown at the Pond, by Cathryn Falwell. (New York: Greenwillow Books, 2001). © 2001 by Greenwillow Books.

Twilight Comes Twice, by Ralph Fletcher. (New York: Clarion Books, Houghton Mifflin Company, 1997). © 1997 by Clarion Books.

Twister, by Darleen Bailey Beard. (New York: Farrar Straus Giroux, 1999). © 1999 by Farrar Straus Giroux.

Up North at the Cabin, by Marsha Wilson Chall. (New York: Lothrop, Lee & Shepard Books, 1992). © 1992 by Lothrop, Lee & Shepard Books.

Uptown, by Bryan Collier. (New York: Henry Holt and Company, LLC., 2000). © 2000 by Brian Collier.

Very Last First Time, by Jan Andrews. (Toronto: A Groundwood Book, 1985). © 1985 by Groundwood Books.

Vroomaloom Zoom, by John Coy. (New York: Crown Publishers, a division of Random House, Inc., 2000). © 2000 by Crown Publishers.

The Wacky Wedding, by Pamela Duncan Edwards, illustrated by Henry Cole. (New York: Hyperion Books for Children, 1999). © 1999 by Hyperion Books for Children.

Walter Was Worried, by Laura Vaccaro Seeger. (New Milford, CT: Roaring Brook Press, a division of Holtzbrinck Publishing Holdings Limited Partnership, 2005). © 2005 by Roaring Brook Press.

Watch William Walk, by Ann Jonas. (New York: Greenwillow Books, 1997). © 1997 by Greenwillow Books.

Water Hole Waiting, by Jane Kurtz and Christopher Kurtz. (New York: Greenwillow Books, an imprint of HarperCollins Publishers, 2002). © 2002 by Greenwillow Books.

Water Music: Poems for Children, by Jane Yolen. (Honesdale, PA: Boyds Mills Press, Inc., 1995). © 1995 by Boyds Mills Press.

Welcome to the Green House, by Jane Yolen, copyright © 1993 by Jane Yolen. Used by permission of G.P. Putnam's Sons, a division of Penguin Young Readers Group, a member of Penguin Group (USA) Inc., 345 Hudson Street, New York, NY 10014. All rights reserved.

What's Up, What's Down?, written by Lola M. Schaefer, illustrated by Barbara Bash. (New York: Greenwillow Books, 2002). © 2002 by Greenwillow Books.

When I Was Little: A Four-Year-Old's Memoir of Her Youth, written by Jamie Lee Curtis. (New York: HarperCollins Publishers, 1993). © 1993 by HarperCollins Publishers.

When Marcus Moore Moved In, by Rebecca Bond. (New York: Megan Tingley Books, an imprint of Little, Brown and Company, 2003). © 2003 by Megan Tingley Books.

When the Fireflies Come, by Jonathan London. (New York: Dutton Children's Books, a division of Penguin Putnam Books, 2003). © 2003 by Dutton Children's Books.

When the Moon Is Full: A Lunar Year, by Penny Pollock. (Boston: Little, Brown and Company, 2001). © 2001 by Little, Brown and Company.

When the Sky Is Like Lace, by Elinor Lander Horwitz, copyright © 1975 by Elinor Lander Horwitz, text. Used by permission of Viking Children's Books, a division of Penguin Young Readers Group, a member of Penguin Group (USA) Inc., 345 Hudson Street, New York, NY 10014. All rights reserved.

Where Once There Was a Wood, by Denise Fleming (New York: Henry Holt and Company, LLC, 1996). © 1996 by Denise Fleming.

White Snow, Bright Snow, by Alvin Tresselt. (New York: Lothrop, Lee & Shepard Books, a division of William Morrow & Company, Inc., 1947). © 1947 by Lothrop, Lee & Shepard Books.

Whoosh Went the Wind, by Sally Derby. (Tarrytown: Marshall Cavendish Corporation, 2006). © 2006 by Marshall Cavendish Corporation.

Winter: An Alphabet Acrostic, by Steven Schnur. (New York: Clarion Books, a Houghton Mifflin Company imprint, 2002). © 2002 by Clarion Books.

The World That We Want, by Kim Michelle Toft. (Watertown, Massachusetts: Charlesbridge, 2005). © 2005 by Charlesbridge. Used with permission by Charlesbridge Publishing, Inc.

The Worrywarts, by Pamela Duncan Edwards. (New York: HarperCollins Publishers, 1999). © 1999 by HarperCollins Publishers.